URBAN FUTURES
Planning for City Foresight and City Visions

Timothy J. Dixon and Mark Tewdwr-Jones

With a foreword by
Sir Alan Wilson

First published in Great Britain in 2023 by

Policy Press, an imprint of
Bristol University Press
University of Bristol
1-9 Old Park Hill
Bristol
BS2 8BB
UK
t: +44 (0)117 374 6645
e: bup-info@bristol.ac.uk

Details of international sales and distribution partners are available at
policy.bristoluniversitypress.co.uk

© Bristol University Press 2023

British Library Cataloguing in Publication Data
A catalogue record for this book is available from the British Library

ISBN 978-1-4473-3093-6 hardcover
ISBN 978-1-4473-7167-0 paperback
ISBN 978-1-4473-3630-3 ePub
ISBN 978-1-4473-3629-7 ePdf

The right of Timothy J. Dixon and Mark Tewdwr-Jones to be identified as authors of this work has been asserted by them in accordance with the Copyright, Designs and Patents Act 1988.

All rights reserved: no part of this publication may be reproduced, stored in a retrieval system, or transmitted in any form or by any means, electronic, mechanical, photocopying, recording, or otherwise without the prior permission of Bristol University Press.

Every reasonable effort has been made to obtain permission to reproduce copyrighted material. If, however, anyone knows of an oversight, please contact the publisher.

The statements and opinions contained within this publication are solely those of the authors and not of the University of Bristol or Bristol University Press. The University of Bristol and Bristol University Press disclaim responsibility for any injury to persons or property resulting from any material published in this publication.

Bristol University Press and Policy Press work to counter discrimination on grounds of gender, race, disability, age and sexuality.

Cover design: Robiin Hawes
Front cover image: iStock/chee gin tan

Excerpt from Under Milk Wood, copyright ©1952 by Dylan Thomas.
Reprinted by permission of New Directions Publishing Corp. The UK copyright holder is The Dylan Thomas Trust.

Contents

List of figures, tables and boxes		iv
Acknowledgements		vi
Foreword		vii
Preface		ix
1	Urban futures: planning for city foresight and city visions	1
2	Cities and integrated urban challenges	17
3	Reimagining the city: views of the future from the past and present	41
4	Planning and governing the future city	65
5	Future narratives for the city: smart *and* sustainable?	79
6	Theoretical approaches to urban futures	101
7	Using city foresight methods to develop city visions	123
8	Shaping the future: city vision case studies	153
9	The innovative and experimental city	181
10	Visioning and planning the city in an urban age: a reality check	201
11	Conclusions: facing the urban future to 2050 and beyond	217
Appendix: selected examples of city visions		233
Notes		239
References		241
Index		283

List of figures, tables and boxes

Figures

1.1	Conceptual framework	15
2.1	Urban and rural populations of the world (1950–2050)	23
2.2	Projected population change 2011–36 for Great Britain, London and by settlement size	26
2.3	Zipf's law for UK cities: log of city population against log of rank order	26
3.1	Plato's Republic and More's Utopia	45
3.2	H.G. Wells' *War of the Worlds*	50
3.3	*Metropolis*	56
3.4	Shanghai and Dubai: inspired by or the inspiration for science fiction and urban futurism?	58
3.5	Ebenezer Howard's *Garden Cities of Tomorrow*: the 'three magnets'	62
6.1	Simplified overview of the multi-level perspective (MLP)	112
6.2	Transition management (TM); governance framework for transitions	113
7.1	City foresight	126
7.2	Backcasting	136
7.3	Three horizons	137
7.4	Reading 2050: visioning process	140
7.5	Reading 2050 workshop activities	142
8.1	Images from Burnham's Chicago Plan (1909) and Cerdàs Barcelona Plan (1855)	155
8.2	Arnstein's ladder of citizen participation	158
8.3	The evolution of city visioning	159
8.4	Examples of city visions	162
8.5	The quadruple helix	164
8.6	Three main elements from the Reading 2050 vision	167
8.7	An example of computerised visualisation	171
9.1	Urban innovation system	185
10.1	Seeing the city: the 'seen' and 'unseen' elements	203
10.2	Annella Olympica, Barcelona	212
11.1	The London cholera outbreak of 1854	225
11.2	Shoppers in face masks during the Spanish flu pandemic (1918, San Francisco) and during the COVID-19 pandemic (2020)	226

Tables

2.1	Overall population growth in the largest 10 UK cities (1981–2014)	25
2.2	Examples of urban challenges	29
5.1	Genealogical classification of city visions	83
5.2	Pillars for achieving urban sustainability	88
6.1	Comparison of sociotechnical transition (STT) and socioecological system (SES) approaches to transitions	110
6.2	Comparison of urban sustainability transition programmes	117
7.1	Futures toolkit	135
7.2	Themes identified in the NCF2065 stakeholder workshop	148
8.1	Key differences between a city masterplan and a city vision	156
8.2	How can Reading deliver its vision? A roadmap to 2050	168
8.3	Quality criteria for a good vision	176
9.1	Examples of UK city vision statements: urban innovation and experimentation	187
11.1	City visions: stages of development, key steps and key questions	220

Boxes

2.1	Sustainable cities and communities (SDG 11) targets	31
6.1	Climate change: a wicked and persistent problem	104
7.1	Ten things we need to know about the future	133
8.1	Reading 2050 vision	165
8.2	City Futures Development Group, Newcastle	172
9.1	Achievements of Newcastle City Futures Urban Living Partnership, 2016–19	197

Acknowledgements

Tim Dixon would like to especially thank Rachel, Sam and Cookie (the cat), but also the rest of his family (including Robin and Jem), for helping and supporting him so much during the first national COVID-19 lockdown and the writing of this book. The book is dedicated to Betty Louise Dixon (1921–2019), beloved wife of Jack, a wonderful mother (and grandma/great grandma), and a huge source of Welsh inspiration and '*hwyl*' to us all whenever we came home to Bristol. 'Time passes. Listen. Time passes. Come closer now. Only you can hear the houses sleeping in the streets in the slow deep salt and silent black, bandaged night' (Dylan Thomas, *Under Milk Wood*).

Mark Tewdwr-Jones would like to thank Robbie for his encouragement, good humour and coffee refills during the writing of this book, and his unflinching support when things got tough during the first national lockdown, especially during the home and job relocation in the middle of it all from one end of the UK to the other. A shared belief in looking towards an optimistic future for all of us proved to be a vital tonic.

Finally, we would both also like to thank all our colleagues and friends in the Reading 2050 and Newcastle City Futures programmes for their help and support along the way, and also Sir Alan Wilson for writing the foreword to this book.

Foreword

Sir Alan Wilson FBA FRS
The Alan Turing Institute

Many years ago, I learned from a distinguished American city planner and good friend, Britton Harris, that planning involved three kinds of thinking: policy, design and analysis. Essentially, what are we trying to achieve or what problems are we trying to solve, how can we invent plans to achieve these goals or solve the problems, and can we root this in good analysis? Harris observed that a problem in planning was that you very rarely found the three kinds of thinking in the same room together. That has been part of my intellectual toolkit ever since; and the gist of that argument still holds. It is the 'design' element that is neglected relative to policy and problem-solving on the one hand and analysis on the other. The authors of this book position themselves perfectly to fill this gap, and indeed, do get all three kinds of thinking into the one room – in this case the book! 'Foresight' is rooted in the articulation of problems and objectives – policy; and 'visioning' is 'design' for the city of the future. Great care is taken here to root this in the science of cities – analysis. To develop this framework is a substantial achievement in itself and this is combined with an ability to draw on the authors' experience to flesh out the substance in innovative ways. In looking forward, the argument is rooted in the works of past thinkers and this provides a platform on which to build a new integrated perspective.

So far so good, but how can this scheme be implemented? The trap of 'futurology' is avoided by emphasising that this is not a book that is offering predictions. There is another key idea here: while the obvious uncertainties rule out predictions, the way forward is to construct alternative scenarios. If some of these can be demonstrated as in principle 'good', and others 'not good', then there is a planning challenge for the present: how can we do things now that will help us to steer towards the 'good' and away from the 'bad'? The authors introduce us to the ideas of 'transformation theory': what are the routes from A to B? From the present to a desirable future? To achieve positive transformations, 'real' community engagement is vital – and very difficult. The authors show how this has been achieved in their two case studies – Reading and Newcastle – and these experiences will serve as a guide for others.

There is, then, an argument running through the book that if we are going to achieve even acceptable futures, radical policies and plans are necessary for the short run. To complete the circle, these actions have to be rooted in visions of the future and the authors offer us a roadmap for developing these. The challenges are investigated through the very helpful concept of 'wicked problems' – those that are of crucial importance, recognised by governments of all colours, and attempts are made to make progress, but they ever present. The problem of 'inequalities' is a good illustration. And of course this book is published in the context of the COVID-19 pandemic, which looks like being an ongoing wicked problem, a transformative shock to the urban system. A bigger and longer-term crisis, a slow-burning shock, is climate change and the associated challenges of sustainability. These kinds of wicked problems are taken head-on.

This is a book that is scholarly, rich in ideas, and offering roadmaps – a toolkit – for city and regional governments and communities to build visions and to explore ways of achieving them. It will be part of the foundations of future city planning.

Preface

The world that we live in is deeply urbanised and this is set to continue to grow over the long term to 2050 and beyond. Cities provide rich and diverse hubs of economic activity and continue to act as magnets for people and industry, yet they also harbour wealth and health inequalities, deplete valuable resources and contribute to continuing climate change. There have been many books written about cities, in fiction and non-fiction, and cities have permeated art and film, but there have been few, if any, previous books that have focused on the practical application and development of 'city visions', or the shared perspectives that can be produced to imagine a city's future.

Part of the inspiration for writing this book came from our strong desire to provide a counterpoint to the argument that 'predictive' city visions are impossible because: (a) of the complexity of cities; and (b) we ourselves, as part of that inherent complexity, are a crucial and unpredictable part of their future creation and design. But, in our view, it is now more important than ever that we look long term and that people help to decide what sort of future they want for individual cities across the world. This is not a prediction of the future and nor is it a generic vision designed by planning visionaries such as Ebenezer Howard and Patrick Geddes, inspirational though they were. What we call 'urban futures' is based on the notion that we need a practical and formal framework to imagine what our cities *could* and *should* be like to live, work and play in, in the long term (beyond 20 years); how they will operate; what infrastructure is needed; and how governance systems will be required to help shape them and ensure their resilience. To do this, we need to develop city visions that are based on participatory city foresight methods (or the science of thinking about the future of cities); and, as we also argue, we need to draw on 'transitions theory,' which emphasises how important city visioning is to the process of managing and planning for a sustainable (and smart) future for cities. In this book we therefore draw on our UK-based research (particularly in Reading and Newcastle) but also highlight international examples of city foresight and city visions.

This view of urban futures acknowledges the complexity of cities and the parallel development of a 'science of cities'. But it focuses not on predictive, or trend-based, visions and plans; instead, it uses a range of city foresight methods (such as visioning and backcasting) to show how different kinds of desirable future can emerge in different cities across the world. In doing this, city visioning must respect the 'eigenart', or unique characteristics of a place, and help us understand the past and present to understand the future. Therefore, participation, co-production and engagement are seen as being crucial to this process, with four main groups working in tandem to develop city visions (that is, government, industry, academia and civil society) in what is termed a 'quadruple helix' approach.

Cities have always been and will remain an important pull for people, despite crises that test their sustainability and resilience, such as the COVID-19 pandemic. As we were writing this book, the full impact of the disease on people's lives in the short to medium term was still to play out, but now more than ever we need city leaders and city stakeholders to think, plan and envision for the long-term future. Climate change impacts continue to have an effect and many cities have declared climate emergencies and set net zero-carbon targets to 2030. Despite its tragic impact on many people, COVID-19 pandemic has offered a view of how a more sustainable and green urban living could work in the future, and as we argue in the concluding chapter of the book, the crisis provides us with a vital opportunity to plan and manage our cities so that we all play our part in tackling climate change to cut emissions even more rapidly, and lead more sustainable lifestyles. The challenges to achieving this, and not 'rebounding' back to how things were before, are considerable and this will require political will across the global north and global south, but we should surely seize this opportunity to change things for the better and use green economic stimuli to kickstart economic recovery. Participatory-based city visions should be at the heart of this, and urban futures thinking is crucial to success. As Greta Thunberg wrote (Thunberg, 2019:22):

> There are no grey areas when it comes to survival. Now we all have a choice. We can create transformational action that will safeguard the living conditions for future generations. Or we can continue with our business as usual and fail. That is up to you and me.

1
Urban futures: planning for city foresight and city visions

Introduction

Throughout history, and in times of continuing uncertainty, writers, artists, film-makers and others have attempted to make sense of the future. Some have argued that, by its very nature, the future is unknowable and unpredictable, whereas others have argued that by taking control of our destiny, and by 'inventing' the future, we can also play an important role in helping to create it. Today, as we stand on the cusp of what many consider to be a future that will present us with our greatest set of perennial challenges, we need more than ever to make sense of what the future holds for humanity. However, living in uncertain times, in an Anthropocene and in an 'urban age', where climate change, environmental impacts, health impacts, political turmoil and socioeconomic upheaval create potentially traumatic perils for both humanity and the natural world (Attenborough, 2020), it is very difficult to even begin to see what the combined impacts of these forces might be, even in the short term, let alone the medium term (10–20 years) and long term (more than 20 years).

What is clear, however, is that, just as cities form the basis of many people's lives today, in all probability, they will also do in the future. Today, some 55 per cent of the world's population live in 'urban settlements' – as defined by the United Nations (UN) – and, by 2030, this will grow to 60 per cent, with one in every three people living in cities of at least half a million inhabitants, and, by 2050, that figure will be 70 per cent (UN, 2018a, 2018b).[1] In some countries, the figure is already higher than this: in England and Wales, for example, 95 per cent of people live in built-up areas (or urban areas) (ONS, 2013). Cities, after all, act as engine houses for wealth creation, employment and human progress, by combining the forces of agglomeration and industrialisation (UN Habitat, 2016). For example, 80 per cent of global Gross Domestic Product (GDP) is generated in cities (World Bank, 2019). On the other hand, rapidly growing cities, particularly in the face of unrelenting globalisation and rapid technological change, can create urban sprawl, slums and areas of poverty and inequality, as well as environmental impacts through resource consumption and climate change. That is not to say that every city suffers the same set of challenges now, or will do in the future. Cities differ in the challenges they face in their global north or global south contexts: for example, rapid urbanisation in South East Asia and Africa (with the growth of more than 100 cities since the early part of the 21st century; Voce and Van Mead, 2019)[2], but stagnation in and shrinkage of some cities in Europe, North America and East Asia (UN, 2018a).

Understanding cities and the way they work, therefore, is key to unlocking our understanding of their future. At an urban scale, there is now an important and growing body of theoretical work that recognises that cities are complex systems, similar to living organisms. This 'science of cities' (Batty, 2013), or 'urban science' (Acuto et al, 2018), originates in the thinking of a number of influential writers, from Patrick Geddes (the 19th century/early 20th century urban planner and biologist) to Jane Jacobs (the mid- to late-20th century journalist and author). Both argued, in different ways, that cities are the result of 'bottom-up' complex interactions and networks, and that urban design and planning need to recognise the intricacy and fragility of this complexity if we are to avoid undesirable outcomes. In its purest form, this new science of cities uses models based on, for example, living cells and networks to understand how cities function in terms of process and their overall form and function (Batty, 2013, 2018; West, 2018).

At the heart of understanding cities as complex systems is a need to recognise their inherent complexity based on the many multiple networks (for example, social and economic) and flows (for example, energy, information and transport) already present in a city (Batty, 2013). As West (2018: 21–2) points out:

> A typical complex system is composed of myriad individual constituents or agents that once aggregated take on collective characteristics that are usually not manifested in, nor could easily be predicted from, the properties of the individual components themselves … The economic output, the buzz, the creativity and culture of a city … all result from the nonlinear nature of the multiple feedback mechanisms embodied in the interactions between its inhabitants, their infrastructure and the environment.

However, Batty (2018) also argues that although models of cities as complex systems can help us understand how cities have evolved and how they behave, the inherent complexity of cities means that we cannot predict their future with any degree of certainty. As Batty writes (2018: 12–13): 'But just as we cannot predict the future, we cannot predict how we might invent it, especially as the future, particularly with respect to cities, is composed of a multiplicity – indeed almost an infinity – of decisions generated from the bottom up by all of us.'

This leads Batty to suggest that, because the future is unknowable, visions of future cities (such as those by Ebenezer Howard, Le Corbusier and others) are simply 'thought experiments', which if implemented would work out very differently from what their creators expected. Indeed, existing forms of urban planning, in Batty's (2018: 103) view, are not fit for purpose:

> [T]he way we have approached cities in the past is largely as though they are timeless; that is, frozen eternally at a moment in time. Although city planning does deal with the city of the future, the kind of master plans that have been the modus operandi of planners for at least a century assume an unspecified temporal future that will be reached at some point, but is invariably a convenient fiction to provide a focus.

However, we support the view that urban planning does have an important role to play in shaping future cities during a time of dynamic urban and technological transformation (Tewdwr-Jones, 2019). Cities are dynamic, as acknowledged in the science of cities, and our urban planning response for dealing with the major environmental and socioeconomic challenges confronting our cities should also be dynamic. Although the future may not be predictable, it is surely a dereliction of duty not to try to grapple with finding other ways of developing desirable and shared visions for our future cities in the light of the many complex and 'wicked' problems that we face.

Therefore, while acknowledging that the 'generic' city visions of utopic visionaries such as Ebenezer Howard and Le Corbusier may be 'thought experiments', we argue in this book that to overcome the disconnection between relatively short-term planning horizons of 5–10 years and longer-term environmental changes (20 years or more), it is vital for cities to develop specific longer-term visions that open up a possibility space to explore multiple futures, and provide a roadmap of how to achieve a shared and desirable future. This does not negate the importance of recognising the inherent complexity of cities, the continued desire for immediate and short-term political decision-making, or the important role that the science of cities plays in our understanding of cities. But it does require us to develop new ways of seeing and planning for a transition to a sustainable urban future.

This book aims to explore the evolution and development of city visions, and to show how important it is to think about the future of cities in objective and strategic ways beyond the short term (5–10 years) and medium term (10–20 years), and into the long term (more than 20 years). To do this, the book draws on two main theoretical lenses: (a) city foresight; and (b) transitions theory. In doing this, the book also examines what the implications are for urban planning (and city visions) now and in the future.

To begin with, in this chapter, we look at how narratives of the city have changed over time, placing the book in the context of other work, before discussing the growing importance of cities and planning for their long-term futures. We then examine the key themes employed and describe the format of the book in more detail.

A growing focus on cities: changing narratives

Since their 'invention' some 6,000 years ago (Smith, 2019), writers, political commentators, urbanists, satirists, film-makers and artists have all been fascinated by cities. The origins of the concept of an 'ideal future city' can be traced back to the writings of Plato, Thomas More (*Utopia*, 1516) and Francis Bacon (*New Atlantis*, 1627), while writers of fiction, such as Charles Dickens, H.G. Wells and Aldous Huxley, have all been heavily influenced by real or imagined cities and their diverse history, culture, characters and environments. More recently, we have seen a plethora of popular non-fiction literature focusing on cities.

We also saw the emergence of what Batty (2018) refers to as 'thought experiments' by urban planning theorists. In the 20th century, this took the form of:

- 'garden cities' or 'social cities', which promoted the idea of a metropolitan, polycentric region (for example, Ebenezer Howard);
- the 'contemporary city' or 'radiant city', which celebrated urban monumentality (for example, Le Corbusier's City of Million);
- 'broadacre City' (by Frank Lloyd Wright); and
- the 'ecological city' or 'spiritual city' ('biopolis') (for example, Patrick Geddes). (Daffara, 2006; Eames and Dixon, 2012; Dixon et al, 2014a)

These proposals for cities were essentially guided by radical and normative new visions for society. Although these helped to provide an intellectual testbed for debate and discussion as to what an ideal city should be like, and what form new cities could take, the reality of urban planning in cities in the mid-20th century was ultimately based very much on a deterministic, rationalist approach to planning existing cities. In other words, planning followed a linear process, from specifying operational objectives and targets through information collection, analysis, plan implementation and evaluation (Wolfram, 2018). Indeed, as Callahan and Ikeda (2014) argue, much of the early utopic tradition in planning (seen as a generic blueprint for the future) was guilty of the same urban rationalism that affected much of 20th century planning – for example, Le Corbusier's plan to create a new Paris was focused solely on 'the plan', which he believed would in itself produce the ideal outcome for society. In contrast, Patrick Geddes (1915), as Batty (2018) acknowledges, took a more nuanced view and highlighted the complexity of cities and their networks.

In the mid-20th century, and in a critical riposte to the utopian tradition in planning, Jane Jacobs (1961) argued for a more organic approach to planning based on local knowledge, which also recognised the importance of people and the complexity of networks and flows in cities. Jacobs argued that, before anyone can think sensibly about what a city should be and how it should work, they needed to understand what a city is and how it actually does work. Consequently, Callahan and Ikeda (2014) refer to Jacobs as an urban physician. As Jacobs (1961: 6) herself noted:

> Cities are an immense laboratory of trial and error, failure and success, in city building and city design. This is the laboratory in which city planning should have been learning and forming and testing its theories. Instead the practitioners and teachers of this discipline have ignored the study of success and failure in real life, have been incurious about the reasons for unexpected success, and are guided instead by principles derived from the behavior and appearance of towns, suburbs, tuberculosis sanatoria, fairs and imaginary dream cities – from anything but the cities themselves.

At the time Jacobs was writing, during the 1950s and 1960s, planners treated the city as a problem of simplicity or disorganised complexity instead of a problem of organised complexity (Callahan and Ikeda,

2014). This worldview of cities was essentially to see them as black-box systems or machines, organised from the top down. But the work of Geddes and Jacobs led to the emergence of a new science of cities, seeing them more as organisms or complex systems, rather than as machines. Moreover, Batty (2018) highlights five main principles, which he suggests can help us understand how cities work and adapt to systemic change (although this still does not enable us to predict their future state with any certainty at all):

- Zipf's law of distribution, which proves that there will be many more small cities than large one.
- Edward Glaeser's (2011) 'paradox of the modern metropolis', founded on his book *Triumph of the City*, which describes how physical proximity to social and economic networks in cities is becoming more important, even though technology has reduced the time and costs of interacting over large distances.
- Johan Heinrich Von Thunen's standard model of land use, which outlines the principles of land-use bands in a city surrounding a central business district (CBD).
- H.G. Wells' proposition in 1902 ('The Probable Diffusion of Great Cities' in *Anticipations*), which suggested that the mode(s) of transportation influence population distribution in a city.
- Waldo R. Tobler's first law of geography, which suggests that locations that are closer to each other create a stronger pull than those farther apart.

Batty's (2018: 1–2) call for a new 'science of cities' is based on the notion 'that to understand place, we must understand flows and to understand flows we must understand networks. In turn, networks suggest relations between people and places, and thus the central principle of our new science depends on defining relations between the objects that comprise our system of interest.' However, this focus on universal principles, data, science and mathematics to understand cities has been typified as being 'techno-scientific urbanism' by Brenner and Schmid (2015). This has formed part of a more general critique that attacks the concept of an 'urban age', and its focus on a universal 'urban form', and therefore simplifies and underplays the complexity and diversity of the 'planetary process' of urbanisation (see, for example, Gleeson, 2012; Brenner and Schmid, 2014; Rickards et al, 2016). Brenner and Schmid (2015) also see much of the literature surrounding smart cities, with the primary focus on technology-led applications and data monitoring to help make cities more efficient, as situated within this category (see, for example, the work of Townsend, 2013).

Alongside this, there has also emerged a literature that has been termed 'urban trumphalism', again reflecting the focus on the urban age in popular non-fiction (Brenner and Schmid, 2015). In this stream of literature, cities are seen as providing exciting possibilities for creative and economic potential through continued urbanisation – see, for example, Glaeser's (2011) *Triumph of the City*, Sanders' (2012) *Arrival City* and Hollis' (2013) *Cities are Good for You*.

Since the 1980s, we have seen a growing body of work that focuses on urban sustainability. Here, cities are viewed as centres for growing environmental and socioeconomic action to counteract the growing threats of climate change, resource depletion and environmental impact (see, for example, Giradet, 2004; Whitehead, 2011; Hodson and Marvin, 2014). The origins of this stream of literature can be seen in the collision of the urban and ecological crises during the 1970s and 1980s (Whitehead, 2011).

Finally, although not directly part of Brenner and Schmid's (2015) critique, there have been several other recent books that have sought to examine what broadly might be termed 'urban futures', including Batty's (2018) *Inventing Future Cities*. This group also includes the development and history of visual future 'urban imaginaries', such as: Marshall's (2016) *Ecotopia 2021*; Dobraszczyk's (2019) *Future Cities: Architecture and the imagination*; and Dunn and Cureton's (2020) *Future Cities: A visual history and critical guide to how we will live next*. Other books, such as Brook's (2013) *A History of Future Cities* and Williams' (2019) *Why Cities Look the Way They Do*, examine the processes of how and why cities have evolved, looking in detail at their history and the complexity of the way they change over time.

This broad description of the changing narratives of cities is not designed to be exhaustive but, rather, is intended at the outset to summarise the main themes that have emerged in relatively recent and relevant literature. The discussion helps situate this book in the context of these different narratives. Although positioned within the theme of urban futures (or more broadly, thinking about future cities), therefore, the book also complements a 'science of cities' narrative by focusing on the practical ways in which we can develop city visions and help establish a sound basis for a more participatory form of futures-based urban planning (Freestone, 2012; Dixon et al, 2018a).

We see a formal vision for an individual (and real-world) city as a shared call to arms and not a generic thought experiment, because it can help mobilise resources and provide us with a roadmap to the long-term future of that city (McPhearson et al, 2016). We acknowledge that within the contested concept of an 'urban age', it is important not only to recognise the real differences and distinctions between cities, but also to acknowledge that the city scale (and city-region scale) offers us real opportunities to tackle the complex urban challenges that we face now and in the future.

The importance of cities in the Anthropocene: planning for their long-term future(s)

The normalisation and widespread acceptance (despite the criticism referred to earlier) of the concept of an 'urban age' also fits with the broader term, 'Anthropocene'. It is now recognised by many commentators that what is termed the 'Anthropocene' represents a new epoch in which humankind plays a dominant role in reshaping the geological dynamics of the earth (Crutzen, 2002; Steffen et al, 2015; Pereira et al, 2018). More recently, the term has been broadened to represent an understanding that this brings with it a diverse range of new challenges such as human-nature tensions, increasing inequalities, the degradation of the natural world, climate change and planetary tipping points (Barnosky et al, 2012; McPhearson et al, 2016). In contrast, it can be argued that, through technological change and better understanding of systemic relationships and risks, this new epoch also offers opportunities to tackle the big challenges we face (Pereira et al, 2018).

In the Anthropocene, urbanisation is a key challenge for humankind because cities and their associated processes impact drastically on the natural world as well as human life (Elmqvist et al, 2018; Wolfram et al, 2019) and, therefore, they have important implications for sustainable development in urban policy and practice. In this sense, sustainable development represents (Brundtland Commission, 1987: 27):

> development that meets the needs of the present without compromising the ability of future generations to meet their own needs. It contains within it two key concepts:
> - The concept of needs, in particular the essential needs of the world's poor, to which overriding priority should be given.
> - The idea of limitations imposed by the state of technology and social organisation on the environment's ability to meet present and future needs.

Many present-day issues and problems, relating to urban sustainability (and sustainable cities), can be viewed through the lens of the triple bottom-line approach, which views the concept in terms of social, economic and environmental sustainability, underpinned by appropriate governance structures (Elkington, 1997). Cities matter not only because of their sustainability impacts but also because they perform four fundamental functions (Knox, 2014). That is, they:

- are centres of decision-making and political and economic power;
- act as centres of transformative capacity because of their size, density and diversity of population;
- can act as mobilisation hubs for labour, capital and raw materials; and
- can act as centres of knowledge, information and innovation exchange.

Just as many of the global sustainability challenges that we face – such as biodiversity decline, climate change, energy supply and environmental justice – are persistent, complex and 'wicked', they are also 'urban scale' problems (Grimm et al, 2008; Wolfram et al, 2019). In other words, wicked problems (for example, the environmental challenges of rapid urbanisation) are those that are difficult or impossible to solve because of incomplete, contradictory and changing requirements that are often difficult to recognise (Rittel and Weber, 1973). This is not surprising given that, already, a majority of the world's population live in cities, and that they consume 75 per cent of global resources, more than two-thirds of energy and are responsible for more than 70 per cent of global greenhouse gas emissions (IEA, 2008). This has led to calls for global-level sustainability 'transformations' in academic work, and allied calls for action in science policy and practice: Wolfram et al (2019), for example, lists the UN 2030 Agenda, the New Urban Agenda and other city-based initiatives such as the C40, 100 Resilient Cities and Covenant of Mayors initiatives, all of which focus on what might broadly be described as 'urban sustainability transformations'. The concept of 'urban transformative capacity' (or the ability to transform cities) also invites us to think about how we can disrupt and adjust current pathways (or 'business as usual') by radically altering structures, cultures and practices (Frantzeskaki et al, 2018; Wolfram et al, 2019). More formally, Wolfram (2016) defines urban transformative capacity as the ability of an urban system (including its physical and human dimensions) to reconfigure and move towards a new and more sustainable state.

This invites the question, if we want to transform our cities and provide a route to a more sustainable future, how can we transition and transform them through urban planning? This question, however, presupposes that, first, we can plan effectively for the long term (and that planning actually works in practice) and, second, that we have some sense of what the long-term future(s) might be, so that we can plan for them.

This, then, is a distinguishing feature of our thinking from Batty (2018): although we acknowledge that the precise nature of our generic urban future may be unknowable (and not predictable in detail), we believe that it is crucial that city stakeholders work in partnership to develop city visions (or shared and desirable expectations of the future) that can act, for example, as the basis for urban sustainability transformations in individual cities. There is a sense in which we agree with the maxim that "the best way to predict the future is to create it".³ For example, by co-creating a specific long-term vision for a city that brings people, government, business and universities in that city together, there is a much better chance that we will be able to mobilise action to tackle the enormous environmental and socioeconomic challenges that we will face in the future.

In turn, this means thinking objectively about the future as a whole, and trying to manage and plan for the long-term future. Urban planning in cities to provide strategic and regulatory direction has traditionally taken one of two routes: planning as a visionary exercise for societal change; and planning as a regulatory and technocratic process (Davoudi, 2001; Wolfram, 2018). As Wolfram (2018: 104) suggests: 'While the former tends to conceive of integrated spatial images for urban futures, explicitly incorporating ideologies and norms, as well as independent and radical thought, the latter is more concerned with practical and specialised solutions for managing urban change through professionalisation and institutionalisation.'

There is also a sense in which longer-term visions might provide the basis for disrupting existing practices and cultures, while regulatory modes might, in the short term, continue to protect existing structures and practices and therefore inhibit change (Wolfram, 2018). Moreover, it is true that the dominant form of planning in most jurisdictions stops well short of 'strategic future oriented activity' (Freestone, 2012: 13). This reflects a number of factors in the context of urban planning, including:

- a common focus on relatively short urban planning horizons;
- a perception that long-term thinking is inherently complex and a luxury in rapidly changing times;

- the relatively short-term nature of electoral cycles; and
- the degree of 'comfort' gained from thinking about the everyday.
(Bai et al, 2010a; Freestone, 2012; Swain, 2016)

In the context of urban planning, the idea of 'city visioning' (or having a clear and formal sense of where a particular city wants to be in the long-term future) emerged during the 1980s and 1990s, particularly in the United States, not only as a way of understanding the future, but also to plan for a desirable, or preferred, set of sustainable outcomes (see, for example, Atlanta and Portland) (McCann, 2001; Myers and Kitsuse, 2000; Gaffikin and Sterrett, 2006; Dixon et al, 2018a). Newman and Jennings (2008) highlight successful examples of city visions in Perth, Vancouver and Chicago during this period. This emergence of thinking about the future of cities reflected a growing body of literature focusing on visioning sustainability in a range of other contexts, such as energy futures (Wiek and Iwaniec, 2014). Since the early 2000s, we have also seen the development of more formal visioning processes (or what might be termed 'city foresight' methods) in cities and urban areas, which have been used to develop city visions – see, for example, Phoenix, Johannesburg and Vancouver (Newman and Jennings, 2008; Iwaniec and Wiek, 2014), or, in the UK, Reading (Dixon et al, 2018a) and Newcastle (Tewdwr-Jones et al, 2015).

In this respect, the field of foresight studies opens up a second front for helping us understand and plan for a variety of possible futures in our cities by creating and implementing city visions (Ravetz, 2020). In the context of studying the future, the *Oxford English Dictionary* defines 'foresight' as 'the ability to predict what will happen or be needed in the future'. For Loveridge (2009: 12), foresight is 'essentially practical and qualitative anticipation'. The European Commission (2001: v) describes foresight as 'a systematic, participatory, future-intelligence-gathering and medium-to-long-term vision-building process aimed at enabling present-day decisions and mobilising joint actions'.

Foresight is part of what might be termed 'futures studies', with the emphasis on multiple futures (Gidley, 2017a). As Gidley (2017a: 136) suggests: 'Future studies is the art and science of taking responsibility for the long-term consequences of our decisions and actions today.' Essentially, as Gidley argues, there is no single predictable future based on modelling trends from the past; instead, we need to be able to imagine alternative futures and work towards those that we prefer. This can involve participatory foresight techniques to develop a vision for a city, using such tools as horizon scanning, backcasting, scenarios and roadmapping (Eames et al, 2013, 2018; Candy et al, 2017). In this way, we can create 'transformative spaces' and open up 'possibility spaces' through facilitated processes with a range of stakeholders to underpin transformative change in our cities (Eames et al, 2018; Pereira et al, 2018).

As an example of this thinking in an urban context, the emergence of the UK Government Office for Science (GOfS) Future of Cities Programme (2013–16) highlighted the importance of 'city foresight', which was founded on the science of thinking about the future of cities, and which can be used to enable city stakeholders to explore urban futures not only in a local and regional context, but also as part of a wider connected network of cities (Cowie et al, 2016; GOfS, 2016a, 2016b, 2016c). A number of UK city visions were created as part of this programme, resulting from partnerships between academia, local authorities, business and civil society (the combination of which form the basis of the 'quadruple helix' model of innovation) (Arnkil et al, 2011; Goddard and Tewdwr-Jones, 2016). Some of these visions have also linked with and underpinned the existing statutory local plans in cities (see, for example, Dixon et al, 2018a).

This concept of 'futures-based urban planning' links closely with the emergence of what is broadly termed 'transitions theory'. Proponents of transitions theory suggest that it can help us understand the complex changes or shifts needed to move societies to more sustainable modes of production and consumption in such areas as transport, energy, housing, agriculture and food (see, for example, Coenen et al, 2011) Transitions theory recognises the importance of persistent, 'wicked' problems in society (for example, energy shortages and food production), or in spatial areas (for example, regions, cities or large-scale development areas), that can only be resolved through a major restructuring of existing systems (Rotmans et al, 2001). A transition is a radical, structural change of a societal subsystem that is the result of a co-evolution of economic, cultural, technological, ecological and institutional developments at different scale levels (Eames et al, 2013; Twomey and Gaziulusoy, 2014, Dixon, 2018a). Transitions theory postulates that successful systems (or sociotechnical regimes) comprising networks of artefacts, actors and institutions become stabilised over time through various processes that can promote lock-in and path dependency (for example, sunk investments in skills, capital equipment and infrastructures, vested interests, organisational capital, shared belief systems, legal frameworks, consumer norms and lifestyles). In this conceptual framework, which also includes a multi-level perspective (MLP), lock-in to existing systems can, however, be overcome and transitions occur as a result of experimentation and the emergence of new sociotechnical configurations (or innovations) (Geels, 2010). The MLP therefore provides a framework for understanding how systemic change can be brought about within society through complex multi-scale sociotechnical pathways for innovations – for example, the idea of interacting alignments between landscape (the overall societal setting within which the innovation occurs), regime (or the dominant culture, structure and practices in place) and niche (where radical innovation and experimentation happens) (Rip and Kemp, 1998; Geels, 2010). Although at a city level it can be difficult to apply the MLP because of complex overlapping regimes across different scales (Naess and Vogel, 2012; Eames et al, 2013), transitions theory can offer a theoretical perspective to understand what needs to be in place to plan and manage an effective urban transition or transformation.

Transitions theory also recognises cities as being complex adaptive systems, which means they have the capacity to change and learn from experience (Crawford, 2016). Based on the conceptual model of the fourth Dutch Environmental Policy Plan, transition management has emerged as a way of deliberately attempting to stimulate transition to a more sustainable future through managing urban processes against agreed societal goals (Eames et al, 2013). For Kemp and Loorbach (2006), the main elements of the process are:

- systems thinking across multiple domains, actors and scales;
- long-term thinking as a frame for short-term policy;
- the use of backcasting and forecasting;
- a focus on learning and experimentation in relation to a variety of options; and
- stakeholder participation and interaction.

Despite the inherent complexity of cities, proponents of transitions theory and transition management argue that urban transition management, which places a strong focus on visioning, developing partnerships and mobilising stakeholders in a participatory way, can provide the opportunity to develop processes that can help planners and decision-makers with what is required to move our cities to a more sustainable future (Rotmans, 2005; Kemp and Loorbach, 2006; Roorda et al, 2014; Frantzeskaki et al, 2018; Wolfram, 2018). This carries resonance with the concept of 'urban transformative capacity', referred to earlier.

Conceptual framework for the book and key themes

In this book, we begin from the standpoint that we are interested in exploring urban futures or, what Moir et al (2014a) term, 'future cities' and what GOfS (2016a) calls the 'future of cities'. Building on this previous work, we define urban futures as follows:

> 'Urban futures' is a term used to imagine what cities and urban areas will be like in the long term, how they will operate, what infrastructure and governance systems will underpin and coordinate them, and how they are best shaped and influenced by their primary stakeholders (civil society, governments, businesses and investors, academia and others). Urban futures thinking should be analytical, investigative, diagnostic and participatory in its ambition by exploring the future through city foresight techniques, including city visioning.

We see city visioning as the formal process (using city foresight techniques) of creating a city vision, or a shared and desirable future for a particular city or urban area. However, in practice, the city vision can either relate to a single preferred urban future, or explore a variety of different and alternative urban futures. City foresight is the 'science of thinking about the future of cities' (GOfS, 2016a). We also recognise that cities have an inherent complexity and that this provides the starting point for how we bring together city foresight and transitions theory to better understand cities, and to actively plan and create visions for them. This inter-relationship is shown in Figure 1.1. In this book, we primarily focus on city foresight and transitions theory, but we acknowledge the important role played by the science of cities in our understanding of cities.

In the book, we explore four main themes:

- **Cities and complex cross-cutting and integrated urban challenges.** A key premise of the book is that, before we examine urban futures, we need to understand what a city is and what different understandings of a city might be. We explore how cities may be formally defined (spatially and temporally, for example), and what cities represent in terms of their inherent characteristics. Is a city a process or a set of processes, or an object, or a system? Cities also present us with a range of important and complex challenges, which we will explore and examine in terms of their nature and

Figure 1.1: Conceptual framework

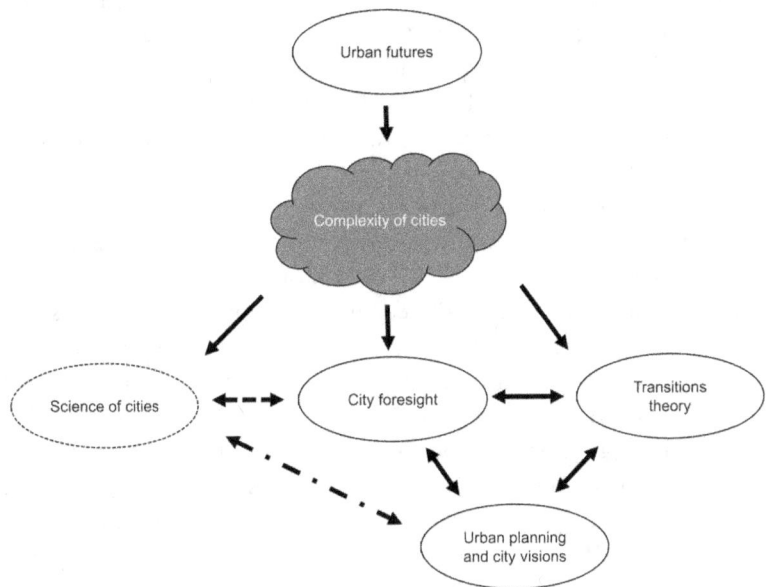

the extent to which they interlink and cross-cut the city and city-region scale and beyond. This is mainly explored and discussed in Chapter 2.
- **Changing narratives of the city.** As we have seen, there is a plethora of literature that has looked at cities through different lenses throughout history. We will explore and analyse the changing narratives and trends, drawing on literature, film (and related art), culture and academic thinking, to see how the development of urban futures and city visions can be traced from its earliest origins to the present day. We will also critically examine the recent academic discourse, drawing on relevant literature and research on eco-cities, green cities, sustainable cities and smart cities. These subthemes are explored in Chapters 3 and 5.
- **City foresight, transitions theory and city visions.** We focus closely on city foresight, or the science of thinking about the future of cities. To do this, we also draw on transitions theory (and transition management) to highlight how important city visions are for the long-term planning of our cities, using previous academic literature and our own recent work on urban futures. We focus on previous examples of city visions from around the world, and how they have been developed and shaped. These examples from the

developed world and the developing world (and global north and global south) are critically reviewed, and the ensuing lessons of good practice are identified. Finally, we explore the emergence of urban innovation and urban experiments, founded on the concept of the 'quadruple helix', which brings key stakeholder groups in a city together. These interlinked subthemes are explored in Chapters 6, 7, 8 and 9.

- **Urban planning and urban governance.** We examine the evolution of urban planning and its response to the sustainability challenges and explore how city visioning can help develop a stronger focus for futures-based urban planning in our cities and urban areas. The links between urban planning and city foresight are explored and the implications of city visioning and long-term strategic planning in cities are highlighted. We focus on exploring the changing role that city visioning and urban foresight play within the future planning and governance of cities, and how place-based leadership can supplement existing governance arrangements. To do this, we draw on good practice, but we also offer a critique of current thinking. This is covered in Chapters 4 and 10.

Finally, in Chapter 11 ('Facing the urban future to 2050 and beyond'), we provide conclusions by refocusing on the policy and practice implications of the main themes emerging from the book, and bring together the lessons learned from the application of the book's conceptual framework to city foresight and transitions theory.

2

Cities and integrated urban challenges

> What is the city but the people?
> William Shakespeare, *Coriolanus*

Introduction

Although Shakespeare seems to focus on the people in a city, Jane Jacobs emphasised the city's overall complexity (Jacobs, 1961: 376): 'No single element in a city is, in truth, the kingpin or the key. The mixture itself is kingpin, and its mutual support is the order'. But both of these quotations invite us to think about the city in different ways: not only as a place influenced and shaped by people and the myriad of relationships and networks they have, but also as a complex system of different but interlinked elements. Both in their different ways implicitly and explicitly acknowledge the complex nature of cities. However, the quotations also invite us to reflect on what we mean by the term 'city'. This is important when we consider that many commentators write about an 'urban age' (Brenner and Schmid, 2014); but what do we really mean when we talk about a city?

In this chapter, we will first explore how cities may be formally defined (spatially and temporally, for example), and what cities represent in terms of their inherent characteristics. Is a city a process or a set of processes, for example, or an object, or a system? Answering these questions is vital if we are to understand how we can move to a more sustainable future. In doing this, we will also explore what is meant by urbanisation, and how past, present and future urban growth has shaped, and will shape, our towns and cities globally, and closer to home in the UK. For example, will London continue to dominate the city landscape in the UK as the national population continues to expand?

The 'urban paradox' of the parallel benefits and challenges of living in cities also raises important questions. Although cities can act as economic engines for growth and attractors for skilled workers, what are the important environmental, social and economic impacts of urban living in an urban age? Moreover, should these challenges be treated in an isolated or an integrated way? We will explore and examine the overall nature and characteristics of these challenges, and the extent to which they interlink and cross-cut the city and city-region scale and beyond. This will require new ways of thinking and planning for the future, and what we term 'city visioning' will be an important part of this process. Finally, we will examine how urban policy and practice have responded and need to evolve to meet these different challenges.

What is a city?

Defining what we mean by the term 'city' is vital if we are to tackle our present and future urban challenges. With its origins in the Latin word, '*civitas*' (meaning citizenship or membership of a community), 'city' can convey different meanings in different contexts. This is problematic given, for example, the recent focus on the Sustainable Development Goals of the United Nations (UN) (UN, 2019), because to monitor progress in achieving environmental and socioeconomic targets at the city level, and compare cities across international boundaries, requires a consistent definition of what constitutes a city.

In one respect, cities could be viewed as objects or entities, or at least as a composition of their most representative characteristics. As Smith and Lobo (2019) note, in his book *Triumph of the City*, the urban economist Ed Glaeser (2011: 6) defines cities as 'the absence of physical space between people and companies. They are proximity, density, closeness.' Although this does have the attraction of simplicity and applicability to many cities past and present, it is, however, not always true that high density is always present in cities (Smith and Lobo, 2019). Moreover, while most people would agree that cities are places where large numbers of people live and work, and form hubs of government, commerce and transportation, the geographical limits of a city are often open to debate (UN, 2018a).

When we use the term 'city' today, this might refer to the spatial form or administrative boundaries of an urban area (for example, a functional approach), or the looser, multidimensional characteristic of urban living, including ecological, cultural, technological, spiritual and socioeconomic elements and interactions (for example, a sociological/demographic approach) (Dixon et al, 2014a; Smith and Lobo, 2019). An example of the former might be the city 'proper', defined by its administrative boundary (UN, 2018c). An example of the latter is used by the sociologist Louis Wirth (1938: 8): 'For sociological purposes a city may be defined as a relatively large, dense, and permanent settlement of socially heterogeneous individuals.'

More recently, building on work by Cottineau et al (2017), Batty (2018) has also sought to define present-day cities in terms of three consistent and measurable criteria:

- density of population;
- the strength of interaction or dependency between geographic populations in the same space (for example, transport flows or commodity flows); and
- geographical proximity or contiguity, based on the units making up the city, whether these are individual people, households, neighbourhoods or districts.

For example, Cottineau et al's (2017) work suggested that density should be 2,000 people per square kilometre.

To add geographic structure to this process, two additional criteria can be used: the minimum size of unit for a city; and the extent of the urban area's administrative boundary, if present. In the United States, for example, the Census Bureau adopts a minimum size of 10,000 people for a 'micropolitan' area and 50,000 people for a 'metropolitan' area, which is similar to the People's Republic of China's definition (Batty, 2018). The UN (2018c) refers to three types of boundary-based definitions:

- the *city proper* (based on the administrative boundary);
- the *urban agglomeration*, based on the contiguous urban areas or built-up areas; and
- the *metropolitan area*, which defines the boundaries of the city according to the degree of economic and social interconnectedness of nearby areas (for example, through commerce and commuting).

The term 'metropolitan area' is also broadly equivalent to the notion of a city-region, defined by Marvin et al (2006: 13) as 'a central urban area, or two or more closely inter-linked urban centres, together with those areas that surround them with which they have significant interaction'.

As an example of how the differences in bounding a city can affect population, in Toronto, Canada, the city proper population was 2.6 million in 2011, but the urban agglomeration was 5.1 million and the metropolitan area population was 5.6 million (UN, 2018c). Similarly, rates of growth differed depending on area: the population within Toronto's city proper grew at an average annual rate of 0.9 per cent, compared with 1.5 per cent for the urban agglomeration and 1.8 per cent for the metropolitan area. It is also worth noting that 'city proper' definitions may underplay the real environmental and socioeconomic impacts of the wider urban area. Therefore, many cities are 'under-bounded', which means their wider impacts, such as carbon footprint, do not map onto the limited administrative boundary (see Dixon et al, 2018a, for example).

Other territorial definitions of the city include the Organisation for Economic Co-operation and Development's (OECD's) 'functional urban area', which consists of a city and its commuting zone. Functional urban areas therefore consist of a densely inhabited city and a less densely populated commuting zone, whose labour market is highly integrated with the city (Dijkstra et al, 2019). In the UK Census (2011), urban areas are currently defined as the connected built-up areas identified by Ordnance Survey mapping that have resident populations above 10,000 people. In contrast, rural areas are those areas that are not urban, that is, consisting of settlements below 10,000 people or open countryside (ONS, 2017). 'Primary urban areas' are sometimes also used to define cities in the UK. The Centre for Cities, for example, an independent think-tank focusing on the UK's 63 largest towns and cities, has defined primary urban areas in its work. It uses data for primary urban areas in its analysis – a measure of the 'built-up' area of a city (that is, the contiguous built-up area of a settlement, where buildings are less than 200 metres apart) – rather than individual local authority districts. This is because they can provide a consistent measure to compare concentrations of economic activity across the UK. This makes them distinct from city-region or combined authority geographies (Centre for Cities, 2019). As the Centre for Cities states (2015: 1):

> A city is the concentration of a large amount of economic activity in a relatively small area. The best performing cities make the most of this density so that the value of what they produce is greater than the value of the inputs (workers, land etc.) that they use to produce it. This process is known as agglomeration.

Although cities may be viewed in this way as entities or objects, cities can also be seen as systems or even as a collection of processes. Indeed, as formal definitions of a city vary between and even within countries, so the metaphorical perspectives of cities have changed and evolved over time. As we saw in Chapter 1, a primary focus in recent years has seen cities as complex systems. Varzi (2019) makes the interesting point that, in fact, since the work of Weber (1921) comparing cities to bazaars, there has been a wealth of work using complex system metaphors. These include: river networks; beehives and insect colonies; stars and galaxies; and machines, fractals, cellular automata and brains. Other perspectives have included the 'city as an ecosystem', and the 'city as a living organism', the health and growth of which depend on their internal organisation as well as the external environment (Geddes, 1915; Jacobs, 1961).

In a philosophical sense, for Varzi (2019), a city is best understood as a collection of processes. As Quine (1950: 210) suggests:

> [A] physical thing … is at any one moment a sum of simultaneously momentary states of spatially scattered atoms or other small physical constituents. Now just as the thing in a moment is a sum of these spatially small parts, so we may think of a thing over a period as a sum of the temporally small parts which are its successive momentary states. Combining these conceptions, we see the thing as extended in time and in space alike.

Varzi therefore argues that cities can be thought of in the same way as a river: they are not enduring objects, but rather a collection of processes that extend in time and in space, meaning that we can walk through a river or a city more than once but experience very different spatiotemporal elements on each occasion.

In contrast, authors such Graham and Marvin (2001) and Hillier (2009) see cities in terms of sociotechnical processes, that is: a physical subsystem, made up of buildings linked by streets, roads and infrastructure; and a human subsystem, made up of movement, interaction and activity. This emphasis on processes within complex systems is also part of the wider understanding that the multi-level perspective (MLP) can potentially bring to city-scale thinking (Hodson and Marvin, 2010), although partly as a result of its disciplinary focus, it is very different in emphasis from Varzi's (2019) conceptualisation of the city.

Ultimately, therefore, much needs to be done to establish a consistent definition of a city for the purpose of international comparison. In a recent survey (UN, 2018d), 104 countries used a single criterion, such as: administrative function (59 countries); population size/density (37 countries); or urban characteristics (eight countries). In 12 cases, there was no definition or an unclear definition of what constitutes an urban environment and in 12 cases the entire population of the country was considered as being urban.

Urbanisation – the past, the present and future trends

For many years, population size, density and heterogeneity have been recognised as key characteristics of urban areas (Smith and Lobo, 2019). For Wirth (1938), size often produced segregation, indifference and social distance for citizens; density caused people to interact in terms of their functional roles, and heterogeneity meant that people participated in different social circles, all of which produced distinct urban lives, differing from the rural context. The concept of 'heterogeneity' and the myriad of social interactions this induces in a city is seen as making urban life distinct, and leading to creative, inventive and innovative possibilities, or a kind of 'energised crowding' through proximity and face-to-face contact (Jacobs, 1961; Kostof, 1991; Storper and Venables, 2004; Smith and Lobo, 2019).

Whatever the true nature of this urban/rural distinction, and there has been much evidence to show that the picture is more nuanced and complex (Urry et al, 2014), it is fair to say that the origins of the world's first cities 4,000 years ago were based on the concept of bringing people together for markets and trade (Knox, 2014; Clark, 2016). Later, other 'foundational' cities, such as Athens, Alexandria and Rome, emerged through a combination of the establishment of extensive trade routes, the establishment of new markets, the thirst for innovation and influence, and emerging geopolitical opportunities (Leontidou and Martinotti, 2014; Clark, 2016). Indeed, a similar combination of forces drove the emergence of medieval and early modern cities, culminating in the industrial revolution of the late 18th century.

Widespread urban living, however, is a relatively recent development. The rapid urbanisation of the 20th and 21st centuries has been complex and transformative, converting rural settlements into cities and shifting the population from the former to the latter, with consequent impacts on demographic and social structures in both areas (UN, 2018e). As we saw in Chapter 1, a large majority of global GDP is also created in cities, making them vital engines or hubs for innovation and economic growth, and is partly influenced and shaped by spatial and urban planning and public and private investments in buildings and infrastructure. The degree or level of urbanisation is therefore typically expressed as the percentage of the population living in urban areas, defined according to the differing criteria used by national governments for distinguishing between urban and rural areas. In practice, therefore, urbanisation 'refers both to the increase in the percentage of population residing in urban areas and to the associated growth in the number of urban dwellers, in the size of cities and in the total area occupied by urban settlements' (UN, 2018e: 10).

In fact, therefore, for many centuries, most people lived in low-density rural areas: for example, before 1600 it is estimated that only 5 per cent of the world's population lived in cities, and by 1800 this had grown to 7 per cent and by 1900, 16 per cent (Ritchie and Roser, 2018). Most of the rapid urban growth occurred during the 20th century, and this continues today. Today, according to UN statistics (UN, 2018e), 55 per cent of people live in urban areas, and this is set to grow to 68 per cent by 2050 (see Figure 2.1). Asia, despite its relatively lower level of urbanisation, is home to 54 per cent of the world's urban population, followed by Europe and Africa with 13 per cent each. Today, the most urbanised regions include North America (with 82 per cent of its population living in urban areas in 2018), Latin America and the Caribbean (81 per cent), Europe (74 per cent) and Oceania (68 per cent). The level of urbanisation in Asia is now approximating 50 per cent. In contrast, Africa remains mostly rural, with 43 per cent of its population living in urban areas (UN, 2018e). However, some cities have also experienced stagnation and decline over recent years, particularly in low-fertility countries in Asia and Europe (for example, Japan, the Republic of Korea and Ukraine).

Figure 2.1: Urban and rural populations of the world (1950–2050)

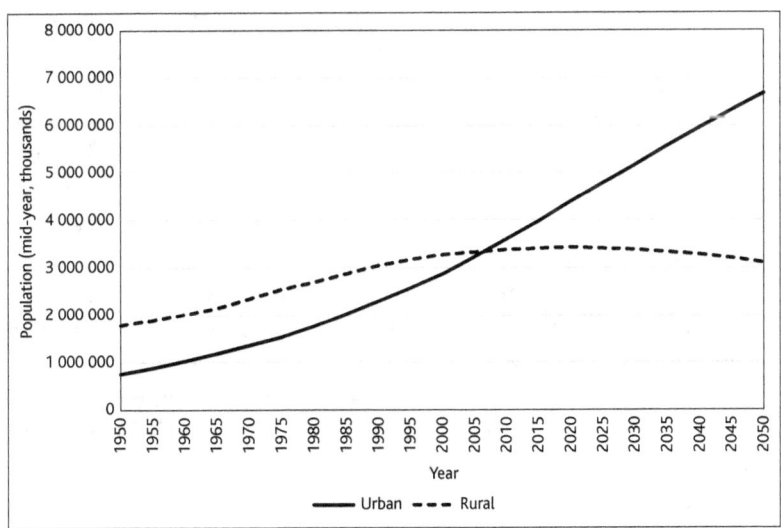

Source: UN (2018e)

According to UN projections, *all* the projected world population growth during 2018–2050 is expected to be in urban areas. During this period, the urban population is expected to rise by 2.5 billion, from 4.2 billion to 6.7 billion, while the total world population is projected to grow by a little less: that is, 2.2 billion, from 7.6 billion in 2018 to 9.8 billion in 2050. This urban growth is the consequence of natural increases in population, migration to cities and the reclassification of urban areas (UN, 2018e). It is notable that China has the largest urban population (837 million), followed by India (461 million), and that these two countries account for 30 per cent of the world's urban population (UN, 2018e). China, India and Nigeria are also expected to account for 35 per cent of the world's urban population between 2018 and 2050.

According to the UN (2018e), by 2030 the world will have 43 megacities (with more than 10 million inhabitants), most of them in developing regions. However, some of the fastest-growing urban agglomerations are smaller cities with fewer than a million inhabitants, many of them located in Asia and Africa. While one in eight people live in 33 megacities worldwide, close to half of the world's urban dwellers reside in much smaller urban areas with fewer than 500,000 inhabitants.

Much of the momentum for the urbanisation phenomenon in Europe and North America has been driven by economic development: in the last two centuries, people moved to cities for education and employment opportunities especially in the industry and services sectors. The end result, however, is not always benign. Since the 1980s, many UK cities have experienced deindustrialisation, as the service sector grew in place of manufacturing, and this led to inner-city deprivation with often rapid population decline, for example, in Merseyside and many traditional coal-mining, steel-making and textile-based towns and cities (Urry et al, 2014). This has been overlaid in the UK by two spatial forces that have also impacted on the performance of UK cities – a north–south drift and an urban–rural shift – although their effect has been dependent on fluctuating business cycles in the economy and the level of growth of service sector jobs in cities (Champion, 2014).

Of course, in contrast to many other countries, the UK has been a heavily urbanised country for many years: data from the UN shows that the country was 79 per cent urban in 1950 (according to the UN definition of 'urban area') and will be 90 per cent urban by 2050 (UN, 2018e). By other measures, despite covering just 9 per cent of land, the top 64 UK urban areas (as measured by primary urban area) account for 54 per cent of the population, 63 per cent of economic output and 71 per cent of knowledge services jobs (Centre for Cities, 2019).

This concentration of the UK economy in particular cities occurs because of the benefits they provide, including access to workers and proximity to other businesses, and because of their scale, they are able to support a diversity of specialisms and a wide range of services. The UK urbanisation rate is also the consequence of a longstanding planning strategy of urban containment to prevent urban sprawl (Hall et al, 1973).

However, Table 2.1 shows a picture of decline for many large UK cities during the 1980s and 1990s, although this decline was reversed after the 1990s, as cities began to grow, with London, in particular, growing strongly (11.5 per cent overall from 2001 to 2011). Certainly, deindustrialisation and the other factors referred to earlier were important in explaining the previous decline and this was underpinned by a rapid expansion in post-war car ownership, which lowered transport costs, and the UK's post-war new towns policy.

Since the 1990s, however, the agglomeration or clustering effects of city centres have attracted workers back into UK cities. London continues to dominate the UK in terms of influence and economic growth, leading to concerns about the future of other towns and cities such as Birmingham, Liverpool, Manchester and Sheffield (Centre for Cities, 2019). As Figure 2.2 shows, the strongest future population growth will be in London and large cities in Britain. London's growth seems likely to be driven by migration, although it is possible that other larger cities may catch up in terms of population growth (NIC, 2016).

Table 2.1: Overall population growth in the largest 10 UK cities (1981–2014)

City	Population 2014	Growth rate (%)				
		1981–91	1991–2001	2001–11	2011–14	1981–2014
London	9,752,000	0.3%	6.9%	11.5%	3.9%	24%
Birmingham	2,471,000	-2.1%	-2.1%	7.0%	2.0%	5%
Manchester	2,412,000	-2.7%	-1.5%	6.9%	1.9%	4%
Glasgow	973,000	-8.0%	-5.2%	1.5%	1.0%	-11%
Newcastle	842,000	-3.5%	-3.1%	3.3%	1.6%	-2%
Sheffield	824,000	-3.4%	-1.6%	6.3%	1.8%	3%
Leeds	766,000	-1.5%	1.3%	4.9%	2.1%	7%
Bristol	714,000	1.7%	3.5%	8.7%	3.3%	18%
Nottingham	656,000	1.7%	-1.1%	6.9%	2.5%	10%
Liverpool	620,000	-8.7%	-6.0%	3.1%	1.3%	-10%

Source: NIC (2016)

Figure 2.2: Projected population change 2011–36 for Great Britain, London and by settlement size

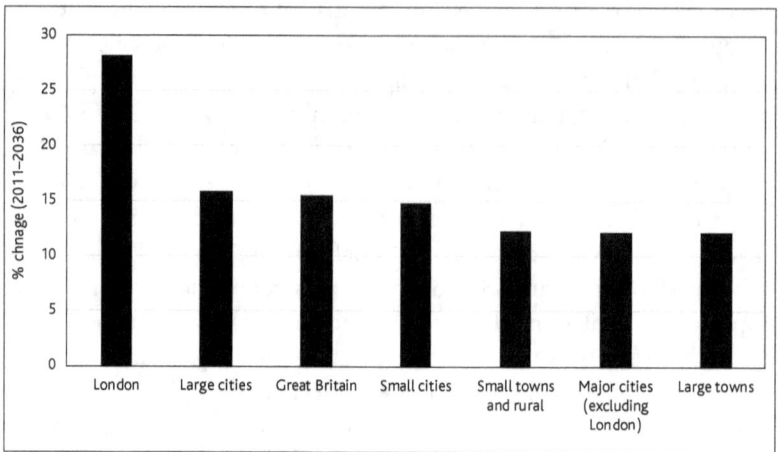

Source: Champion (2014)

Figure 2.3: Zipf's law for UK cities: log of city population against log of rank order

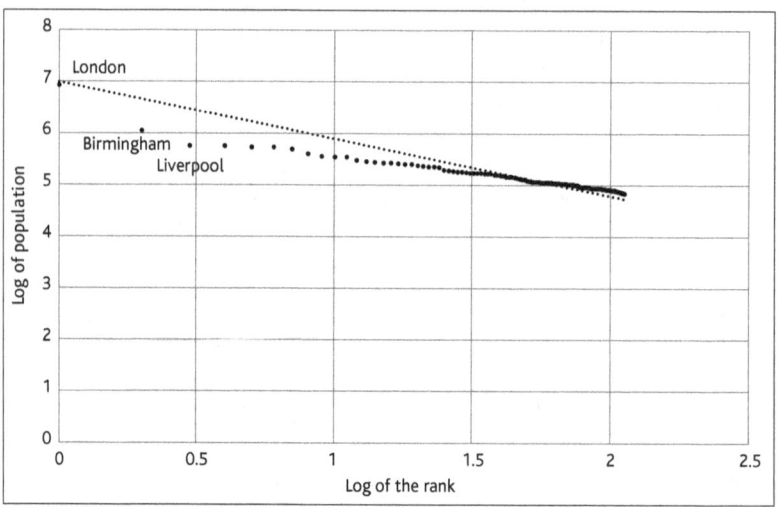

Source: ONS (2018)

The dominance of London is shown in Figure 2.3. Zipf's law is a statistical relationship, which is found to be broadly true between a city's size and its rank order by size in a particular country. Put simply, we would expect the second-largest city to be half the size of the largest, and the third-largest to be a third of the size of the largest, and so on. As Batty (2018) points out, this law holds true in many instances throughout the world, although in some countries there are exceptions. One of these is the UK where, as shown in Figure 2.3, London dominates, and many of the UK's larger cities are smaller than might be expected. Perhaps England's long history of political centralisation around London has re-enforced its dominance. Despite their scale, as the Centre for Cities (2019) suggests, many of the UK's biggest cities 'punch below their weight': for example, cities such as Birmingham, Liverpool, Manchester and Sheffield lag behind the national average on productivity and a range of other indicators.

It is also true that cities exist within interdependent regional, national and continental systems of cities, which impact on a city's specialisms, function and future growth (Moir et al, 2014b; GOfS, 2016b). At a national scale, systems of cities might be polycentric (organised around a number of political, social or financial centres) or dominated by a single city (Hall and Pain, 2006). A country's size, its economic development and infrastructure, and the underlying political and governance systems, all play their part in determining the shape and form of these systems. Therefore, although London dominates the systems of UK cities, it draws on a wider network of smaller towns and cities, including Milton Keynes, Oxford and Reading, and UK cities themselves are part of a wider global network of cities (GOfS, 2016b).

In an era of rapid urbanisation, the future of cities therefore matters globally for a number of reasons (GOfS, 2016b). First, cities will be where the majority of population and economic growth occurs, and this matters to policy-makers across scales. Second, there is now a good understanding of more than 150 years of urbanisation, especially in the developed world, and this has raised awareness of not wanting to repeat the mistakes of the past, with regard to over-specialisation, negative path dependency and infrastructure lock-in. Third, the growing awareness of climate change and environmental issues places a firm emphasis on cities to think about the long term and develop visions of the future. Fourth, cities are also appreciating the need to provide for transformative infrastructure, retrofit and renewal projects.

An urban paradox? Integrated challenges for cities

Paradoxically, although cities act as engines for economic growth and hubs of innovation (the 'urban advantage'), they also face a wide range of challenges, ranging from climate change and environmental degradation, to crime, traffic congestion, health problems and socioeconomic inequalities, giving rise to the term 'urban paradox'

(EU, 2016, Iossifova et al, 2018). This concept of the paradoxical nature of the parallel benefits and challenges to people who live in cities is fundamental to understanding the urban challenges that we face today, and in the future, and therefore calls for a more integrated approach to their assessment have been made (Dawson et al, 2014; GOfS, 2016b).

Moreover, cities themselves both have an impact on and create these challenges. For example, although urban areas form only 3 per cent of the world's land area (6 per cent in the UK) (University of Sheffield, 2017), they can have a significant impact on global warming through their effect on urban consumption, which has ramifications beyond their immediate geographic boundaries. For example, when products or services are purchased in a city, resource extraction, manufacturing and transportation have already generated emissions along every link of a global supply chain, and these consumption-based emissions add up to a total climate impact that is approximately 60 per cent higher than production-based emissions (C40 Cities, 2019). As the same research points out, to avoid climate breakdown, emissions from global urban consumption must halve by 2030, which means that emissions from consumption in high-income cities must decrease by two-thirds within the next decade. Similarly, fast-growing economies in the developing world will also need to adopt sustainable consumption patterns.

The current and future urban challenges that cities face globally in their own right were first formally identified in the 1976 UN Conference on Human Settlements in Vancouver, which established the Vancouver Declaration, urging countries to commit to human settlement policies to alleviate 'uncontrolled urbanisation' and led to the establishment of the UN Commission on Human Settlements in December 1977 (UN, 1976). Since then, further UN initiatives, such as Local Agenda 21 in 1992 and the Habitat II conference in 1996, have brought cities centre-stage, based on a broad principle of sustainable human settlements (UN-Habitat, 2016). Today, the UN-Habitat Urban Settlements Programme (UN-Habitat, 2016) identifies what it terms *persistent* challenges, such as urban growth and changing family structures, and *emerging* urban issues, such as climate change, exclusion, insecurity and migration (see Table 2.2). Many of these challenges are created by an unsustainable and uncontrolled urbanisation model: for example, environmentally low-density urbanisation, which is dependent on car ownership, is energy intensive and contributes to climate change. Socially, the urbanisation model creates inequalities, exclusion and deprivation and promotes gated communities and slums, often exacerbated by migration. Economically, urbanisation can also create widespread unemployment among young people and economic

Table 2.2: Examples of urban challenges

International urban challenges (source: UN-Habitat, 2016)	European urban challenges (source: EC, 2019)	UK urban challenges (source: GOfS, 2016b)
Persistent: Urban growth Change in family patterns Increased residency in slums and informal settlements Challenges in providing urban services *Emerging:* Climate change Exclusion and rising inequality Insecurity Upsurge in international migration	Affordable housing provision Mobility and environmental impacts Provision of services Ageing populations Urban health Social segregation Environmental footprint Climate action	Availability of data on city processes Changing demographics Ageing population Divergent economic performance High-skilled labour mobility and productivity Integrating systems to make cities liveable Managing risks to city environments and resource supply Increasing housing pressure Differential transport connectivity between cities Changing ideas about decision-making and accountability

hardship among the low paid, with unequal access to services and poor quality of life, including slum development (UN-Habitat, 2016).

At a European level, a number of similar urban challenges focusing on housing, mobility, public and commercial services, demographics, health and climate change have been identified (EC, 2019) (see Table 2.2). In the UK, the Future of Cities programme (Moir et al, 2014b; GOfS, 2016b) also identified important challenges, noting that a number of the challenges were diffuse in nature and would require whole-system approaches to city planning and governance.

It would be dangerous to see these urban challenges in isolation from each other, as the opportunities for assessing them in an integrated way would be lost. A purely sectoral approach can lead to fragmented thinking and failure in policy (Hunt and Watkiss, 2011; Dawson et al, 2014). Recently, there have been calls for a more integrated approach to urban challenges. Using Birmingham UK as an example, Leach et al (2019) argue for an 'urban diagnostics' approach to the identification of urban challenges. In their work, they used workshops and other research methods to identify four cross-cutting challenges (the 'critical challenges nexus'): connectivity, economy, energy, and health and wellbeing.

An example of a cross-cutting theme in this respect is health, where human decisions and choices are strongly affected by urban contexts and provide important public health challenges (GOfS, 2016b). For example, the design of cities through housing, green space and transport infrastructure can have an important effect on health and wellbeing. In cities where the fewest people exercise, there is twice the housing density and 20 per cent less green space than in cities with the most active population (RIBA, 2013).

However, the concept of 'integration' is used by different people in different ways (Kelly et al, 2013; Rode et al, 2017). The term can be used with reference to issues or challenges, but also with regard to stakeholders, for example in terms of stakeholder engagement with particular groups. The term can also be used in relation to integrating disciplines and working together on urban challenges in an academic or practice sense, or across scales (for example, building, neighbourhood, district or city and city-region) or in terms of combining particular models of urban systems, or institutional and policy processes (Healey, 2007).

This growing focus on urban challenges has been underpinned at an international level by a number of other important UN-led international agreements with a particular emphasis on sustainable development and climate change (Acuto et al, 2018). For example, the Sustainable Development Goals (SDGs), also known as the Global Goals, were adopted by all UN member states in 2015 as a universal call to action to end poverty, protect the planet and ensure that all people enjoy peace and prosperity by 2030 (UN, 2019). The 17 SDGs, which form part of the UN's Agenda 2030 and cover the period 2016–30, are integrated – that is, they recognise that action in one area will affect outcomes in others, and that development must balance social, economic and environmental sustainability. The goals, each of which have a number of targets and indicators, are as follows:

Goal 1: No poverty
Goal 2: Zero hunger
Goal 3: Good health and wellbeing
Goal 4: Quality education
Goal 5: Gender equality
Goal 6: Clean water and sanitation
Goal 7: Affordable and clean energy
Goal 8: Decent work and economic growth
Goal 9: Industry, innovation and infrastructure
Goal 10: Reduced inequality
Goal 11: Sustainable cities and communities
Goal 12: Responsible consumption and production

Goal 13: Climate action
Goal 14: Life below water
Goal 15: Life on land
Goal 16: Peace, justice and strong institutions
Goal 17: Partnerships for the goals.

Alongside these goals, the New Urban Agenda (NUA) was adopted by heads of government in 2016, and while the explicit links between the NUA and SDGs continue to remain relatively weak, their combined force is important in recognising the essential role of regional and local governments in achieving sustainable development (Valencia et al, 2019). As far as cities are concerned, Goal 11 of the SDGs is particularly important, with the ambition of making cities and human settlements inclusive, safe, resilient and sustainable (see Box 2.1).

Box 2.1: Sustainable cities and communities (SDG 11) targets

More than half of us live in cities. By 2050, two-thirds of all humanity – 6.5 billion people – will be urban. Sustainable development cannot be achieved without significantly transforming the way we build and manage our urban spaces.

The rapid growth of cities – a result of rising populations and increasing migration – has led to a boom in megacities, especially in the developing world, and slums are becoming a more significant feature of urban life.

Making cities sustainable means creating career and business opportunities, providing safe and affordable housing, and building resilient societies and economies. It involves investment in public transport, creating green public spaces and improving urban planning and management in participatory and inclusive ways. The following are targets under SDG11:

11.1 By 2030, ensure access for all to adequate, safe and affordable housing and basic services and upgrade slums.
11.2 By 2030, provide access to safe, affordable, accessible and sustainable transport systems for all, improving road safety, notably by expanding public transport, with special attention to the needs of those in vulnerable situations, women, children, persons with disabilities and older persons.
11.3 By 2030, enhance inclusive and sustainable urbanization and capacity for participatory, integrated and sustainable human settlement planning and management in all countries.

11.4　Strengthen efforts to protect and safeguard the world's cultural and natural heritage.

11.5　By 2030, significantly reduce the number of deaths and the number of people affected and substantially decrease the direct economic losses relative to global gross domestic product caused by disasters, including water-related disasters, with a focus on protecting the poor and people in vulnerable situations.

11.6　By 2030, reduce the adverse per capita environmental impact of cities, including by paying special attention to air quality and municipal and other waste management.

11.7　By 2030, provide universal access to safe, inclusive and accessible, green and public spaces, in particular for women and children, older persons and persons with disabilities.

11.A　Support positive economic, social and environmental links between urban, peri-urban and rural areas by strengthening national and regional development planning.

11.B　By 2020, substantially increase the number of cities and human settlements adopting and implementing integrated policies and plans towards inclusion, resource efficiency, mitigation and adaptation to climate change, resilience to disasters, and develop and implement, in line with the Sendai Framework for Disaster Risk Reduction 2015–2030, holistic disaster risk management at all levels.

11.C　Support least developed countries, including through financial and technical assistance, in building sustainable and resilient buildings utilizing local materials.

Source: UN (2019)

There has therefore been an increasing awareness of and growing focus on sustainable cities and urban sustainability. The concept of 'sustainable cities' and its links with sustainable development have been discussed since the early 1990s. As Sattherwaite (1992: 3) suggests, sustainable cities should meet their 'inhabitants' development needs without imposing unsustainable demands on local or global natural resources and systems'. Essentially, in working towards urban sustainability as an end goal, sustainable cities need to integrate social development, economic development, environmental management and urban governance in a coherent and integrated way (UN, 2013b). This agenda finds its roots in a number of the initiatives discussed earlier, including Agenda 21, but more recently, particularly in view of the dramatic impacts that climate change is having, resilience has also been a primary element in the urban agenda. For example, the Rockefeller Foundation (2020) describes urban resilience as the 'capacity of individuals, communities, institutions, businesses, and systems within a city to survive, adapt, and grow no matter what kinds of chronic stresses and acute shocks they experience'. This agility or ability to bounce back is a response to shocks or sudden events such as earthquakes, floods, pandemics and terrorist attacks.

Other city-based networks, such as the C40 Cities Climate Leadership Group, the ICLEI Local Governments for Sustainability network and the United Cities and Local Governments Group, have re-enforced the efforts made by cities and local authorities to respond to the emergent urban challenges (Acuto et al, 2018). For example, the C40 group includes 96 of the world's largest, most politically active cities, and is a network and platform designed to bring together the best policy and practice on climate change responses and low-carbon transitions in cities. The roles of cities, metropolitan areas and local governments have therefore strengthened since the 1990s, as the impacts of urbanisation and globalisation have grown at a local level. This has also posed increasing challenges for current urban governance and financing models as cities are required to become more resilient to environmental and socioeconomic shocks and impacts. On a practical level, although the regional challenges differ between developed and developing countries, a lack of long-term city visions, budget constraints, a lack of leadership and uncoordinated governance structures have often hampered attempts to take a more coordinated long-term approach to planning urban transformation (WEF, 2016).

However, in the UK, there has so far been little attempt at implementing and embedding the SDGs in national policy planning frameworks. Geraghty (2019) highlights the lack of progress, particularly in relation to the revised National Planning Policy Framework of 2019. In contrast to this void nationally, it is at city level that momentum has developed, spurred on by the recent spate of climate emergency declarations and zero-carbon targets in more than 300 English local councils (Bramah, 2019). For example, in Bristol, the Bristol SDG Alliance has been developed to discuss and review the implementation of SDGs in the local plan, and in York, the SDGs are very much at the heart of the city's One Planet vision for the future.

Individual cities responding to such forces for change is an emerging and growing trend and this highlights the individuality of response in the absence of concerted national actions. Indeed, there is no one-size-fits-all rule here. As Moir et al (2014b: 51) suggest, there is no single 'future of cities':

Cities of different sizes, in different locations, are facing unique and distinctive futures. The populations of various cities are shrinking, growing, becoming richer, poorer, older, younger, more spread out and more concentrated. Accordingly, they face different challenges in securing the liveability and economic development outcomes that our new urban age demands.

Despite this, there are several broad challenges that Moir et al (2014b) suggest all cities will face in the future:

- Growth and change challenges and the need to respond to changing global markets.
- Infrastructure challenges and the need to retrofit or create new systems.
- Environmental and social challenges, with a particular focus on climate change, urban sustainability and resilience.
- Governance deficits and challenges, as cities grow, and the need to evolve open and transparent systems that engage with people and operate across scales and tiers of government.
- Financial challenges and the ability of cities to be financially sustainable to address the key challenges.

Tackling these challenges will require strategic long-term planning, greater devolution of powers to the city and metropolitan level, building partnerships and coalitions, sharing ideas and building capacity. Developing and articulating clear and tangible city visions will be key to this (GOfS, 2016a).

Urban planning and practice

We have seen through this chapter that the story of cities is one of ebbs and flows. Cities as agglomerations of people and services have been a matter of fact for centuries, but equally so long as cities have existed there has been a need to attempt to deal with major externalities associated with change in cities, as they grow and contract. Rapid periods of urbanisation, a desire for more and better housing, achieving improvements to cities' infrastructure and generating employment opportunities have all necessitated a form of managed change where this is possible and desirable. In some instances, and in some historic contexts, this attempt to manage city change has been seriously lacking, with concomitant externalities. And in other instances, the challenges of managing the urban have been compounded by the way multiple problems can co-exist in individual places; that is, how the systems of a city intertwine and manifest themselves in different ways, and to differing degrees, geographically.

The task of defining, understanding and managing cities has rested, since the start of the 20th century in global north countries, on forms of urban and regional planning (Hall and Tewdwr-Jones, 2020). This modernising, and principally state-based, project sought to analyse the trends and trajectories, and develop a political and resourced programme of action to remedy them, often through interventionist instruments led by government institutions, and sometimes summarised in the form of a plan applicable to a city's administrative area. The degree to which nations and cities have relied on and utilised forms of urban and regional planning, to manage urbanisation and the drivers of change affecting cities, has been dependent on the form of governmental, constitutional and legal settlement evident in any one city, and the prevailing political and land-ownership forms that shape those activities. At the start of the 1900s, the garden city movement in the UK and the city beautiful movement in North America (see Chapter 8, for example) influenced the overall form of city planning in design terms, by attempting to integrate the best features of the rural into urban development, for wider societal wellbeing. For the first half of the century, urban and regional planning in many nations was characterised by the role of the expert, a visionary leader, who stood metaphorically over the city, offering generic visions and trajectories for change.

Figures such as Patrick Geddes and Patrick Abercombie in Britain and its then dependent nations, Daniel Burnham and Clarence Perry in the United States, Le Corbusier in France, Arturo Soria y Mata in Spain and Ernst May in Germany, all advocated new models of urban form and stylised forms of urban and regional planning as a way to deal with urban trends and manage cities. At a time when there was little in the way of public involvement in city change other than through increasing direct representative democracy, these pivotal figures became important, almost mystical, visionaries for urban development and management, acting – in the words of Gold and Ward (1997) – as 'planning wizards'.

As the 20th century progressed across North America, Europe, Australasia and parts of Asia, this planning approach developed into a more formalised and institutionalised activity of the state. This was in response to emerging urban change (for example, through post-war reconstruction, the rise of personal mobility through car ownership, deindustrialisation, population growth and housing need), but also to begin to deal with the complexity and convergence of different issues (essentially competing demands) in the same geographical space (Batty, 2018).

In this regard, as the planning wizards gave way to more bureaucratic and institutionalised strategies of professional urban planning teams, so too did questions on the legitimacy and form of the most appropriate ways forward for a city and region. In more pluralistic and democratically transparent times, as the 20th century progressed, it became apparent that a high-level vision (or long-term plan) for a city was heavily determined by political contexts for decision-making, and on agreement as to the validity of the evidence base and the options informing that political vision. After the 1980s, as the market (rather than the state) began to take the lead in urban development and regeneration matters, so there was less reliance on strategic plans and long-term planning for cities. The pace of urban change was much faster than the speed at which the set and established planning tasks could be performed, and the market – increasingly global rather than localised – demanded more immediate and pragmatic responses from governments.

The challenge of addressing a multitude of urban issues, represented by the array of UN SDGs, while coming to terms with the complexity and pace of urban change, may suggest an inability to plan formally. Indeed, some politicians across the globe have expressed a view that urban and regional planning is now either an archaic irrelevance to 21st century requirements, or else a state impediment to economic growth. The alternative to not using any form of urban planning to manage change in cities would certainly allow the market to rip, but at what additional environmental and social cost? Behaving pragmatically, picking up the pieces reactively after one urban crisis after another, rather than attempting to proactively manage and coordinate systemic analyses and phased processes of intervention, however, is popular – indeed populist – among some nations in the 2020s. But this is not a new viewpoint: in the 19th century, politicians and business people used similar arguments to resist intervention to deal with the social impacts of unplanned rapid urbanisation and install better-designed places for wider benefits. But the costs of not intervening could be far more than the temporary impediments caused by planned state intervention. Having said that, we know that the form of urban and regional planning that has been devised and implemented for much of the past 120 years in the global north, may no longer be fit for purpose to address urban challenges of the 21st century (Harrison et al, 2020).

The reality today is that cities are becoming more complex, technologically shaped and increasingly difficult to plan for. As we saw earlier in this chapter, as a result of increasing urbanisation, most of the world now live in cities, a process that is going to continue and at a greater pace in some parts, and that will have even greater disruptive effects that we may, as yet, not know about. The world faces an array of near-constant crises (COVID-19 being a recent example) that have an identifiable urban footprint, from economic uncertainty, health and ageing concerns, and demographic change, to climate change, social polarisation and political upheaval. It is difficult to consider what impact these crises will have on cities both in the immediate future and longer term, but that makes it all the more vital that we try to develop a coherent view of the future for our cities even in times of uncertainty.

21st century smart cities and the 'internet of things', which embeds digital technology in cities, are now having a pervasive impact on our lives (Clark, 2020). These developments will have important consequences for the way we plan, manage and govern future cities, but in what respect they will do so is also more uncertain. The digital world may transform places, democratic involvement and elected governance – and of course more traditional urban planning processes – in ways that have to date not really been considered. The way we have managed and regulated places, using tools and processes that were designed in another century, with defined state institutions and with set systems, seems to jar with what the immediate future holds, as we noted in relation to Batty's (2008) work in Chapter 1.

Urban planning still has a role to play in this different future, however. There remains a need to legitimise new urban processes and regulate externalities, to allow communities a democratic voice in urban change, and to communicate change through novel forms of visual methods. But existing forms of urban planning, even the use of geographical maps, may not meet our future needs. New technology, alongside a myriad of new digitised ways in which people can interact in cities and with governments, makes the case for a different style of planning across urban spaces (Future Cities Catapult, 2016; NESTA, 2019). A future form of urban planning is needed that can facilitate the SDGs in practice, but one that is able to harness new intelligence and data, different models of citizen interaction and a multitude of organisations that, together, shape cities. Taking advantage of the benefits of smart technologies in an inclusive and participatory way will therefore be crucial.

Attempting to develop a trajectory for any city is never an easy task. The key issues that will shape planning in cities are these days often outside the direct control of political leaders, or even city governments themselves. But it is possible to identify pathways to possibilities that create a set of principles for enactment by different agencies of change. These principles relate to the relevance, usability, legitimacy, funding and agility of competing city visions. The idea of a specific vision for a particular city (or city visioning) is now more relevant than ever, and that vision should be set beyond election cycles. It can also relate to the style and agenda of an elected political leader, but in this sense it is more to do with having a sense of direction, a roadmap, that is just as relevant as a form of certainty for business interests, as it is to give a clear message to citizens that a city has a purpose and a mission.

The need for alignment across sectors, agencies, time and space remains a necessity, irrespective of the political context within which decisions are being made. Alignment is a more preferable word here than integration; as we discussed earlier, integration implies different elements coming together, sometimes against their will, to secede roles for a common good. We might, instead, have to face the fact that those elements will not change their own positions fundamentally even if we expect them to join forces with others; the alignment that occurs between actors and agencies is one of temporality, for a specific project or place need, rather than to produce a single all-encompassing grand plan. A future successful mission for cities will be one developed from a plethora of different and diverse voices, addressing a multitude of challenges, in novel and innovative ways, legitimised politically but also one sufficiently agile to enable adaptability.

Summary

As we have seen in this chapter, we live in an urban world, and cities dominate and shape the lives of many people globally now and will do so even more in the future. Understanding what is meant by the term 'city' is key to how we explore the influence of urbanisation in our globalised world. Cities offer us exciting opportunities and benefits but can produce some of the most challenging problems humankind faces, as the COVID-19 pandemic highlights. Indeed, the 'urban paradox' has shaped and influenced the way that urban policy and practice have evolved and responded to changing thinking about cities since the late 19th century and early 20th centuries. Today, planning in cities has to deal with messy and complex elements, but new technologies and new ways of thinking about the future provide us with potentially powerful tools to democratise and open up planning processes, and to help us think longer term about the way in which cities could and should evolve over the next 25 years and beyond. In the next chapter, we will look at the evolution and origins of city visioning in more detail.

3

Reimagining the city: views of the future from the past and present

> A map of the world that does not include Utopia is not worth even glancing at, for it leaves out the one country at which Humanity is always landing. And when Humanity lands there, it looks out, and, seeing a better country, sets sail. Progress is the realisation of Utopias.
>
> Oscar Wilde, 1891

Introduction

Humankind's capacity to envision the future and to be able to imagine alternative futures is a relatively recent development, relating directly to the age of enlightenment (Gidley, 2017a). Thus, 'utopian' thinking, founded on the work of writers such as Plato and Thomas More, was transformed during this period into 'euchronia' (or a time of perfect social, technological and ecological harmony), which enabled different places in different times to be imagined. The city has often been at the heart of much of the utopian and euchronian literature, film and related art that has emerged since then. As Clarke suggested: 'For at least the past five centuries ... the make-believe city has been the benchmark of all imaginary societies' (Clarke, 1992: 702). Moreover, the resultant 'urban imaginaries' that have been developed have been founded on both utopic ('good') and dystopic ('bad') futures. In turn, this body of work has helped shape and influence the nature of urban design and urban planning.

In this chapter, we will first examine what is meant by the term 'vision' and how writers such as Plato and Thomas More have influenced our thinking about the future, through their utopian ideas. We then compare and contrast utopian and dystopian views of the future, drawing on literature and film (and related art) to examine questions such as what sort of 'urban imaginaries' emerge from literature and film, and do these imaginaries shape the way our cities look and feel today (and will do in the future), and vice versa? Finally, we look at the way in which utopian thinking has influenced and shaped urban planning through the visionary thinking of early thinkers such as Geddes, Howard and others.

It is important to note, however, that the chapter is not intended to be a comprehensive or exhaustive inventory or critique of all futures-based thinkers or writers – for this the reader is referred in the general literature to authors such as Claeys (2010, 2011, 2017) and in the planning and urban design literature to other writers such as Eaton (2001), Rosenau (2010) and Hall (2014). Instead, the chapter seeks to show the links and interconnections between real cities and imagined urban futures and 'ideal cities', drawing on whom we believe to be some (but not all) of the exemplary thinkers in the field.

Visions – shared expectations of the future?

Thinking about the future is perhaps now more important than it ever has been in the history of humanity, as we face the potentially devastating effects of climate change, environmental degradation, biodiversity loss and resource depletion. The English word 'future' seems to have been first used in the 14th century, and has its roots in the Latin word '*futura/futurus*', meaning 'going to be, yet to be' (Gidley, 2017a). Yet the act of imagining and even foretelling the future is much older. Before the 14th century, 'specialists of the future' included prophets, diviners, seers, oracles, witches, sages and wizards, often drawing on specific bodies of expert knowledge and combining a mixture of spiritual and secular elements. If these experts mis-told the future or provided the wrong news, they were often punished or even killed (Urry, 2016).

It is interesting to note that, in much of Greek mythology, fate was predetermined, and so although the Delphi Oracle could know the future, it could not be changed through intervention – this gave rise to the idea of a Greek tragedy (for example, the Trojan Horse) where the future is known but cannot be changed (Adam and Groves, 2007; Urry, 2016). Other examples of historic interpretations of the future include the Druids, who were regarded as prophets and magicians, and the prophecies from the Old Testament, which foretold of events such as Christ's birth. Indeed, the word 'prophet' means 'forespeaker' (Greek) and 'delegate or mouthpiece of another' (Hebrew), and the future in Judaeo-Christian and Persian culture was seen as being very much in the hands of God, as a part of God's divine plan (Gidley, 2017a). Therefore prophets, who people thought could hear and mediate God's revelations, were very powerful.

Often, these early prophets would focus on a vision of some kind. Again, the use of this word is perhaps surprisingly recent. The *Online Entymological Dictionary* suggests that it was first used around 1300, as 'something seen in the imagination or in the supernatural', from the Anglo-French word, '*visioun*', from the Old French word '*vision*' ('presence, sight; view, look, appearance; dream, supernatural sight') (12c.) and from the Latin '*visionem*', or the 'act of seeing, sight, thing seen'. The alternative meaning of 'sense of sight' is first recorded in the late 15th century and the meaning 'statesman-like foresight, political sagacity' is evidenced from 1926.

Van der Helm (2009) suggests a helpful typology of visions. Religious or eschatological visions are the oldest form of visions of the future. They draw on concepts of life and death and are at the heart of many of the world's religions. But visions can also be humanistic, based on a philosophy that concerns itself with the human race, perhaps in relation to an ideal human society. Examples of this kind of vision include social utopias (for example, Thomas More and Francis Bacon). Political visions of the future are closely linked with what are known as ideologies, which, although not in themselves necessarily defined as futures-oriented, often provide particular visions of the future. We have also seen:

- *visions developed for communities*, through an interactive group process;
- *business visions for organisations*, often based on visionary leadership (Mintzberg, 1994);
- *policy visions*, often based on a hybridisation of political, business and community visions, which may also contain elements of humanistic visions (for example, sustainable development visions);
- *personal visions*, which help to provide meaning to individuals' lives.

Visions are therefore fundamental to thinking about the future and these different types of vision share common elements. First, a vision, by default, is a vision of the future, related to an individual, or collective, worldview or point of view, and by its very nature is referring to something that is not yet existing. Second, a vision is also often seen in the light of an idealised future or even an ideal future. Visions are often therefore seen as preferred futures as opposed to possible futures or likely futures, and it may be that visions may be multiple, with one a preferred choice (van der Helm, 2009). Third, visions are underpinned by the assumption that the vision itself is needed to help bring together actions into a desired direction, with a normative idealisation often the preferred outcome. Finally, a vision also seeks to engender both ideational change through the development of new ideas and new ways of thinking, and transformational change to replace old and outdated structures. The latter is often required to overturn undesirable structures or as an answer to external forces to redirect change. Van der Helm (2009: 100) therefore defines a vision as 'the more or less explicit claim or expression of a future that is idealized in order to mobilise present potential to move into the direction of this future'.

As part of the humanistic tradition of visionary thinking, both Plato (writing in the 4th century BC) and Thomas More (writing in the 16th century) are both examples of visionary thinkers who focused on a worldview based on utopic thinking (see Figure 3.1). For example, Plato's *Republic* (360 BC) addressed important questions about education and the role of men and women in society and is the closest vision possible to an ideal society (Sargent, 2010). Plato's society in his *Republic* had three classes, which correspond to three fundamental elements of the soul or psyche: (a) philosopher-kings (or 'reason'); (b) the auxiliaries (or the 'spirited element'); and (c) the artisans (who represent 'moderation'). The focus of *Republic* and its ideal urban society (the '*polis*') is primarily the first two classes (otherwise known as the guardians), and each person is seen as fitting the role or vocation that best suits them, and so as a result everyone is happy. However, importantly, Plato also recognised that corruption can undermine and destroy utopian societies (Claeys, 2010, 2011).

The word 'utopia' is, of course, synonymous with the work of Thomas More, who wrote the book that carries the same name in 1516 (More, 1516). At the time, the word 'utopia' was a neologism, or a new word, to name a new concept, but, over time, it has been widely accepted and used to form new words such as dystopia, euchronia and ecotopia (Claeys, 2010). As Claeys (2010) notes, More had originally called his imaginary island, *Nusquama*, which is Latin for 'nowhere', but rather than curtail possibilities by imagining a place that could not exist, but rather one that could, More developed a more positive neologism. This reflected the humanistic ideal of the Renaissance period, during which More wrote, and which was based on the premise that human beings did not have to accept their fate but could use reason in order to plan and build for the future. This burgeoning of the will and capacity of individuals was partly brought about by the expansion in humans' geographical view of the wider world through exploration and endeavour (for example, Vespucci, Columbus and Poliziano). More's concept of a new or other space was

Figure 3.1: Plato's Republic and More's Utopia

Sources: Wikimedia Commons, Metropolitan Museum of Art

founded on the combination of the Greek for 'not' (*ou*) and 'place' (*topos*) – or literally 'not a place' – but the word 'utopia' can also be derived from 'good' (*eu*), so the term came to have a dual meaning: 'no place' and 'good place'.

More's Utopia was an isolated place set apart from the wider world (or somewhere in the New World), but was also designed to rival

Plato's city as it was described as achieved and completed, whereas *polis* had only been outlined in a plan. More's Utopia was very much a city-based vision. As he wrote (More, 1516: 83–5):

> The island of Utopia is in the middle just 200 miles broad, and holds almost at the same breadth over a great part of it; but it grows narrower towards both ends … There are 54 cities in the island, all large and well-built: the manners, customs, and laws of which are the same, and they are all contrived as near in the same manner as the ground on which they stand will allow. The nearest lie at least 24 miles distance from one another, and the most remote are not so far distant, but that a man can go on foot in one day from it, to that which lies next it. Every city sends three of their wisest senators once a year to Amaurot [the capital] to consult about their common concerns; for that is chief town of the island, being situated near the centre of it, so that it is the most convenient place for their assemblies.

In More's Utopia, each of the 54 cities were made up of 6,000 households with 10 to 16 adults, and so that the numbers were approximately equal, populations were redistributed (or exchanged) between households and towns, and if the island experienced over-population, new colonies were established (Urry, 2016). This contrasts with Plato's limit of 5,040 citizens in the *polis*, the ideal number for a single orator to address. It is also interesting to note that the population of Amaurot, the utopian capital, was between 70,000 and 100,000, which approximates the population of London in 1515 (80,000), and More's description elicits a regular grid pattern (Eylers, 2015). Indeed, this description echoes some of the earlier thinking on the 'ideal city' by Francesc Eiximenis, a late-14th century Franciscan monk from Catalonia who suggested a regular grid pattern and central plaza as being the best way to lay out a new city. In turn, this influenced the development of the ideal city that emerged from Renaissance Italy a hundred years later and led to 'bastide' towns and extensions to towns (Messina, 2008).

Over time, the concept of 'utopia' came to be associated with one of four characteristics (Levitas, 1990; Claeys, 2011):

- the concept of an 'imagined society' (or 'good place');
- the literary form into which utopian writing fits (although this may limit what might be broader work that does not necessarily connect with More's model utopia);

- the function of utopia, which impacts on the reader and creates action and activity in the reader's mind; and
- desire for a better life caused by discontent with the present life, or the feeling that individuals absorb feelings of hope through the influence of utopia.

Plato's thinking clearly had some influence over More, but More's vision of a new society was one anchored on self-sufficiency, and where social cohesion and equality are the foundation for happiness (Eylers, 2015). More's work also acted as a bridge between the old order and chaos of the Middle Ages to the new order of the Renaissance (Mumford, 1924). Private property is renounced and there is freedom of religion, so it is perhaps not surprising that most commentators believe that More's work forms the foundation for a long line of 'social futures', including Marx, although others such as H.G. Wells consider Francis Bacon's incomplete *New Atlantis* of 1627 to be more influential as the first modern utopia (Urry, 2016).

More's utopic thinking has directly and indirectly inspired subsequent architects and planners to think about urban design in an idealistic way, and was important for influencing thinking about ideal cities in the 17th and 18th centuries, and more recent urban visions such as Etienne Cabet's (1840) *Voyage en Icarie* and Ebenezer Howard's (1898) garden city (Eylers, 2015) (see later in this chapter).

There is, however, one important distinction between More's and Plato's work and this later thinking. The early utopias were based on an 'other place' so that their potential to influence the future (or other time) was through implication rather than direct reference. It was only at the end of the 18th century that utopian thinking started to consider the future explicitly, as thoughts turned from thinking about a different place at the same time to the same place at a different time (or the concept of *euchronia*) (Gidley, 2017a). This has led to more dystopian thinking or more disturbing and negative futures. The next section of the book therefore explores how thinking about the future has evolved over time.

Seeing into the future: a short history

As Gidley (2017a) suggests, we commonly assume that the human race has always had a three-part conception of time: the past, the present and the future. But this is not the case and, indeed, is not how all cultures see time, even today. This linear approach to time came into being about 2,500 years ago, at the time of Plato, as Western philosophy emerged in ancient Greece. Before this point, humans perceived time as cyclical and embedded in the astronomical, seasonal and everyday scale of life. Key to understanding was the widening of horizons through literature and art, and a change in belief that time could be thought of as the measurement of change, rather than eternal and permanent, or the 'eternal now' (Milojevic, 2002). However, it also true that different metaphors for time influence the way in which different cultures and religions understand the future: the variation in time over cycles is important in Hindu and Buddhist thinking (for example, 'cosmic eras'), whereas in Graeco-Roman and Judaeo-Christian culture, time is perceived as a trajectory towards accomplishment through God (Milojevic, 2002).

For writers such as Gebser (1985), 'time consciousness' developed with other forms of consciousness throughout history, as humankind moved from nature-based 'timelessness' towards a 'mythical consciousness' (founded on cyclical time and the development of language systems to enable story-telling and myths), which paralleled a shift from nomadic life to more settled agri-villages and the world's first cities (Gidley, 2017a). Subsequently, the development of 'mental-rational' consciousness during the ancient Greek period led to advances in knowledge of all kinds, and the development of linear time prior to the age of 'integral consciousness' from the Renaissance, exemplified by higher forms of reasoning, and multiple perspectives on time.

Schultz (2016) offers an alternative (and sometimes light-hearted) perspective on the development of what might broadly be termed 'futures studies', or 'foresight' or 'anticipatory studies'. Schulz (2016) suggests five 'waves of futures':

- first wave: the oral tradition;
- second wave: early written age;
- third wave: enlightenment and extraction;
- fourth wave: systems and cybernetics;
- fifth wave: complexity and emergence.

The first wave of futures was exemplified by the oral tradition of shamans and mystics, and characterised by often seeing particular future events as inevitable and unchangeable. In the second wave of futures studies, scholars such as Sima Qian (a Chinese historian who lived during the 2nd century BCE) and Ibn Khaldun (a Tunisian Arab historian, 1332–1406) looked at the past and the emerging patterns of history, and tried to see how a better understanding of events could help explain how similar situations might influence the future. Their macro view of history was fundamental in shaping subsequent historians such as Hegel, Comte and

Eisler. Ibn Khaldun, for example, charted five typical main stages in the rise and fall of political power in his major work, *Muqaddimah* (1989). As we have seen with the work of Plato and More, visionary thinkers outlined their ideas of imagined societies, which although future-neutral and anchored as alternatives to the present, have nonetheless influenced other visionaries. For example, Nostradamus (1503–1566) was a French astrologer, physician and visionary or seer, who is best known for his book *Les Prophéties*, a collection of 942 poetic quatrains (or four-lined poems) allegedly predicting future events (Reading, 2015). To Schultz's list we might also add Augustine's (344–430 AD) *City of God* (in AD 427) as another visionary contrasting an ideal, heavenly city of God founded on love with an earthly city founded on contemptible self-love (Dodds, 2014), and Francis Bacon's (1561–1626) *New Atlantis* (1627), where Bacon adopted a more scientific approach to visioning and an idealistic view of humankind founded on state-funded scientific research. Finally, Schultz includes Robert Boyle (1627–1691), the Anglo-Irish scientist who, as well as Boyles' Law, developed a future 'wishlist' of scientific problems to be solved.

In the third wave of enlightenment and extraction, Schultz suggests that we see thinkers such as the Marquis de Condorcet (1743–1794), a French philosopher and mathematician, and Auguste Comte (1798–1857), a French writer and philosopher, emerging to highlight scientific rationalism and progress through science and technology. The late 19th century saw early science fiction literature exploring different futures – for example, in 1870, Jules Verne's *20,000 Leagues Under the Sea*, and its focus on an ecological utopia, suggests, to some at least, an anticipation of the environmental movement. H.G. Wells' work – including *The Time Machine* (1895) and *The War of the Worlds* (1898) (see Figure 3.2) – was highly influential in employing futures thinking, and indeed Batty (2018) acknowledges Wells' importance in highlighting the links between population distribution and transport links between cities in his work *Anticipations* (Wells, 1902). In turn, such literature also inspired early film-makers to explore futuristic science fiction themes, for example: George Meliere's affectionate *A Trip to the Moon* (1902) and Fritz Lang's darker and moodier *Metropolis* (1927). These dual themes of literature and film are explored in more detail later in this chapter.

The fourth wave of systems and cybernetics was founded on continued industrial expansion and scientific progress. An early form of planning and futures-based thinking was the Soviet Union's first five-year plan in 1928, for example, and, in the United States, Herbert Hoover's appointment of the Research Committee on Social Trends, and its landmark report in 1933 entitled *Recent Social Trends in the United*

Figure 3.2: H.G. Wells' *War of the Worlds*

The heat-ray in the Chobham Road.

Source: Wikimedia Commons

States. Schultz also highlights the emergence of formal futures thinking during this period. During the last phases of the Second World War, the RAND Corporation was established in 1945 as a leading think-tank to help with the United States' war planning. Its focus was very much on military technology, strategy, operations and curtailing the spread of communism (Gidley, 2017a). During this wave, as Gidley notes, in the 1940s to 1960s, futures thinking was dominated by the idea of one predictable future linked to the concept of 'scientific positivism'. This was anchored on empiricism and modelling the future, often based on trend analysis, and was used by the RAND Corporation and other organisations in the United States such as the Institute for the Future as well as the Soviet Union, often in the Cold War setting.

However, as Schultz (2015) and Gidley (2017a) acknowledge, through the work of writers such as de Jouvenel (1964) and Rescher (1967), it became clear that relying on past trends to extrapolate future trends was fraught with danger. Although analytical prediction might help in science, using the same techniques for complex social systems was unrealistic. Rescher (1967) suggested, for example, that expert opinion and speculation (using a Delphi approach) was an alternative and viable method to adopt. Moreover, Rescher suggested we are impotent in shaping the future because it is complex and beyond our control. These criticisms were aimed at what Gidley (2017a: 50) calls the 'predictive approach', where 'trend is destiny', although this approach still often dominates futures thinking and the general media view of futures studies.

So, if we cannot predict the future and cannot control it – as argued by Rescher (1967) and Batty (2018) – what other options are there for us in futures studies? During the fourth wave and what Schultz refers to as the fifth wave (of complexity and emergence), we have seen a growing focus on human-centred and multiple futures to address these criticisms. The seeds for the first were sown in the 1950s with authors such as Fred Polak's *The Image of the Future* (Dutch, 1955), and the establishment of European futures institutions such as the Peace Research Institute in Oslo in 1959. Thus, as Andersson (2012) (referenced in Gidley, 2017a) suggests, by the end of the 1960s, there were two movements of futures studies: the empirically based predictive futures studies movement in North America; and the more critical, sociological futures studies movement in Europe and elsewhere.

In parallel with these movements, there was a trend away from positivism (a single body of scientifically proven knowledge) towards pluralism (diverse sets of scientific knowledge) in the sciences, and this was mirrored in the range of qualitative methods that came to be used in the social sciences. This also led to a focus on multiple futures – in other words, that there is not one single predictable future but a range of different futures. Perhaps the current diversity of techniques used, from 'causal layered analysis' (linking different layers in the future; Inayatullah, 2014) to 'integral futures' (an overarching approach that links individuals and broader groups/collectives), are indicative of the complexity and emergent techniques that Schultz suggests form the basis for present-day futures studies (including experiential futures and anticipatory studies).

In summary, therefore, modern 'futures studies' (or the multidisciplinary and systematic field of inquiry of probable, possible and preferable futures) today are characterised by the following key features (Milojevic, 2002):

- The future is not predetermined and cannot be known or predicted.
- The future is determined partly by history, social structures and reality and partly by chance, innovation and human choice.
- There is a range of alternative futures that can be forecasted.
- Future outcomes can be influenced by human choices.
- Early intervention enables planning and design, while in crisis response, people can only try to adapt and/or react.
- Ideas and images of the future shape our actions and decisions in the present.
- Our visions of preferred futures are shaped by our values.
- Humanity does not make choices as a whole nor are we motivated by the same values, aspirations and projects.

The tradition of futures thinking, as we have seen, therefore stretches back to pre-history, and Son (2015), in an interesting review of futures studies, suggests that five main intellectual traditions pervade and inform the more recent movements:

- Futures studies thoughts are embedded in all religions, as we have already noted.
- The utopic tradition has underpinned much of the work in futures studies.
- Historicism (or historically based prediction), although criticised by authors such as Popper (1957), has often pervaded futures studies.
- Science fiction literature (and art and film) has often influenced the way in which we think about the future.
- Futures studies have been influenced by systems thinking, which sees the relationship between elements in our world as connected and complex.

Son's five intellectual traditions are also helpful in making the link between futures studies and city visions. Certainly, it is true that the city visions and city foresight that emerged during the 1980s and 1990s were influenced not only by the strong utopic tradition of urban planning but also by the emergence of new types of futures studies during that time. We have seen how important it is to recognise the nature of complexity in urban systems, and to acknowledge this in constructing any vision for a city (see Chapter 1). Moreover, in this chapter, it has been intimated how important previous literature (particularly science fiction) has been in influencing and shaping thoughts and ideas about the future. Is there a sense in which life imitates art and our urban areas are shaped by perceptions of the written word or, indeed, film? Or do the cities that we live in (and will do in the future) influence the literature and the films that are produced?

To take a connected example from urban studies, terms such as 'smart city', 'resilient city' and 'green city' conjure up for us a normative vision of a place that we may not necessarily have ever seen. In the case of a smart city, this might even be based on a techno-utopian future (Bina et al, 2020). Such terminology can produce a spatial imaginary, which may over time be embedded as a particular representation of cities or, indeed, a particular type of city (Davoudi, 2018). Visionary planners and urban designers such as Ebenezer Howard, Le Corbusier and Frank Lloyd Wright all used their imagination to develop urban visions anchored on a strong sense of place and spatiality. These were essentially individual imaginaries, but philosophy and sociology have taught us that collective imagination or collective consciousness is also very powerful (Said, 1994). As Davoudi (2018: 101) argues:

> Spatial imaginaries are deeply held, collective understandings of socio-spatial relations that are performed by, give sense to, make possible and change collective socio-spatial practices. They are produced through political struggles over the conceptions, perceptions and lived experiences of place. They are circulated and propagated through images, stories, texts, data, algorithms and performances. They are infused by relations of power in which contestation and resistance are ever-present.

For Davoudi (2018), spatial imaginaries (which can include city visions where there is a collectively held sense of spatiality in the vision) are characterised by a clear sense of background understanding of, for example, a city and its role in a wider polycentric network (Granqvist et al, 2019); their emergent nature as novel ideas, which become embedded realities (for example, Patrick Abercrombie's green belt and Albert Plasman's *randstat* or ring city); their collective belief, which strengthens their embeddedness in current thinking; and their performative nature, as ideas are translated into practice (for example, in Le Corbusier's 'skyscrapers in the park'). Moreover, spatial imaginaries are epistemic and normative: they describe both how things are and how they should be. An example of this is the concept of Detroit as a decaying city, but one that is being reborn and futurised into a place that can grow and evolve into something better, for example through urban food production and urban villages on derelict and vacant land (Millington, 2013; Kinney, 2016; Doucet, 2017). In a different context, Beckert (2013, 2016) has shown how imaginaries (or 'fictional expectations') about the future (for example, 'the American Dream') have influenced and shaped economic decision-making at a variety of levels. The question arises, therefore, what sort of urban imaginaries emerge from literature and film, and do these shape the way our cities look and feel today (and will do in the future), and vice versa?

Utopic and dystopic visions: the role and influence of the city in literature and film

So far in this chapter we have predominantly focused on the concept of 'utopic futures'. The counterpoint to this kind of future is a dystopic one. The word 'dystopia' conjures up disturbing and frightening images of death, destruction and collapsed and derelict cities. As Claeys (2017) points out, the word 'dystopia' is derived from two Greek words, *dus* and *topos,* meaning a diseased, bad or unfavourable place, and first appeared in the mid-18th century, but was not widely used until the 20th century. Today, the word can carry fictional connotations of a dystopic imagined future, and real futures, based on the known, for example the ravages of climate change and environmental destruction in the Amazon and elsewhere across the world. Moreover, there is a sense that utopia and dystopia are inexorably linked: for example, More's utopia is a fortified island, was an imperial powerbase, and when overpopulation results, colonisation of neighbouring land occurs.

Certainly, there are plenty of examples of dystopic literature over the past 200 years where cities have played a major role in the narrative, ranging from Mary Shelley's *The Last Man* (1826), through E.M. Forster's *The Machine Stops* (1909), to Aldous Huxley's *Brave New World* (1932), George Orwell's *Nineteen Eighty Four* (1949) and Ray Bradbury's *Fahrenheit 451* (1953). Urry (2016) and Claeys (2017) both provide comprehensive analyses of this literature. What is important and valuable about this dystopic literature (and associated visualisations of future cities) is that it carries warnings for us in a range of imagined futures, challenging our conceptions of continued existence, freedom and privacy and the impact of technology on our lives (Eames and Dixon, 2012). More recently, Jones (2019a: 68), in *Stillicide* (a collection of short stories), imagines a future where water is commodified, and which challenges the concepts of 'utopia' and 'dystopia': ' "People get on with it. People have always got on with it. Dystopia is as a ridiculous concept as Utopia. Ultimately, we're animals," I say, thinking of the nature discs. "And animals find ways."'

Nonetheless, science fiction in literature and film has played a major role in art and culture, and future imaginaries, often through its dystopic imageries. In science fiction, as Sobchak (2004) and Collie (2011) argue, the very act of imagining futures in an unfettered way can create an imaginary architecture that grounds imaginary cities of the imagination in the narrative action – in effect to help conjure up an urban imaginary (Soja, 1996). A number of films have emerged that connect science fiction and cities in powerful ways: for example, Fritz Lang's *Metropolis* (1927), Ridley Scott's *Blade Runner* (1982), Wachowski Brothers' *Matrix Trilogy* (1999 and 2003) and Alex Proyas' *Dark City* (1998). Gerlacj and Hamilton (2003) highlight a number of common issues that such films explore as being:

- the conflict between utopian and dystopian elements;
- the alienation produced by the built environment in such cities;
- the relationships between the built environment and nature;
- the effects of a centralised power on individual freedom;
- the relationships between time and space;
- the powerful role of technology in future cities.

Clarke (1992) and Gold (2001) also provide interesting perspectives on the role of the city in science fiction film, observing the emergence of different types of filmic city. As Gold (2001) notes, Fritz Lang's dystopic *Metropolis* (set in 2026; see the images in Figure 3.3) drew on the growing belief that 1920s New York was the face of the new 'vertical city' of the future, with the super-rich living high above poor workers toiling at lower levels (drawing on the analogous Biblical Tower of Babel). In contrast, the H.G. Wells-inspired film, *Things to Come* (1936), was based on an underground city called Everytown, with high-rise buildings and interconnecting walkways but with a utopic ambiance underlying the film. For Gold, Ridley Scott's *Blade Runner* (1982) was a metaphor for the future 'noir city', based on visual images of Los Angeles in the year 2019, in a future city where genetically engineered organic robots called replicants must be hunted down. A third type of city was imagined in films such as *The Matrix* (1999 and 2003) where a virtual city is seen through the lens of hyperreality, where re-creations are so life-like they are more authentic than the real ones and where parallel worlds co-exist.

Figure 3.3: *Metropolis*

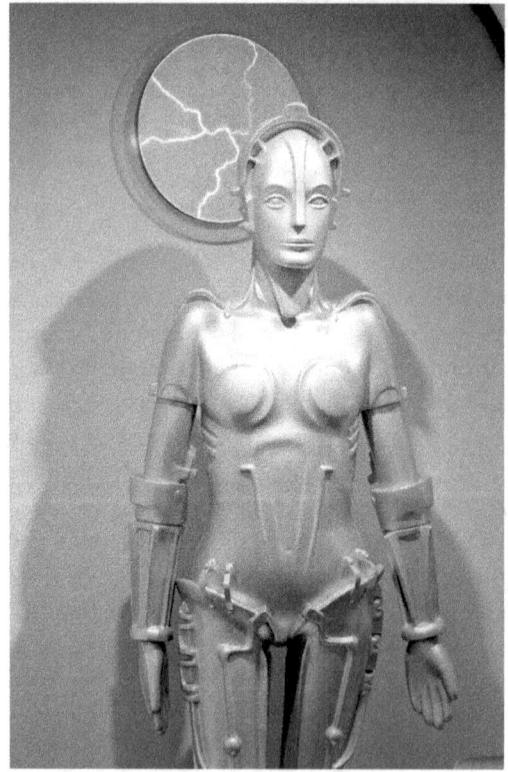

Source: Wikimedia Commons

It is no accident that the outpouring of literature focusing on existing cities in the 19th century (from, for example, Dickens, Zola, Hugo and others) coincided with the rapid growth of cities such as London, Paris and New York (Dobraszczyk, 2019). It is clear that film and literature during the early 20th century found its way into urban design principles – for example, we can draw parallels between *Metropolis* and its swarms of aerial vehicles and Broadacre, Frank Lloyd Wright's suburban utopia of 1932, the vertical city in *Metropolis* and Le Corbusier's *Radiant City* concept city of 1933.

Other commentators have argued that film has directly influenced urban design. In a recent interview (Carmichael, 2016), Stephen Graham, the author of *Vertical* (2016a), suggests that Syd Mead, the visual designer who set the designs for *Blade Runner* (and was an architectural draftsman by training and had travelled a lot in the Middle East to discuss futurist architecture) emphasised 'gulf futurism' architecture in the film and this found its way into reality, particularly through tall buildings and grandiose plans for new cities.[1] Similarly, Adrian Smith, the architect for the Burj Khalifa in Dubai, was inspired by the *Wizard of Oz* and the Emerald City as a child. Graham refers to Shanghai's Pudong district and urban development in China (see Figure 3.4), which he believes is shaped by *Blade Runner*'s visual concept of 'urban futurism'. As Graham (2016b: 395) writes:

> Built projects, material cities, sci-fi texts, imaginary futures, architectural schemes and urban theories mingle and resonate together in complex and unpredictable ways. This occurs within broader 'postmodern' cultures dominated by multiple circuits of mediation, prediction and simulation. These, in turn, fatally undermine remaining notions of an 'authentic' urban life which exists in advance of its representation in fiction and media.

There is, therefore, a reciprocity in film, art, literature and urban design (Graham, 2016a, 2016b; Butt, 2018; Bina et al, 2020). It is no coincidence that the designs seen in Dubai and Shanghai echo the designs of films such as *Blade Runner*, which then provide the focus for new films, which in turn come to exemplify the future, helping to brand such cities as futuristic places (Carmichael, 2016). This reciprocity is acknowledged by Dobraszczyk (2019: 9) in his book on architecture and imagination: 'Thus imagination can be said to prepare the ground for the "real" and is always at work trying to transform it. Here, what is real and what is imagined are not two separate worlds, but ones that are always informing and transforming each other.'

Figure 3.4: Shanghai and Dubai: inspired by or the inspiration for science fiction and urban futurism?

Source: Wikimedia Commons

Other writers have provided helpful analyses of how city visions have been visualised and how they can be classified. For example, Dunn et al (2014) point to the duality of what they refer to as the 'city of visions'. They are both allusive and elusive in so far as they typically seek to show how people may live, work and move in a city but are often not ultimately translated into built conditions, although there are exceptions such as Robert Owen's New Lanark. Visualisations of future cities are important because they provide a powerful way of reimagining the future, contribute to our 'social imaginary' and provide new insights and a better understanding of what shapes the present and ultimately the future (Barbrook, 2007; Dunn et al, 2014; Dobraszczyk, 2019). Such images or representations of the future also emphasise the nature of power and agency as they represent the ideas, aspirations and hopes of those who have constructed them. As Urry (2016: 17) suggests, quoting the science fiction writer, William Gibson: 'The future is already here – it's just not very evenly distributed.' Dunn et al (2014) propose that there are six dominant visual paradigms for future cities:

- *regulated cities*, which have developed urban visions that integrate aspects of rural living;
- *layered cities*, which are based on multiple levels of different kinds of urban mobility;
- *flexible cities*, which are urban depictions that allow for change and 'plug-ins', but are still fixed in some way;
- *informal cities*, which present visions that imply some degree of transience or are itinerant in some way, and so might include walking, nomadic and non-permanent cities;
- *ecological cities*, which explicitly state ecological concerns, renewable energies and low- or zero-carbon ambitions;
- *hybrid cities*, which blur the distinction between physical and digital space including smart cities and augmented reality.

Using this categorisation suggests that the garden city movement (based on the thinking of Ebenezer Howard), which has dominated much of the thinking in urban planning in the UK, could be positioned not only within the ecological city paradigm, but also within the regulated city.

What is clear is that literature and film (and related art) have influenced and been influenced by the cities we have built, are building now and will build in our cities of the future. The next section explores how the utopian tradition has influenced and shaped modern urban planning.

The utopic tradition in urban planning

The utopic tradition had an influence in the formative years of modern urban planning thought and practice. The writers and thinkers about urban problems throughout the 19th century were certainly influenced by these utopian ideas, even if their own ideas only found niche audiences at the time. But, in retrospect, their influence on urban planning, and indeed on the shape of cities, has been incalculable and, tellingly, it still continues. The individuals who took the ideas of More and others were regarded as visionaries; there was no one ideology here that leapt in a linear way from early thinkers to 19th and 20th century practical application. Rather, we can identify a series of closely woven, sequential ideas that shaped the formative years of urban planning over a 100-year period up to the middle of the 20th century. They are not the only people or events that shaped the course of urban planning, both in those formative years or since that time, but they did shape the activity demonstrably, and for that they are worthy of mention.

Ebenezer Howard

The most influential thinker at this time was Ebenezer Howard (1850–1928). His book *Garden Cities of Tomorrow* was published in 1898 but republished in revised form in 1902 (Howard, 1898, 1902). Despite its age, it remains relevant to many modern urban problems covering the garden city movement and, more lately, the planning and design of new housing settlements. Howard was a shorthand writer in the courts but one who liked to speculate about the future. He travelled and spent a number of years in the United States when it was undergoing rapid urban growth, but returned to the UK to write his book.

At that time, several pioneer industrialists and philanthropists had already started new 'ideal communities' in association with their large new factories. They had, perhaps, ulterior motives beyond creating small utopian communities: they built factories cheaply on undeveloped rural land and needed to provide their workforce with homes; they also needed to have fit and productive workers in better housing and health. These early examples include Robert Owen's settlement at New Lanark in Scotland (1800–10), Titus Salt's Saltaire town built around a textile mill in Yorkshire (1853–63), George Cadbury's Bournville on the edge of Birmingham (1879–95) and Lord Lever's Port Sunlight on Merseyside (1888). But the experiment was also underway elsewhere in the world. In Germany, the engineering and armaments company Krupp built a number of settlements at Essen in the Ruhr, while in the United States, the railroad company Pullman built a model town near Chicago in the 1880s.

All these examples can be characterised by a relatively standard approach: to separate industry from homes, parcel up and segregate the different uses of land, create a range of housing types and sizes to meet different needs and family sizes, and create central services in the middle of the settlements so that they would be accessible to the greatest number of people.

Howard generalised the idea from these early model villages into a general planned movement of people and industry, in stark contrast to the industrialised and over-urbanised 19th century city. But Howard was also influenced by some key 19th century writers. These included Edward Gibbon Wakefield, who had advocated the planned movement of population, and James Silk Buckingham, who had developed the idea of a model city. The greatest influence on Howard, however, was from economist Alfred Marshall, who had argued in 1884 that much industry was footloose and could locate anywhere if the workforce was available, thus allowing new settlements to form with an economic base. But Marshall also recognised that society was paying the social costs of inadequate health and housing, these being higher in the largest cities.

Howard developed the idea into a practical call for action through his well-recognised 'three magnets' diagram (see Figure 3.5). Its essence was to take the best features of the countryside and best features of the city and combine them into a new ideal settlement. The advantages of urban living comprised accessibility to jobs and services, whereas the disadvantages were in the externalities and costs for people in poverty and the environment. The countryside, by contrast, offered much better, cleaner, environments but little in the way of opportunities for employment or services. The new settlement, which he termed 'towncountry', or 'garden city', could be achieved by a planned decentralisation of workers and jobs to the new settlement. This also included generous housing densities, and the settlement was to be located outside the traditional travel-to-work area of the existing urban centre. But the size of the settlement would be relatively small, perhaps only 30,000 people, surrounded by a green belt that would be accessible to all. The utopian element also included a belief that the new urban areas had an optimal size; once that population size was reached, rather than continue to expand the town, Howard (1902) argued that the additional population should be accommodated in another brand-new town close by. The settlements would be characterised by a green backcloth of open countryside and connected by transport routes. This

Figure 3.5: Ebenezer Howard's *Garden Cities of Tomorrow*: the 'three magnets'

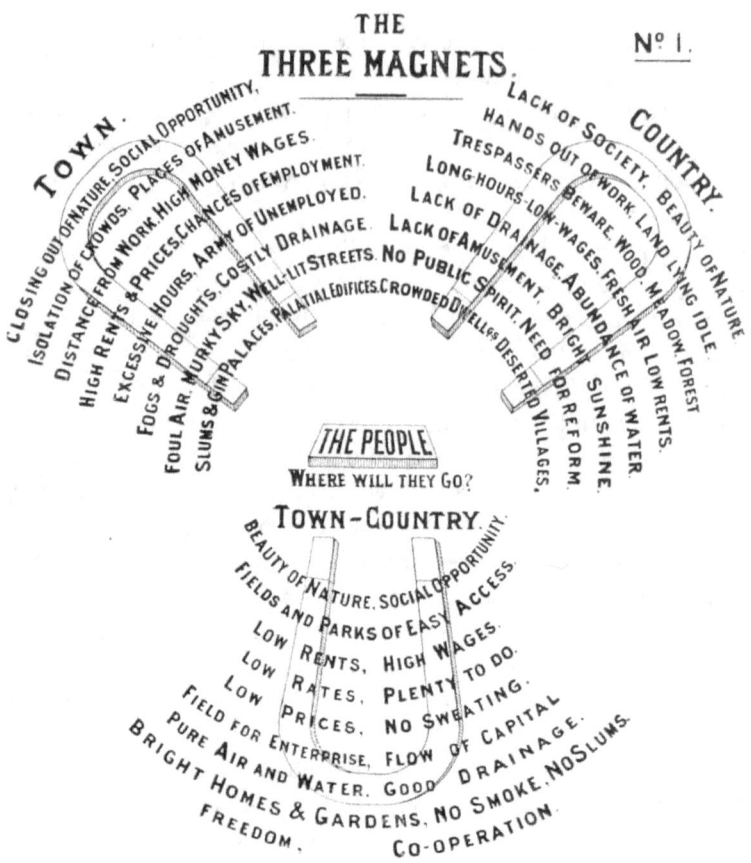

Source: Wikimedia Commons

feature, once repeated across a wider region, could form what Howard referred to as a 'social city' and a maximum population of 250,000.

Howard (1902) was interested in the model and how it could be turned into a practical reality. Shortly after the publication of his ideas, two garden cities were started, both north of London: Letchworth (1903) and Welwyn Garden City in Hertfordshire (1920). Both were built on the lines he had advocated, and were located within green belts. But creating these new settlements in an existing setting was not without problems, and both places suffered financial troubles and proved not to be the start of a larger social city movement.

Patrick Geddes

The second key figure who played a pivotal role in developing the utopic tradition in early modern planning was a Scottish biologist, Patrick Geddes (1854–1932). Geddes developed an area of study that we now recognise as human ecology: the relationship between humans and their environment. He undertook a systematic study of the forces that were shaping the growth of modern cities, which resulted in his book *Cities in Evolution* (Geddes, 1915). Geddes stressed the importance of considering, in a geography tradition, the relationships that exist between human settlement and land, through the local economy.

Geddes' contribution to the birth of modern planning was to analyse the broader context of settlement patterns and the local economic environment, way beyond the limits of a single town or city, and to stress the 'natural region' as the basic framework for planning. This tallied, of course, with Howard's idea of the social city. Geddes' method translated into a principle that underlined urban planning throughout the 20th century: first, survey the region and identify its characteristics and trends; second, analyse the survey; and third, produce and adopt a plan. Geddes, by taking Howard's ideas and adding in a wider geographical and more ecological element, gave what became known as urban and regional planning a logical structure.

By the mid-20th century, Geddes' and Howard's utopian ideas had developed into a powerful political and economic call for action, to deal with economically lagging regions in both the UK and the United States. These regions had been affected by the decline of those heavy manufacturing industries that had given rise to rapid 19th century urbanisation in the first place. Indeed, an American follower of Geddes, Lewis Mumford (1895–1990) produced a work in the 1930s, *The Culture of Cities* (Mumford, 1938), which became the guidebook of the regional planning movement to such an extent that planners started to apply Howard's ideas to the large-scale decentralisation of people and jobs from London to satellite towns in the surrounding home counties of England from the 1940s through to the 1970s (Hall and Tewdwr-Jones, 2020).

It was during this period, in the midst of a global crisis brought about by war, that these initially utopic ideas had direct and practical application. A convert to both Howard's and Geddes' ideas in the UK, Patrick Abercrombie (1879–1957) gave them shape in his seminal wartime plan for London's future, the Greater London Plan of 1944 (Abercrombie and Forshaw, 1943; Abercrombie, 1945), produced at the direct request of the UK government. Extraordinary events required extraordinary responses and, at a time when existing governmental structures nationally and locally were no longer in place, it was delegated to an urban visionary to respond to the planning and city reconstruction challenge. Abercrombie's achievement was to weld together the complex ideas of Howard and Geddes and turn them into a graphic plan for the future development of a region that extended for 30 miles and encompassed more than 10 million people. The broad aim of the Greater London Plan was essentially Howard's; it called for the planned decentralisation of half a million people from the overcrowded central area of London into a series of new planned communities, which would be self-contained towns for living and working. The commitment to and realisation of this objective came about because of the dire condition that London and the UK found itself in during the war, with an urgent need for new housing and the need to rebuild existing infrastructure. The method of how to achieve this, by contrast, was essentially Geddes', and his survey analysis plan approach. Nevertheless, it was Abercrombie who fused it into a political and visionary plan for the future.

Summary

Visionary thinking and the construction of visions (or shared expectations about the future) have permeated the world's literature, art and, more latterly, film for many centuries. The early writings of thinkers such as Plato and More gave rise to a long tradition of futures thinking, culminating in the more formal foresight techniques that we see in operation today. As art and literature have changed our perceptions of the future, so cities have come to be shaped by (and shape) our views of the future. In parallel, urban planning also saw the emergence of visionaries such as Ebenezer Howard and Patrick Geddes, whose work influenced and helped to form the inspiration for the ideals of modern-day planning, and the way we think about future cities. In the next chapter, we will look in more detail at how planning has evolved to engage with and plan the city in an urban age.

4

Planning and governing the future city

Introduction

We have seen through the course of the previous chapters of this book that the story of creating urban futures, from the development of visions to the employment of urban and regional planning as governmental intent and action, has been one of ebbs and flows. The case for initiating any long-term urban vision for a city, whatever its size and form, and at whatever moment in history it happens to be situated, has necessitated a political programme to deal with major complexities and externalities associated with the growth or decline of places – whether this has involved, for example, attempting to stymie rapid uncontrollable urbanisation, rolling out better and decent housing for those in need of shelter, providing adequate infrastructure to meet people's mobility needs and energy consumption, committing a city to green growth and sustainable practices, or ensuring good standards of health provision to address an urban society's basic human needs and survival. These issues, common as they are across time and space as a hallmark of urban living and urban trends, manifest themselves in different ways in different places. But the ways in which these issues are recognised, analysed and addressed within cities and nations have been the identifiable features of urban planning movements, enacted as functions of city governments.

The task of utilising urban and regional planning to examine all the changing aspects of urban life, by analysing problematic trends and trajectories and then ensuring a political and resourced programme of action to remedy them, is never a straightforward or easy process. Discussion of, and commitment to, an appropriate way forward for a city and region are heavily dependent on agreement on the validity of the intelligence and evidence base, on the various options available to think about the future, and on the political, economic, regulatory, social and environmental contexts for decision-making. As the task of planning proceeds even within a single nation, the world is forever changing, thus rendering agreed action plans potentially outdated by the time they are implemented. Ensuring that a city's political commitments are 'future-proof' is just one of the many requirements of shaping urban futures.

As cities across the globe have undergone cycles of structural change, and have developed, grown and declined, and as the range of urban issues has exploded and become, seemingly, more complex as the centuries have passed, so too has debate about the shape, form and adequacy of urban planning regimes to manage and address urban futures. This has been accompanied by an exceptionally fluid political and governmental context that has also been subject to questions about a range of related issues. These include matters concerning institutional design, the state's role and power over people's lives, and calls for either greater or less regulation of markets. As we shall see later in this chapter, there has also been consternation over who finances urban improvements and for whose benefit. Wrapped around these debates is the question of whether representative democracy, through state and city elections, provides an adequate voice for citizens who have to live with the implications of political and planning decisions.

Invariably, urban and regional planning, as the common means through which urban futures are given shape and a trajectory as an urban and governmental project, has been subject to a prolonged attack from various quarters in numerous countries for its perceived interventionist approach. There is now a large body of work that seeks to understand the evolution of planning approaches across the globe, particularly the adaptation of planning under varying forms of neoliberalism and pro-market agendas. Some of this research attempts to consider empirical insights into new state spaces and the actors that are shaping them. Other writers have made theoretical explanation of the reform agenda (planning, governmental, political) their goal (Gleeson and Low, 2007; Booth, 2009; Gurran et al, 2014). Much of the literature of the 20th century points to an academic understanding of government policies on planning as being characterised as a seismic new, or at least different, moment, and as part of a post-political debate on what the fundamental objectives of the activity of urban planning should, or could, be in a very different context to the one that saw the rise of urban planning as a utopic model a century earlier.

In this chapter, we examine the more recent evolution of urban planning and its response to these contextual, state and neoliberal pressures, and explore how city visioning can still help develop a stronger focus for an activity that we might refer to as futures-based urban planning in and for our cities and urban areas. The links between urban planning, city foresight and wider state theory are explored and the implications of city visioning and long-term strategic planning in cities are highlighted. We focus on exploring the changing role that planning and city foresight might play within the future governance of cities, and how place-based leadership and place management can reinvigorate urban planning approaches.

How we govern the urban

For most of the 20th century, the way we governed cities could be characterised as depending on the constitutional settlement of individual nations (Kornberger, 2012). For example, in some countries, strong national (or central) governments possessed both tax-raising and tax-spending powers, legislating for urban planning regimes that were operated by subnational governments in uniform ways (such as in China), irrespective of geographical difference or distinctive place-based problems. In other nations, such as in federal countries (Germany or the United States, for example), both the national government and individual states may have possessed tax-raising powers and distinctive planning arrangements to address problems in different parts of their countries. In yet other countries (such as in the UK), government has been split between central government and local government, although finances have been determined principally at the national level, and planning – although created nationally – has been implemented by local authorities acting as de facto agents of central government (Rhodes, 1988). These different styles of government give rise to different styles of legal planning processes, as well as setting the parameters (constraints, discretion) for individual scales of government and planning to be able to respond to various inter- and intra-urban challenges.

During the period since the 1980s, these governance approaches have been shaped and reshaped continuously (Buck et al, 2005). This may be the consequence of nation state governments embarking on restructuring models, but also because there may have been pressure within some nations from regions and cities for greater self-government, or at least the devolution of government responsibilities to subnational areas. In other cases, governments have attempted to change the administrative boundaries of cities, or to constitute new governing forms to reflect changing urbanisation patterns (such as the rise of edge cities in the United States; see, for example, Phelps, 2012). In another hallmark of the ideological preference for governing cities, some nations have also instituted new governing arrangements by establishing ad hoc governance bodies for specific tasks alongside elected subnational government. These have included special-purpose governance vehicles (for the delivery of the 2012 Olympic Games in London, for example; see Brown et al, 2012), commercial and property companies for urban regeneration (such as business improvement districts in the United States and the UK; see, for example, Justice and Skelcher, 2009) and even public–private joint ventures.

All these governance forms have reshaped the 20th century urban government model, to the point that we can now say that cities are characterised by somewhat messy, fixed and incremental institutional arrangements and governing forms, involving both the state and business interests, and sometimes a mixture of them operating in partnership, which employ strategies and resources that affect urban development. Consequently, when we think of how governments manage cities through urban planning, it is no longer a singular activity that we are referring to, but a myriad of institutional, partnership and quasi-public organisations that, combined, reshape the form and feel of cities. Formal legal urban planning arrangements may still exist in and for cities, but the question is whether the more ad hoc governance arrangements replicate or override the urban planning systems, or whether they sit in a parallel world to them. One distinctive feature of this myriad governance form for cities, though, is a tendency to adopt ad hoc institutional initiatives for more short-term periods, and returns, rather than address long-term trajectories.

We need to be concerned about this government and governance mix within any given urban area since it is politics – and the context for political decision-making – that will determine the existence and status of urban planning, and the call for city visions for long-term change. In the literature since the 1990s, this governance and planning churn has received considerable attention (see, for example, Jessop, 2000; Tewdwr-Jones and Allmendinger, 2006; Jones, 2019b; Sturzaker and Nurse, 2020). Governmental and institutional changes within any nation state demonstrate a heavy political steer in the type of scalar politics desirable, and often complete disagreement politically, on the appropriate governmental structure to deal with city-wide or subnational issues. The different preferences reveal debates on the ongoing relationships between different political tiers of the state but are also affected by global governance trends (Herrschel and Newman, 2002). Urban planning, as one manifestation of the fluid, changing and changeable forms of state restructuring, remains a deeply contested process. It is stretched vertically and horizontally across the various politically axes of the state and attempts to mediate between different interest groups and address sectoral policy concerns that, often, pull in opposite directions. As the governmental and institutional structures are amended politically, so urban planning is seen as a construct of those structures.

The governance frame itself is not a static construct, even though it comprises layers of institutions possessing differential roles and power. The political process constantly re-layers governance, removes discretion from some governmental scales, adds to others, and changes the balance of relationships between the institutions, in a way described by Agnew (1999) as a 'jostling of power'. These changes are as much affected by forces outside a nation as inside it, with global economic ebbs and flows, climate change, demographics, migration and mobility all driving the need for change and state reaction. Urban planning, by implication, is utilised by the state, and by different layers of the state, to recognise the forces of change, and their implications for the status quo, and to manage tensions and expectations. It is a delicate balancing act, with no guarantee of certainty of outcome or results to meet all those expectations. Carving out long-term city visions is therefore often susceptible to more short-term political concerns.

Aspects of the ongoing and emerging relationships between pre-existing and new scalar politics of the state (MacKinnon, 2011), with responsibility for urban planning, form a contested and malleable framework of territorial governance and management (Haughton et al, 2010). Within this understanding of territorial governance, different levels of government and new forms of governance 'flex their muscles' and claim ownership of responsibility for urban planning and strategic coordination across and within government (Tewdwr-Jones, 2012). In some nations, such as the UK, a push towards decentralisation from nation states to cities and regions has created new devolved governmental structures and institutions (Shaw and Tewdwr-Jones, 2017). Many of these have been accompanied by new forms of planning, or at least the reawakening of metropolitan or strategic planning processes that may or may not be intended to be city-wide (Zimmermann et al, 2020). In some cases, this has also created a patchwork of governance styles that differ from city to city within individual nation states, do not necessarily cover all the sectoral areas and governmental functions one would expect to see, and privilege certain institutions and pro-economic growth agendas over social and sustainability issues (Etherington and Jones, 2018). To some, this era has been characterised as the 'post-political' (Swyngedouw, 2018), where more progressive forms of politics (including traditional democratic government and even planning) are replaced by more managerial forms that work towards consensual governance.

In this context, attempts to empower local political leaders in crafting locally defined and coordinated approaches to economic growth and service delivery in cities are 'being developed in the context of unclear rationales, complex geographies, centre-local deal-making, public sector restructuring and expenditure reductions' (Pike et al, 2016: 39). It also means that the role and desirability of a city to have a singular and uniform long-term city vision in this melee is much more challenging. Urban planning is no longer the preserve of government-appointed planners or, for that matter, elected city leaders, but rather performs the role of facilitating and delivering growth agendas of the market.

The fact that planning still survives at all in these contexts is, perhaps, surprising, given that it is a relic of 20th century idealism and was intended as a progressive function of national, regional and local states (Harrison et al, 2020). Urban governments used to have the power, finances and professional personnel to carve out a trajectory for cities, formulate plans and commit to action over years if not decades (Hall, 1998). In the 21st century, we still find cities and nations around the globe that are designed to function in this way; parts of Asia, the Middle East and Africa still retain strong nation states and are committed to subnational (local, city or metropolitan) elected government, embarking on state-led urban planning exercises (Wu, 2015; De Satgi and Watson, 2018; Hashim, 2019). But in parts of Europe, the United States and Australasia, the picture is much more mixed, in terms of the role of both the state and the market in shaping cities, in the use of urban planning mechanisms that may be more focused on short-term implementation and development delivery rather than on strategic policy and plan-making, and in embracing more diverse voices beyond government, and beyond traditional planning consultation modes, in discussing and executing urban change. Cities are becoming more contradictory (Beauregard, 2018).

Positively, these changing roles for the state and for urban governments do move the agendas away from what may be seen as the narrow agendas of the ruling political elite, and open up debate about cities to wider constituencies of interests; they also tend to disrupt the heavy hand and machinery of bureaucratised government in favour of localised or community responses to urban problems. But, negatively, these changing roles for the state and for cities may also allow in globalised capitalist interests, and serve to neoliberalise cities, deregulate and privatise public services, undermine place distinctiveness and lead to a polarisation of agendas between markets and citizens (Peck and Tickell, 2002). It amounts to a 'hollowing out' of the state and its replacement with non-state actors, a process that has been underway for more than two decades (Patterson and Pinch, 1995). The consequence may well be even greater urban contention and the need for urban governments to resolve differences across cities that are more fragmented, between disparate actors, short-term and long-term perspectives, and pro-growth and more sustainable agendas. This brokerage is achieved through democratic and less-democratic means, short-term investment sweeteners and compromises, selective alliances and developing incremental partnerships for infrastructure delivery; it is what has been referred to as 'city statecraft' (Peck, 2015; Pike et al, 2019).

Aspects of these trends are not new: Harvey's (1989) discussion of urban entrepreneurialism highlighted how urban governance had shifted from local service delivery to more creative uses of local resources to boost local growth through new partnerships. The key question to emerge from this kaleidoscopic institutional urban landscape is, what role is there – if any – for urban planning and the adoption of urban visions and city foresight in a series of politicised processes that are essentially undermining the props on which progressive planning regimes are built?

Selecting the form of urban planning in a new 'urban age'

Within the urban planning discipline there have been several related theoretical developments, each attempting to understand the present and future role of planning and of urban governance in emerging forms of subnational scales and a post-political context. In parallel to the literature emerging in political science and geography, planning literature concepts have also varied in substance and reflect the lack of consensus academically on the form and trajectory of theory within planning.

The writings include, among others, notions of:

- Collaborative planning (Healey, 1997) and spatial strategy and governance (Vigar et al, 2000; Healey, 2007), which emphasise aspects of spatial coordination and integration across agencies within regional and urban partnerships.
- Spatial planning and governance (Tewdwr-Jones and Allmendinger, 2006; Tewdwr-Jones, 2012), where planning is viewed as a function

of vested interests and spatial flows within the political arena of both government and governance.
- City-regionalism and governance (Herrschel and Newman, 2002), where spatial strategy is one of the outcomes of increasing city- and metropolitan-scale reactions of European and global trends.
- Sustainable development (Pinderhughes, 2004).
- The development of agonism within planning, following Mouffe's work, which discusses how to work with conflict in cities as part of pluralistic democracy (Hillier, 2003).
- Soft spaces and fuzzy boundaries (see, for example, Allmendinger and Haughton, 2010; Haughton et al, 2013), where spatial planning is characterised as enabling the emergence of spaces for experimentation that benefit neoliberal pro-growth agendas.

What characterises many of these conceptual debates is acknowledgement of a move to a post-political order, and an ongoing frustration with what urban planning has become, in the midst of a series of urban and regional crises. This includes concern with urban planning's complicit role in furthering neoliberal agendas aimed at economic growth at all costs. Furthermore, there is a dichotomy between planning within fixed local or metropolitan governmental boundaries (a hallmark of 20th century planning) and planning as form to cater for fluid or agile spatial change (which does not and cannot respect administrative lines on a map) (Massey, 2005). We might also identify selectivity in the way planning involves narrow sectional interests, pandering to ruling political elites and pro-development interests at a time when the world is concerned about those at the margins of society, excluded from decision-making and at the mercy of the political elite's policies (Carmon and Fainstein, 2013). Given the complexity, it is little wonder that planning sometimes struggles to align all the various interests and organisations within the same spatial scale that, together, remain necessary to shape and deliver change for urban areas. There is frustration with the ongoing failure of nation and local states to get to grips with the climate change emergency and address, and give force to, truly urban sustainable practice. More lately, led by populist forces, there has been the continuous undermining of democratic planning processes by economic and political forces, portraying them as a socialist construct, outmoded for present-day concerns.

Underneath most of these concerns, in part, is a belief that the tools and methods available for effective urban planning are no longer fit for purpose. As Allmendinger and Haughton (2012: 101) argue, 'what we are witnessing appears to be a new moment in the post-political management of dissent and the continuing selective displacement of the handling of controversial issues to alternative modes and scales of planning', and the terms of what is now possible for urban planning to achieve have been deliberately limited (MacLeod, 2013; O'Callaghan et al, 2014; Haughton et al, 2016).

A variety of contemporary complex urban issues, and the pace with which change occurs, have also undermined the case for fixed long-term plans. Demographic change and economic cycles serve to amend the assumptions on which urban plans have been based, resulting in plans becoming overly or insufficiently ambitious by the time they have been adopted by political leaders. Fixing the limits of an urban plan to the administrative boundaries of city government can ignore the actual spatial flows occurring, particularly between the city and its hinterland and neighbouring cities. As we noted earlier, it is no longer city government alone that manages and acts on city change, nor is it professional planners employed in city governments alone who have full control over urban management; many would argue that that is a good outcome. The process of plan-making can also take too long, such is the requirement to address so many issues affecting the city, harnessing all the data and intelligence necessary to understand what is happening, develop scenarios and alternative courses of action, perhaps model those choices, and then seek political, market and democratic legitimacy to adopt a course of action. These requirements, by themselves, are not necessarily the fault of professional planners and urbanists, or of political leaders; in fact, these components of urban planning are still promoted by protagonists for specific ends (see, for example, Healey, 2007; Beauregard, 2015; Goodspeed, 2020). They are merely the components of good planning necessary to manage change in and across the city. However, it is little surprise to learn that in a fast-paced world, with global economic and investment flows, questions of speed, timeliness and relevance have, with some justification, become the reasons for urban plans – indeed urban planning more generally – to be sidelined or even ignored.

Global flows and national and regional change are now so short term and immediate that it becomes difficult to spatially fix the problem in a geographically bounded way. Nations that have rigid urban planning processes, or even a defined constitution with set powers and responsibilities, or federal tax regimes, may not be so ready to sideline their urban planning regimes. On the other hand, for other nations, with looser and changeable governmental structures, and political discretion at their disposal, eager to respond to changing economic conditions with pace, urban planning may be seen as a long-term luxury that is no longer appropriate to shape the future of cities that aspire to be globally agile and highly competitive. The irony is that, in some cases, it is urban government itself, often aided by national governments, that has sought to downplay its own urban plans to create a more flexible and incremental form of city policy context that can adjust to rapidly changing circumstances and new investment opportunities. So, what opportunities are there for urban planning to play a role in shaping the future of cities?

The 21st century case for urban planning

The case for planning has not diminished, but has increased, over time. In the contemporary world, we are witnessing cities responding to ongoing concerns and crises with proactive displays of urban planning. In the wake of the COVID-19 pandemic, the rapidity with which urban areas changed their transport priorities in many cities away from the car and to more pedestrian and cycle-friendly places (Nurse and Dunning, 2020) has been a belated acknowledgement of something that planners have been advocating for decades. Later in the pandemic experience, people reacted to the threat of contagion by avoiding public transport, working from home more frequently and shopping in localised rather than urban centre locations. How we shape cities needs to be about a balanced sustainable form of urban living, rather than a focus on development parcels, global economic growth or over-engineered transport schemes (Lall and Wahba, 2020).

A heightened awareness of the importance of parks and gardens in urban areas for health and wellbeing purposes has seen the rise of pop-up or pocket parks in cities, a feature that can be traced back well before the garden city movement of 120 years ago (Ward Thompson et al, 2016). Lockdown has demonstrated for some communities the pleasure of using local and independent shops and cafes, rather than big supermarkets and international chains (Rudlin, 2020). Shop closures have occurred and temporary uses have developed (Crump, 2020), while shopping itself has not stopped people ordering goods online and seeing them being delivered directly to their door by courier. Logistic services have expanded with pressure placed on goods and services. Airports globally have become quiet hubs, as people are either unable to travel or else think twice about the consequences, with ramifications for emission targets and commitments to sustainability. People are commuting less from their home to sites of work in urban areas, with an acknowledgement from employees and employers that perhaps not everyone needs to travel into a place of work each day, particularly if they are fortunate enough to have good wifi access in their home (Baker, 2020). Local areas of attraction are now busier than they have ever been as international travel and tourism have been affected.

All these issues require some form of urban planning, not only in the way changing patterns of behaviour are supported, but also because for every change there will be consequential negative implications for those agencies and individuals that had benefited from the pre-COVID-19 world (Howie, 2020). Planning's function is also to assess what works and what does not work, and to map and analyse how these changes manifest themselves in different places. These changing times require urban planning to come into its own again, because it is more about assessing the changing patterns of urban living rather than building development and devising growth strategies (Matthews, 2020). Ultimately, it is not only the effects of the pandemic on cities that require positive planning responses.

Climate change and extreme weather events are now much more frequently wreaking havoc in urban areas, with the flooding of homes, businesses and infrastructure. Good planning means identifying locations that are more prone to inundation and limiting or prohibiting new development that might be affected in the medium term. This is a terrible occurrence for anyone who is affected, but there are implications for wider organisations. The insurance industry is one service that expects good planning to help insurance companies assess urban risks and resilience, the vulnerability of some cities over others, and likely claims for compensation. National security agencies also need to know what the infrastructure vulnerabilities are and where they are sited in the event of climatic impact. The consequential effects of these changes relate to the availability of technology, essential utilities and mobility services. In the future, cities will still function and provide essential services. But disruptions to infrastructure and energy supplies may not only affect how cities function; they may also affect the degree to which entire nations become vulnerable to insecurities outside their direct control.

Technological change since the 1980s has demonstrably affected urban areas, in the way we interact with services, in trade and business flows, in our work patterns, in our ability to control our home, in our navigation through places, in the way we shop and pay for goods and access finances, and in our ability to stay connected to friends and family. Planning has had to respond to the need for our demand for greater connectivity, with new infrastructure but also an awareness that technology changes our demand for spaces in cities. Increasing roll-outs of innovation districts and clusters, for incubation spaces, from small digital start-ups, have jarred with the traditional way the real estate market and aspects of urban planning have thought of service sector employment in cities. As cities across the globe have behaved competitively to attract large office-centred companies to their areas, urban planning has had to adapt by ensuring the steady supply of what is often referred to as 'grade A' office space. Thanks to the COVID-19 pandemic, as well as the emergence of the digital creative sector, we might begin to question whether this paradigm is suitable in the future to the same degree. Will the demand for large offices in prime urban centre locations survive these changes?

Two examples from the UK show what is and what is not possible with urban regeneration. Manchester's 'Northern Quarter' is a city-centre location that has an agglomeration of independent coffee shops and bars, and is the home of start-up creative and digital companies (O'Connor and Gu, 2010). Manchester City Council did not impose a plan on the area, but rather allowed the area to flourish without intervention. It is now one of the most popular places in the city. By contrast, 'Silicon Roundabout' was the branded name for a creative and digital cluster at Old Street, just to the north of the world financial centre, the City of London. It expanded with tech firms, marketing and web companies, and hot-desking spaces. As it occurred, it was lauded by national and regional politicians, with planning policies enacted to support its expansion (Volpicelli, 2020). Very quickly, property developers sought permission in the vicinity for grade A offices, high-end hotels, restaurants and loft-living that pushed rents up, gentrified the area and caused the smaller businesses to move further out of the city. The lessons from these experiences is that, sometimes, urban planning's role is to recognise when urban planning is not needed.

These examples demonstrate that the importance of urban planning is not to reproduce successful development from elsewhere and create identikit cities. Rather it is to understand places – place uniqueness – and the need to harness intelligence about how places are changing beyond the expectations of politicians and businesses, to keep the best features of the past that people have an emotional place connection to, and to develop scenarios for the future that highlight good trajectories. Above all, urban planning is there to promote urban liveability, not as a commodified desirable luxury lifestyle based on property acquisition, but as a principle of living well, in health, in sustainable limits, in ways that maximise benefits for all. In the words of Hall (2014), 'good cities, better lives'.

Summary

To make urban planning work effectively to support and shape the cities of the future, there has to be some compromise in what planning is, what it can do, what it should avoid doing and who is involved with it. That means avoiding thinking solely in terms of fixed long-term static plans and excluding large sections of urban communities from having a direct say in how places change, overcoming a fixation with administrative and governmental boundaries, adopting and returning technological, mapping and analytical modelling back into urban planning processes, and encouraging innovative community-led projects. Urban planning could still happen at different scales, and so it should be, since localised change can be felt more strategically and vice versa; it could also still be enacted by a whole host of different sorts of actors across and within cities. However, the context for urban planning now is vastly different from the 20th century tools that have been relied on to date.

This changing mindset will be as much of a challenge for urban planners as it will be for cities. In reality, the form that urban planning takes was already being subject to scrutiny with the accusation that it was not delivering for all sections of urban society even before COVID-19, and even from voices within planning (see, for example, Watson, 2009; Agyeman, 2020; Keil and Hertel, 2020). It is necessary to think of urban planning as a series of components, or even as a toolkit, from which techniques are drawn and used, according to the needs of a specific place. This approach places less focus on the idea of a single all-encompassing urban plan, drawn up and implemented by the local state, and more emphasis on urban planning as a continuous wave of intelligence and flows, analysed in real time, employed for use by a range of actors and agencies in a city. We might refer to this style as a more 'agile' form of urban planning (Hall and Tewdwr-Jones, 2020; Tewdwr-Jones and Galland, 2020), which still necessitates, critically, the need for an urban vision, as a trajectory of desirable outcomes, and applies across long time periods, but involves – essentially – a requirement for programme and project management rather than an institutionalised and rigid system. Employing urban planning and seeing it as a changeable and flexible inclusive process does require an emphasis on understanding places, while also developing the idea of a pluralistic style of place-based leadership beyond urban government itself.

Alongside urban planning debates, and somewhat separate from them, has been a growing academic interest in the role of leadership in local and regional development. Instead of focusing concern on the attributes and style of political leadership or the capacity of professional urban planners to manage cities, the literature has instead addressed what is referred to as 'place-based leadership' as a product of relationships between a range of actors and agencies within the urban realm. This includes those representing local or regional government, but also incorporates a variety of state, business, community, voluntary, educational and civic organisations.

Hambleton and Howard (2013) suggest that responsibility for place-based leadership is shared between local elected politicians, professionals employed in the public sector or community sector, and citizens who may be representative of wider business or civil society sectors. The leadership deploys different forms of power, deriving from institutions, and some control over resources, using expert knowledge and webs of social networks (Sotarauta, 2016). But because the actors are drawn from different institutional settings, the style of leadership is relational; this means that it requires interaction across different types of organisational, professional, sectoral and territorial boundaries to make it relevant (Gibney et al, 2009; Horlings et al, 2017).

As others have argued, we agree that the strategic leadership of place is therefore needed to respond to the demands of cities, which is:

> concerned with facilitating interdisciplinarity across institutional boundaries, technology themes, sub-territories and professional cultures in order to promote the development of innovation across the public and private sector domain ... [but also] to ensure the comprehensive engagement of local communities so that they can both contribute to and benefit fully from the outcomes. (Gibney et al, 2009: 10)

5

Future narratives for the city: smart *and* sustainable?

Introduction

The intense, politicised and highly divisive debate over whether the UK should leave membership of the European Union between 2016 and 2020 (so-called Brexit) highlighted the fact that those offering competing visions of the future can become locked in an intractable battle. Similarly, the devastating COVID-19 pandemic has resulted in a great deal of soul-searching about creating a vision of what sort of place people want the UK to be in the future. In the world of cities and urban studies, we have seen a similarly important, but perhaps less brutal, battle of ideas, thoughts and visions as conceptualisations of the ideal city have been promoted in literature, art, academic discourse and policy and practice throughout history. This debate and discourse also have profound effects for the way we see and experience cities in the UK and elsewhere now, and in the future.

The two main strands of thinking, or narratives, that have emerged during the late 20th and early 21st centuries, and which build on previous historic principles, debates and discourses about cities, have been focused on sustainable cities and smart cities – both of which have been underpinned and strengthened by the emergence of international networks that promote dialogue and learning about the implementation of such cities. These two 'signifiers' or 'leitmotifs' have been highlighted and promoted not only by national governments, but also by city and municipal governments seeking to compete for investment and globalised capital.

In this chapter, we will begin by discussing and analysing how cities can be typified and conceptualised in terms of their 'ideal' characteristics. To do this, we will examine how new theories, such as actor network theory (ANT) and 'urban assemblage' theory, can help inform our thinking about cities. We then discuss and critically review the emergence of sustainable cities and smart cities before looking at the concept of 'smart *and* sustainable cities', and why visions lie at the heart of urban futures. Ultimately, as we will argue, if we are to re-imagine the future of our cities and create a solid basis for exploring and developing urban futures thinking, part of that process requires the co-production of coherent, participatory city visions that recognise the innate value of a place's character, and the needs of the people who live, work and play there.

Conceptualising and typifying the city: the evolution of thinking about cities

As we saw in Chapter 1, the way in which we have viewed the city has shifted and changed over time as writers, thinkers, academics and urban visionaries have influenced and been influenced by the past, present and future urban environment. Analysing the nature and form of this shift often depends on the disciplinary or practice perspective we might adopt (for example, sociology, geography, ecology, engineering and so on). As Iossifova et al (2018) point out, the city can be viewed as:

- *a clearly delineated entity*, for example in the form of a bounded space or analogous to a living organism (in the urban metabolism literature);
- *a counterpart of nature*, distinct from the natural or rural world;
- *the outcome of capitalist accumulation*, particularly in the fields of sociology and geography where the city is seen as rendered space that is consumed and produced;
- *a process*, which reflects, for example, different social structures or perhaps interrelated natural, social, economic, cultural and material flows; or
- *a complex adaptive system*, where complexity prevails and structures affect and are affected by individuals and collective agents.

Taking a different perspective, but with a focus still on cities, Farias (2009) suggests that there are three major understandings of cities that can be traced back to the early days of urban studies in the last century. These are broadly understanding the city as spatial forms, economic units and cultural formations.

First, for example, the ecological approach of the early Chicago School of Urban Sociology – see, for example, Burgess (1925) and Park (1952) – was that cities constitute a defined and definite spatial environment in which people and communities settle within, as a result of ecological processes such as competition for space; in this respect, therefore, the city is seen as a spatially bounded and delimited place.

Second, Christaller's (1933) central place theory and Weber's (1921) work on the role of cities in capitalism, both understand the city as an economic unit, and the more recent work of writers such as Florida (2002) see creative cities and global cities as economic actors – in a global city perspective, the city is seen not as a spatial object but as a network object that has a relationship with other cities. However, by using a collective description of a city such as 'London's success', we create a 'synecdothe', which treats a part of the object as the object, and ends up describing a collective belief or description of a city that may well fail to capture the many complex views and relationships that help shape that city (Farias, 2009).

Third, Farias (2009) suggests that we can trace back the concept of a city as being shaped and influenced by cultural formations to the work of Louis Wirth (1938) and others. Here, the city is seen as the outcome of the product of human nature and human culture, which invites a focus on communities and neighbourhoods (see, for example, the work of Lefebvre, 1991).

These three understandings of cities reflect a strong focus on thinking about them as single, or unified, objects. In reality, the situation is more complex, as writers such as Jane Jacobs and Michael Batty, in their different ways, have recognised. Cities are messy and complex and are made up of a myriad of different actors and relationships. As Amin and Thrift (2002: 27) note: '[T]he city is made up of potential and actual entities/associations/togetherness ... The accumulation of these entities can produce new becomings – because they encounter each other in so many ways, because they can be comprehended in so many ways, and because they exhibit "concrescence"'.

This concrescence means that people experience different kinds of urban reality so that we need to think of cities as multiple objects rather than a single object. As Latour and Hermant (1998) suggest, there is not one Paris but multiple Parises, which different people experience. This has given rise to a call for different understandings of the city to be deployed to recognise this complex set of experiences. For example, authors such as McFarlane (2011) and Ingeborgrud (2018a) suggest that the related concepts of 'actor network theory' (ANT) and 'urban assemblages' offer a more powerful way of providing insights into how cities can really be understood than object-related studies. ANT, for example, which provides insights for describing social relationships and the relationship between technology and people, was used by Graham and Marvin (2001) to unravel and unpack the hidden relationships between people and infrastructure in the context of urban areas. The idea of an assemblage was first introduced by Deleuze and Guattari (1987) to highlight the way in which human and non-human components are linked through a rhiozomatic network with multiple and complex connections. In essence, the proponents of assemblage theory suggest that objects (or things) can only be understood as a diverse whole constructed from heterogeneous parts. This includes everything from atoms and molecules to ecosystems and cities. As a practice theory, the main focus of assemblage theory is not to interpret phenomena or things, but to explain how human and non-human parts function together to drive our experiences of the phenomena or things (Sesay et al, 2016). As DeLanda (2006) suggests, as social justice movements are assemblages of several networked communities, so cities are assemblages of people, networks and organisations. Researchers have therefore applied assemblage theory to the urban context to understand, for example, how city visioning processes or the creation of city visions can be seen as representing the construction of different types of assemblage as the vision was created and defined (Ingeborgrud, 2018b).

Similarly, as Batty argues, cities should be understood as complex systems within what is described as the science of cities. As Batty (2013: 7) suggests:

> To do this, we adopt the contemporary approach of complexity theory, which treats systems as being constructed from the bottom up, in a hierarchical fashion in which their basic components – functions that relate to how populations interact with one another – determine the networks on which individuals and groups engage with each other through social and economic exchange.

There is, today, a clear sense in which the inherent complexity of cities is recognised more readily in both the sciences and social sciences (Keith et al, 2020). However, as we suggested earlier in this book, the complexity of cities does not mean that we cannot or should not try to plan and manage our path to a more sustainable urban future.

Moreover, just as the academic thinking about the way in which we need to conceptualise the city has changed ad morphed over the past 100 years, the way in which we have typified the ideal city' has also changed throughout history (Eames and Dixon, 2012) (see Chapter 3). Lynch (1981) saw three main types of urban form that have arisen from antiquity, and from more recent urban forms:

- *cosmic* – highly monumental and anchored in cosmology (for example Babylon);

- *organic* – freeform and anti-geometric, balanced and in tune with nature (for example, Athens); and
- *mechanistic* – simplicity, productive efficiency, autonomous parts linked by well-defined dynamic connections (for example, Le Corbusier's modern city designs).

Building on this, Daffara (2006) used these three metaphors to develop a useful and extended genealogical classification or typology of city visions throughout history (see Table 5.1). Daffara (2006) sees four main strands running through this thinking: cosmic, organic, mechanistic and eclectic hybrid (the last of these a product of academic and policy/practice discourse in the 20th century). For example, Thomas More's Utopian capital Amaurot (which did incorporate elements of control and regulation) is seen as a direct predecessor of a more modern technocity or smart cit driven by technology. In contrast, more modern visions of eco cities or green cities' (or sustainable cities) have their origins in the Greek *polis*, or city state.

Table 5.1: Genealogical classification of city visions

City archetype	Antiquity	Pre-modern	Modern	Post-modern
Cosmic	• Temple city • Atlantis	• Renaissance city • City of the sun	• City beautiful (US)	• New urban monumentality
Organic	• Greek polis	• Medieval city	• Garden/social city (Ebenezer Howard) • 'Biopolis' (Patrick Geddes)	• Eco-city (or sustainable city); • Green city
Mechanistic	• Imperial city	• Amaurot (capital of More's Utopia)	• Cité Industrielle • Broadcare city (Frank Lloyd Wright) • Radiant city (Le Corbusier)	• Non-place • Technocity • Technoburbia
Eclectic hybrid				• Cultural city • Heritage city • Global city • Informational city • Creative city • Cosmopolis • Ecumemopolis

Source: Adapted from Daffara (2006)

For Daffara (2004), much of the thinking behind the post-modern typology of the city, and city visions, was linked with the growth of the sustainability agenda since the 1970s and 1980s. For example, he suggests that four futures are linked to this agenda but with very different outcomes:

- a *technocity*, or a place where urban problems remain unresolved and is an antecedent to ecological and cultural collapse;
- a *smart city*, where people are trying to resolve the contradictions of urban sprawl and its negative systemic impacts through the management of growth;
- an *eco-city*, where people reconstruct their lives to achieve the goal of sustainability through sustainable development; and
- a *Gaian city*, where all urban contradictions and problems are solved within a sustainable and holistic culture.

Huxley (2006) offers a different typology to identify three types of spatial rationality that links different types of spatial organisations and environmental qualities to more general schemes of urban and social reform in the 19th and early 20th century. These comprise:

- disposable spatial rationalities, which attempt to impose order and draw boundaries (for example, Ebenezer Howard's 'garden city');
- generative spatial rationality, which combines medical and biological metaphors with modern technology to combat disease and moral decay (for example, Benjamin Ward Richardson's *Hygeia: A city of health* of 1876); and
- vitalist spatial rationality, which focuses on social and spiritual development (for example, Patrick Geddes' planning theories of social cohesion and harmony).

Such typologies or classifications are attempts to identify thematic similarities in the emerging practice, policy and discourse about urban futures. As Griggs et al (2017) suggest, discourses are practices in that they are produced by actors, who join together a series of heterogeneous elements into a cohesive whole, although the resultant formations also help to structure and shape actions, social behaviour and institutions. Therefore, the types of city vision defined earlier are not material objects nor necessarily in existence beyond or before the discourse. Often such badges are a signifier that is brought into existence through discursive practices. They may be empty, in the sense that they are used to galvanise support that is lacking, or floating, because they can be articulated in different ways by a range of hegemonic projects. However, policy and practice through institutional involvement can also underpin and strengthen these dominant discourses (Hodson and Marvin, 2014).

Just as academic discourse and debate have helped shape our conceptualisations of the city, so, in alliance with policy and practice, they have been interwoven and interlinked to provide sustenance and succour to the emergence of two dominant city futures (or signifiers): the sustainable city and the smart city (Whitehead, 2003; Cugurullo, 2018; Martin et al, 2018). The focus has been not only on whether existing cities meet the requirements of such leitmotifs, but also on how new urban futures may be constructed to meet the normative aspirations of an idealised urban future. The evidence for this is to be found not only in a range of national and international programmes and projects directed by institutions that have focused on these urban futures (for example, the Habitat II conference in 1996 and the EU Smart Cities and Communities Programme via the Horizon 2020 programme), but also in the plethora of academic and grey literature that has been focused on them.

In turn, the discourses promote and strengthen the process of urban policy mobilities, which assist in enabling the transfer and integration of these city futures in different contexts internationally; as Joss et al (2019) suggest, the smart city is a 'global discourse network', or a collection of locally contextualised but globally connected and interwoven discourses. This internationalisation of both the concept and policy and practice of sustainable cities and smart cities has also often been founded on international actors delivering city projects and the networked learning of bringing the actors together (Caprotti, 2019). The next two sections therefore examine the shape and form of these two distinctive, but linked, conceptualisations.

Sustainable cities

The origins of the term 'sustainable city' (or 'eco city') can be found in previous 'organic' city visions such as Patrick Geddes' biopolis and Ebenezer Howard's garden city. Howard's vision, as we discussed in Chapter 3, was a blend of the best elements of town and country, brought to life through a series of interconnected and self-contained garden cities, surrounded by green-belt areas. In turn, Geddes suggested that planning must start with a survey of the resources of a natural region, how humans respond to those resources and the cultural landscapes created by the interaction of this relationship. The thinking from these visionaries subsequently helped shape urban and regional planning in the UK, the United States and elsewhere (Zhou and Williams, 2013; Hall, 2014; see also Chapter 3).

It was not until the 1960s and 1970s, however, that the concept of what a sustainable city might be started to permeate the world of urban studies. Whitehead (2003; 2011) suggests that this increasing focus was the result of the interweaving of an ecological crisis and the urban crisis. The former had been spawned by the rapid post-war growth and development of urban areas in the United States and elsewhere: writers such as Rachel Carson (1962) in *Silent Spring* had already alerted the world to the importance of environmentalism and the interactions between human activities and ecosystem health. The urban crisis had also been increasingly recognised as an important issue for the quality of life of those living in cities, particularly those in the global south. As a result, and as other texts – such as the Club of Rome's *Limits to Growth* report (Meadows et al, 1972), which highlighted the unstable relationship between population growth and resource use – were published, there was a growing focus on the role of cities in the growing ecological crisis (Hodson and Marvin, 2014). There had also been some pioneering moves to develop alternative eco-communities, set physically away from from cities: for example, the Findhorn project in 1962 in Scotland and the Arcosanti complex built in the Arizona desert in 1970. Although initially sporadic, these gained traction and Arcosnati and its emphasis on 'arcology' (or the relationship between archaeology and ecology through the thinking of Paolo Soleri) influenced subsequent thinking about sustainable cities (Zhou and Williams, 2013).

These growing concerns about cities were first addressed in a systematic way in the United Nations (UN) Centre for Human Settlements (Habitat) Conference in Vancouver in 1976, which laid the foundations for the principles of sustainable urban development. Although the conference did not formally define the term 'sustainable city', it was important for debating crucial issues such as the challenges of providing clean water and sanitation, the migration to cities, slum living and the potential that lay behind a more sustainable approach to urban development.

As the ramifications of the Brundtland Report (1987) also became clearer, writers, academics and practitioners began to bring different strands of thinking together (de Jong et al, 2015). Richard Register (1987) is credited with first using the term 'eco-city' in which he outlined the eco-city as one built according to the principles of living within environmental limits (set within the ecological capacity of the city's bioregion). The emphasis in using the term was very much on the environmental impact of cities and Register had been influenced by the 1960s and 1970s counterculture of projects such as Arcosanti by Paolo Soleri. As he wrote quite directly (Register, 1987: 1): 'An ecocity is an ecologically healthy city. No such city exists.'

However, as Whitehead (2003) notes, during the 1990s there was also a further urban policy focus at the global level, which built on the 1976 conference and Brundtland to move towards an explicit focus on sustainable cities. He suggests that there was a growing number of major international and European-level policies and initiatives that underscored the growing emphasis on sustainable cities. These included:

- The UN Sustainable Cities Programme (1990) – this integrated the sustainable development remits of the United Nations Centre for Human Settlements and the United Nations Environment Programme.
- The European Commission's 1990 Green Paper on the Urban Environment (European Commission, 1990) – this was a response by the European Commission and leading European cities to the perceived neglect of urban environmental issues relative to those of rural areas.
- The European Commission's Expert Group on the Urban Environment (1991) – an independent group composed of national representatives and experts to consider how future planning could influence the urban environmental aspects of the European Commission's Environmental Programme.
- The UN Conference on Environment and Development (1992), *Agenda 21*, Chapter 7, 'Promoting sustainable human settlement development'.
- The European Sustainable Communities Programme (1993) – launched by the European Commission's Expert Panel on the Urban Environment.
- The European Sustainable Cities Campaign (1994) – a coalition of 80 urban and regional authorities implementing sustainable urban policies.
- Habitat II – 'The City Summit' (1996) – with a focus on the implementation of Local Agenda 21 in urban areas. Local Agenda 21 (LA21) is a voluntary process of local community consultation with the aim of creating local policies and programmes that work towards achieving sustainable development. LA21 focuses on awareness raising, capacity building, community participation and partnership development.

Definitions as to what a sustainable city really is differ in range and diversity. The UN Human Settlement Programme defined such a city as (UN, 2002: 4):

a city where achievements in social, economic and physical development are made to last. A sustainable city has a lasting supply of natural resources on which its development depends (using them only at a level of sustainable yield). A sustainable city maintains a lasting security from environmental hazards which may threaten development achievements (allowing only for acceptable risks).

The UN also developed a summary of the main elements of urban sustainability that characterised the three pillars of sustainability (social, economic and environment) underpinned by governance structures (see Table 5.2).

In contrast to these prescriptive conceptualisations, Rogers (1998) (and Rogers and Power, 2000) suggested that a sustainable city is a place where high quality of life is realised in partnership with policies that effectively create and promote self-sufficiency; in other words, making them more compact, better connected and less damaging to the environment. For Whitehead (2003), sustainable cities are never finished objects, however, whether as visions or blueprints, or artefacts, but are rather in a constant state of becoming.

The term 'sustainable city' has also been echoed in the use of alternative signifiers or leitmotifs, such as eco-city, green city, liveable city and resilient city (Zhou and Williams, 2013; Martin et al, 2018). For example, the term 'eco-city' has been used practically in the shaping of newly built South East Asian cities such as the Sino-Singapore

Table 5.2: Pillars for achieving urban sustainability

Social development	Economic development	Environmental management	Urban governance
• Education and health	• Green productive growth	• Forest and soil management	• Planning and decentralisation
• Food and nutrition	• Creation of decent employment	• Waste and recycling management	• Reduction of inequalities
• Green housing and buildings	• Production and distribution of renewable energy	• Energy efficiency	• Strengthening of civil and political rights
• Water and sanitation	• Technology and innovation (R & D)	• Water management (including freshwater)	• Support of national, regional and global links
• Green public transportation		• Air quality conservation	
• Green energy access		• Adaptation to and mitigation of climate change	
• Recreation areas and community support			

Source: UN (2013a)

Tianjin project, a city planned for 350,000 people and due for completion by the mid-2020s (Caprotti, 2019). While there may be subtle differences between these terms, the term 'sustainable city' is the dominant typology for envisioning a city or urban area that has the ultimate goal of sustainability.

Besides the sustainable development agenda, the sustainable city has also been driven by the concept of 'ecological modernisation' in both discourse and policy (Hodson and Marvin, 2017). This places a particular emphasis on balancing current and future economic growth with the efficient use of natural and ecological resources. This includes activities such as better energy and resource efficiency through technological innovation such as renewables and better environmentally friendly product design. Therefore, as processes and production become greener, the nature and rationale for industrial production are changed. A recent example of this thinking is the Green New Deal, promoted in both the United States and the UK, as a way of creating investment and jobs through new energy and built environment projects in cities.

The mainstreaming of the concept of the sustainable city can be understood in terms of the specific outcomes of regulatory processes, which themselves have been interwoven from their origins in political, economic and ecological history and traditions. The sustainable city must also be understood within the wider regional, national and international regulatory orders in which it is positioned and sustained (Whitehead, 2003). In other words, there is a sense in which, despite their name, sustainable cities are not necessarily equally sustainable for everyone. For example, in reality, is a sustainable city able to provide affordable and sustainable housing for all, or just privileged groups in 'eco-enclaves'?

The growth of the sustainable city agenda was fostered by a strong emphasis on a managerialism role for the city in boosting economic growth, so that cities were positioned as attractors for inward investment and also promoted as acting as the centres for innovation to tackle the ecological crisis (Hodson and Marvin, 2014). This was promoted not only through the neoliberalisation of policies in a global context, but also by an increasing emphasis on a 'carbon discourse' (targeting a reduction in emissions), which was underpinned by the Kyoto protocol in 1997. Cities therefore became the focus for thinking about a low (or net-zero) carbon future through the reduction of carbon emissions (Fu and Zhang, 2017a, 2017b).

In what became a growing period of austerity in the UK during the post-2008 recession, and the continued focus on sustainable cities, cities faced additional pressures, as the reality of climate change continued to hit home, and environmental movements such as Extinction

Rebellion forced many city authorities to act in the UK and elsewhere. Therefore, within the overall aegis of sustainable cities, the focus has shifted towards a growing emphasis on resilience and achieving net-zero carbon emissions many cities by 2030. If this is the case, what are the implications for the sustainable cities agenda, and how will issues of social justice and social equity play out? How realistic are net-zero carbon targets by 2030? These are certainly important questions to address.

It is also noteworthy that, at the same time that the sustainable city discourse was gaining traction during the 1990s and 2000s, there were moves in urban planning to look beyond the short term to the long term through the formation of city visions (see Chapter 1). For example, Parrad and Goux-Baudiment (2001) showed how important sustainable development, alongside competitive strategy, and the formulation of territorial projects were in driving cities towards developing long-term visions. An early example of the importance of sustainable development was seen in the Gothenburg 2050 vision of 2002, and later on, similar developments were also underway in the United States, underpinned by continuing academic discourse (Gaffikin and Sterrett, 2006; Iwaniec and Wiek, 2014). The link between visioning and the sustainable (and smart) cities agenda(s) is one to which we will return later in this chapter.

Certainly, the sustainable city discourse, and the continuing emergence of city visions playing out to the sustainable development theme, have been strengthened by initiatives such as the UN Sustainable Development Goals (Goal 11) (see Chapter 2). Here, making cities sustainable (UN, 2019) 'means creating career and business opportunities, safe and affordable housing, and building resilient societies and economies. It involves investment in public transport, creating green public spaces, and improving urban planning and management in participatory and inclusive ways'. We have also seen a parallel move to measure, evaluate, assess and benchmark the progress of cities towards the end goal of urban sustainability. This is part of a wider move to assess city performance. For example, there are now more than 150 city benchmarking initiatives that seek to compare and contrast hundreds of cities globally across a range of indicators, including economic performance (Moonen and Clark, 2013). In urban sustainability, there has been a plethora of tools and measurement systems relating to indicators and indices of various descriptions, each seeking to measure the three main pillars of urban sustainability, although differentiated according to whether they are citizen-led or expert-led. Recent 'leading' sustainable cities, measured according to their urban sustainability, include London and Stockholm (Arcadis, 2018).

Smart cities

Although the 'sustainable city' concept continues to run strongly through policy and practice discourses, over the past decade the smart city has gained traction as a major leitmotif, or 'global discourse network' in urban development (Joss et al, 2019). Essentially, the smart city discourse relates to a normative view of the future founded on a technology-led ecological modernisation (Trencher and Karvonen, 2017).

There is a very large number of definitions for smart city, which not only reflects the differing origins of the term, but also the varying disciplinary and institutional lenses through which a city can be viewed (Kitchin, 2015). For example, some highlight the smart city as an urban environment that is idealistic, alluring and more liveable than the complex, messy environments that we inhabit today. For others, the smart city provides a new market for urban management systems and an opportunity to sell technology-led solutions to city authorities facing environmental, economic and social challenges.

This lack of consensus, as in the case of sustainable cities, has led to a growing critical literature on smart cities, particularly as issues over the role of citizens, privacy and security are raised. Other critics have suggested that the concept is an 'empty signifier', which means discourses are fragmented and diverse as it is difficult to pin down what the concept means (Caprotti and Cowley, 2019). There have therefore been a variety of attempts at defining what a smart city is. For example (ISO, 2014: 2):

> Smart Cities [is] a new concept and a new model, which applies the new generation of information technologies, such as the internet of things, cloud computing, big data and space/geographical information integration, to facilitate the planning, construction, management and smart services of cities. Developing smart cities can benefit synchronized development, industrialization, informationization, urbanization and agricultural modernization and sustainability of cities development.

The term 'smart city' can be broadly related to two distinct understandings of what makes a city smart (Kitchin, 2015). First, the term 'smart city' is often used to focus on the increasing extent to which cities are composed of pervasive and ubiquitous information and communications technology (ICT) embedded in the urban fabric (for example, fixed and wireless telecoms networks, sensor and camera networks, and building management systems) (Townsend, 2013). In a smart city, these are used to monitor, manage and regulate real-time data flows and processes as people in the city move around, interact and use mobile devices. By connecting up, integrating and analysing this *'everyware'* technology, a more cohesive and better understanding of the city can be developed, it is argued by smart city advocates, which can help cities provide not only more effective and efficient governance to benefit their citizens, but also a better and 'smarter' understanding of how data can be used to analyse processes and outcomes in a city. Second, the term 'smart city' has been used to refer to the wider economic and innovation benefits that can be gained by developing and enhancing the knowledge economy in a city region. In this view of smart cities, ICT is seen as a platform for bringing together ideas and innovations, especially with regard to professional services. The focus, however, is not on ICT in its own right, but rather on how networked technology infrastructures can provide a platform for innovation and creativity in a city, and therefore facilitate social, environmental, economic and cultural development.

The concept of a 'smart city' is not new, however. For example, Angelidou (2015) suggests that the origins of smart cities can be found within two strands of thinking. First, there is an *urban futures* strand,[1] with its origins in the thinking of early urban visionaries such as Ebenezer Howard, Garnier and Le Corbusier, leading to more recent work in the 1960s, 1970s and 1980s to 'wired cities', 'information cities' and 'network cities'. In essence, in many of these visions of urban futures, technology is seen as a key driver in creating modern and healthy environments and democratic governance, although research has questioned whether the smart cities movement now being promoted is itself a strategic vision for the future rather than a reality. Second, there is also a *knowledge and innovation* strand of thinking, which is based on ideas that emerged in the second half of the 20th century and which sees knowledge and innovation as assets that underpin creative competitive advantage in a city (or indeed an organisation or company).

In contrast, other authors (for example, Townsend, 2013, and Goodspeed, 2015) see the origins of the smart city in the emergence of *urban cybernetics*, based on the concept of using computer programs to understand cities, and how to model and plan them, which emerged in the 1960s (building on the earlier systems theory work of Wiener, 1948). This perspective sees smart cities emerging from urban science, as personified, for example, by the quantitative revolution in geography that emerged in the 1950s and 1960s, and the scientific RAND-based urban planning approaches to cities in the United States during the same period (see Chapter 3).

Smart cities come in a range of types, sizes and with different characteristics. Not only is the concept a broad one in itself, but understanding the particular context is also important, as some smart city projects are new, greenfield cities while many others apply smart city concepts and embed smart city projects within existing cities. Again, as Zegras et al (2015) point out, in some of the biggest cities in the world, such as Dhaka in Bangladesh, something as simple as a transit map is not available: what is 'smart' for one city may already be available in another therefore. According to Lee et al (2014), there were 143 ongoing or completed self-designated smart city projects globally in 2012, divided between Europe (47 projects), North America (35 projects), Asia (40 projects), South America (11 projects) and the Middle East/Africa (10 projects). Much depends on definition, of course, and recent research within the EU-28 (Directorate General for Internal Policies, 2014) identified 240 cities with significant and verifiable smart city activity, with particular hotspots in Italy, Spain and the UK. Joss et al (2019) indicated that there is a close relationship between whether existing world or global cities are also found to be 'smart' – their analysis of 5,533 cities suggested that 27 global cities (including Barcelona, London and Singapore) were leading smart cities.

Recently, there has been a particular emphasis in the so-called BRIC countries (Brazil, Russia, India and China) on developing smart cities. For example, up to the year 2015 there were 296 large-scale and ongoing smart city projects in China (Yu and Xu, 2018). These are primarily technology-focused, often with a strong focus on environment. A number of South East Asian countries such as Hong Kong, Singapore, South Korea and Taiwan are following a similar path, promoting economic growth through smart city programmes. These include Singapore's IT2000 plan to create an 'intelligent island' and Taoyuan's E-Taoyaun and U-Taoyaun projects. In India, there are plans to create 100 smart cities at a cost of £445 billion (UK Trade and Investment, 2015). Several of these projects have already been started, including Kochi Smart City and Naya Raipur Smart City. The Indian government plans to develop these as satellite towns of larger cities and by retrofitting existing medium-sized cities, which are planned to act as magnets for investment and development.

The majority of smart city projects tend to be based on existing cities rather than greenfield cities, although in India, the Middle East and South East Asia, new smart city projects are more commonplace than in the rest of the world. For example, in the United Arab Emirates, Masdar City has been promoted as a smart and sustainable city, and in Korea, Songdo is a new smart city built over the past decade to house 75,000 people at a cost of $35 billion (Albino et al, 2015). In the UK, the majority of smart city projects have been developed through 'bottom-up' approaches using new technologies and new data to enable stakeholders to develop solutions, and these initiatives include open data platforms. Leading examples of UK smart cities include Bristol, London and Milton Keynes.

The smart city arena is being shaped by two distinct forces (Angelidou, 2015): first, the *technology push* of new supply-side solutions; and second, the *demand pull* of solutions/products being driven by scientific research and innovation responding to demand. On the supply side, for example, there have been an increasing number of transport, energy, health care, water and waste solutions and products being delivered to assist in urban management. Technology vendors and consultancies have therefore responded, driven by other stakeholders such as global forums, academic research groups and local and global policy-making institutions and their funding streams. On the demand side, the growth of interest in smart cities has been driven by increasing urbanisation and an increasing recognition that city authorities need to do more to tackle climate change and resource depletion issues. In an increasingly globalised world there is also increasing recognition that cities need to compete for skilled labour and investment, so having a more effective and efficient city government can potentially offer a better service for those the city is seeking to impress. This is being driven and enhanced by grassroots movements of local technology applications and software developer specialists, as well as public and non-profit organisations such as the World Bank. For example, there are a wide range of models promoted through industry consultants including IBM's Smarter City model and Cisco's Smart City and Communities.

Despite these drivers, there have been, and continue to be, important barriers in the development of smart cities. Policy Exchange (2016) highlights key barriers relating to policy. For example, divided political authority continues to rein in the UK: 26 of the UK's largest towns and cities fall under the remit of more than one local authority, which makes an integrated approach to transport, housing, energy and the built environment very difficult. Budgets are frequently siloed between different local authorities (and other public sector bodies) in a city, and often between teams with the same local authority. Finally, budget cuts in an era of austerity (where according to the Local Government Association, councils in England face a £20 billion shortfall by 2020) (Proctor, 2020), means it is difficult for cities to find the upfront costs required for smart city projects. The smart city has also been a particular focus in European policy and practice. A report from the European Parliament's Directorate General for Internal Policies (2014) highlighted six main smart city characteristics:

- smart governance, including within and across city governance;
- smart economy, including e-commerce, e-business and ICT-enabled innovation;
- smart mobility, meaning ICT-supported and integrated transport and logistics systems;
- smart environment, including smart energy, renewables, buildings, planning and urban service provision;
- smart people, including skilled workers;
- smart living, including ICT-enabled lifestyles, behaviour and consumption.

Similarly, these characteristics require components for them to be operationalised. For example, if a key characteristic of an initiative is smart environment, the components may be various green environmental technologies. If a key characteristic is smart mobility, then new sustainable transport technologies are required. European Union policies, such as the European Innovation Partnership on Smart Cities and Communities (EIP-SCC), have helped channel funding to a large number of smart city projects, particularly in Germany, Italy, Spain and the UK, which have frequently focused on experiments in energy and the wider environmental agenda. Neirotti et al (2014) provide a helpful summary of smart city domains from the literature. These can be defined as 'hard' or 'soft', in relation to the importance that ICT systems have as a key enabler. So hard domains (where ICT is a key enabler) might include energy grids, public street lighting, transport, buildings and health care, and soft domains would include education, culture, economy and governance (where ICT is more limited in use).

Despite the allure of smart cities, there has been a groundswell of critical narrative focusing on the command and control aspects of the smart city, and its emblematic nature, shaped by power relations (Marvin et al, 2016, Martin et al, 2018). For example, Greenfield's (2013) work, which focuses on Masdar City, Songdo International Business District and the Living PlanIT project in Portugal, suggests that we should be wary of the allure of a neoliberal ideology, which, in his view, mixes technocratic governance with mass surveillance. Townsend (2013) argues for a more socially inclusive notion of a smart city, with is more important for bottom-up innovation driven by citizens themselves instead of a one-size-fits-all approach from technology companies and consultants. Certainly, the idea that 'one size does not fit all' can apply to smart cities and, for Goodspeed (2015), information technology itself can often be fundamentally ambivalent and evolve in different directions in cities over time. Therefore, private companies may not understand local contexts and conditions. This means that bottom-up community-driven and experimental projects may offer cities better opportunities to help address what ultimately are 'wicked' problems in an urban context.

Other criticisms revolve around the fact that smart city strategies are driven by corporate sector interests, or that they do not fully involve all stakeholders. Certainly, for some large multinational firms seeking to take over a city's smart infrastructure, there are immense long-term benefits of procuring local government contracts in terms of the access they provide to the public realm and its street-scene paraphernalia (such as lampposts and waste bins) and the data they generate; but for local authorities, there are difficult long-term lock-in contractual obligations with a firm that may do harm to local or bottom-up innovation. This may also oblige them to take the digital public platforms from a single company, even if the procurement has been accompanied by a single one-off cash payment to the local municipality of millions of pounds. As with the emblematic use of sustainable city, perhaps the smart city is another example of an empty signifier that merely provides the opportunity for different actors who hold power and resources to exert a very narrow and prescriptive 'right to the city' (Haarstad, 2017). Finally, research in the UK has found that so-called smart cities have often lacked visions and strategies (Dixon et al, 2017).

Certainly, the growth of the smart city agenda has been dramatic within the policy-making community. Haarstad (2017) argues that this is the result of three main forces. First, the smart city is attractive because it appeals to a future where technology can help solve societal challenges; this makes sense to cash-strapped cities where the public sector may struggle to provide resources, in which case the corporate sector (for example, IBM, Siemens and Cisco) can step in. Second, the smart city appeals to cities because it promises new ways of collaboration, problem-solving and new governance models. Smart projects, and the idea of projects or experiments in 'urban living labs', open up possibilities for developing new networks to help solve urban challenges. Third, the smart city appeals to consensus-based politics around a desirable goal, and against which it is difficult to argue. As a result, 'smartness' has also become a key area for sustainability-based action and policy in cities.

Smart and sustainable thinking: projects, experiments and the role of city visions

In comparing the two discourses, it is probably fair to say that while the sustainable city has concentrated more on the social, environmental and economic realms, the smart city has had a more technological emphasis, and has focused more closely on socioeconomic roles (Fu and Zhang, 2017). As we saw earlier in this chapter, the evolution of both sustainable cities and, latterly, smart cities has been driven by international networks and coalitions, and the outcomes of these discourses in particular cities are the result of not only these networks, but also the localised understandings of the discourses within particular cities (Haarstad, 2017). As it has evolved, the smart city signifier has been used to 'wrap up' and link with ongoing and existing sustainable city activities and projects in a city (Martin et al, 2018).

However, from the mid-2010s onwards, we have seen the emergence of a new term, the 'smart and sustainable city', as a result of growing sustainability awareness, continued urban growth and technological development (Bibri and Krogstie, 2017; Dixon, 2018b). This relabelling is intended to highlight the fact that not every smart city is necessarily a sustainable city – for example, smart transport technologies may continue to promote car use at the expense of more sustainable modes of transport such as taking the bus, walking and cycling (Dixon, 2018b). There is also a sense in which smart cities may lack ecological wisdom'because of the very nature of their technological focus, and therefore combining the elements is intended to strengthen the whole (Young and Lieberknecht, 2017). The International Telecommunications Union (ITU, 2014: 3) defines the term 'smart and sustainable city' as 'an innovative city that uses information and communication technologies (ICTs) and other means to improve quality of life, efficiency of urban operation and services, and competitiveness, whilst ensuring that it meets the needs of the present and future generations with respect to economic, social and environmental aspects'.

The main goal of a smart and sustainable city is therefore to enhance the quality of life for its citizens across inter-related areas such as water resources, energy, transport and mobility, education, environment, waste management and housing. The revised focus highlights the fact that, in themselves, smart cities are heavily focused on technology, and in a recent study by Yigitcantlar and Kamruzzaman (2018) it was found that there is little evidence to suggest that sustainability targets (such as reduced emissions and technology uptake/sustainable outcomes) are achieved in recognised UK smart cities. Colding et al (2018) points to the inherent complexity of smart cities and the potential danger of them actually increasing resource consumption through, for example, 'energy rebound' or the increased use of energy by ICT through, for example, excessive online ordering.

However, there are critical elements to this revised and rebranded discourse of smart and sustainable cities. Evans et al (2019) point out that smart-sustainable applications need to be aligned with neighbourhood and city scales rather than simply focusing on economic growth agendas. This, in turn, highlights the importance of collective visions to focus on particular issues that are relevant at the local and city level: historical development patterns in cities, the prevailing cultural norms and practices, and political structures, all play a role in shaping the roll-out of smart and sustainable cities in particular places. Ultimately, the implementation of a range of digitally based sensors, smart phone apps, urban dashboards, digital platforms and internet-of-things technologies could potentially change the way that cities are planned and governed, as decentralised and post-networked forms of governance start to gain traction. Specific smart-sustainability tensions may also arise within cities: for example, how sustainable is continued economic growth? How will the benefits of digital innovation be distributed? How can technology protect and enhance the environment (Martin et al, 2018)?

The 'smart city' and 'smart and sustainable city' concepts have both promoted urban experimentation within cities, or the understanding that cities can become smart or smart and sustainable by allowing technology-based experiments (for example, on energy, mobility or waste and water) to be conducted (Cugurillo, 2017). This has given rise to the emergence of 'urban living labs', with cities as testbeds for a range of experiments (or 'sites devised to design, test and learn from social and technical innovation in real time'; Marvin et al, 2018: 1) (see Chapter 9). Frequently, the moves towards promoting cities as testbeds or as sites for urban experimentation are founded on a homogenous plan of action or a vision that is designed to make a city smart or smart and sustainable. Often, the reality does not match the rhetoric in real cities: as Cugurillo (2017) argues in a study of Hong Kong and Masdar City, cities of all kinds are 'disorganic', so that applying a singular and homogenous vision to a place that attempts to apply smart and sustainable principles may produce an undesirable, fragmented and disjointed 'Frankenstein urbanism'.

Despite such criticisms, in practical terms, we would argue that it is possible to use a smart and sustainable city framework (or overlay), provided that the framework fits with the ambitions and aspirations of those living, working and playing in the city (Dixon et al, 2018a). However, it also means that we need to have a clear long-term vision for the city as a place (not just as a testbed or a lab for experiments), that we recognise its individual characteristics and the different needs of the people who live there, and that we understand the city's past and its present in order to understand its future. Different kinds of vision suit different kinds of circumstances. For example, in an interesting study of the Norwegian Cities of the Future programme, Ingeborgrud (2018b) highlights the importance of recognising the complexity of multi-level governance that can underlie visions for cities – in Norway, two different but inter-related visions of the city have emerged: the 'attractive city' and the 'complex city', shaped and influenced by the different interests of local, regional and national government stakeholders. In this sense, visions can become 'trading zones' for the negotiations over future directions in urban sustainability.

Summary

Understanding the dominant discourses of the city in relation to sustainability and smartness, and how they have shaped and influenced our thinking about cities, is vital because of the consequences for vision-making and urban planning. This means engaging with key stakeholders in a city to develop a participatory vision of the long term. This is not a corporatist vision applied from the top down and imposed on a city. Positive visions are needed for cities in order to guide urban planning, to underpin and inspire actions – more dystopic visions instead rule out and exclude creativity and innovation. Visions therefore should point to a desirable future state. As McPhearson et al (2016: 38) suggest: 'Positive visioning processes are an opportunity to dig deeply into the key tensions and challenges to bring communities together to create shared visions, or even to create pluralistic visions within which to reveal underlying conflicts, tradeoffs and tensions.'

Participatory visioning must be at the heart of developing urban futures-based re-imagining and planning in our cities. In the next chapter, we will examine how visioning is fundamental to understanding how we can manage and plan for transformative change in our cities to 2050 and beyond.

6

Theoretical approaches to urban futures

Introduction

The rapid growth of climate emergency declarations in cities across the world in the latter 2010s and early 2020s throws into focus the major structural and institutional changes that will be required in our urban areas to tackle the impacts of climate change. Scientific evidence tells us that, to keep global temperatures from rising by more than 1.5°C, cities have to achieve net-zero emissions by mid-century (Bazaz et al, 2018). This has potentially transformative impacts not only for city economies and people's lifestyles, but also for the multi-level governance structures we see currently at play at national and subnational levels in jurisdictions across the world. As Lord Stern wrote:

> We are at a unique moment in human history. The policies and investments made in the next two decades will determine the quality of life on this planet for generations to come. We need cities with net-zero emissions by mid-century to have a reasonable chance of staying close to 1.5°C. Such a transition will need big investments, and quickly, but they are very productive, attractive investments. (CUT, 2019: 4)

The risks of climate change present a clear and present danger to cities. For example, much of the world's population lives in low-lying coastal areas susceptible to flooding by sea-level rise; as a measure of the scale of the risks involved, in Europe 70 per cent of the largest cities have areas that are fewer than 10 metres above sea level, and recent work has shown that people living in poverty, older people and people who are economically vulnerable are likely to be impacted the most by climate change (Kamal-Chaoui and Robert, 2009; Matsumoto et al, 2019). Climate change, therefore, can entrench and deepen systemic and structural inequalities in cities.

Add into the mix the continuing socioeconomic pressures in cities caused by migration, population growth and pandemics, and there is a potent cocktail of urban challenges to be addressed (see Chapter 2). Yet cities also offer great potential for tackling climate change and other environmental issues. For example, it has been calculated that deploying low-carbon measures in cities could reduce greenhouse gas emissions from urban buildings, materials, transport and waste by nearly 90 per cent by 2050. These measures would have a net present value of US$23.9 trillion – greater than the biggest economy in the world, the United States (CUT, 2019).

If cities are to play an important role in tackling such challenges, then we need to understand the pathways (or development paths) to the goal of urban sustainability by 2050 or sooner. What will be the nature of such pathways and how can we develop our critical understanding of how transformative change can be managed and planned for, given that cities are complex systems, as we saw earlier in this book?

In this chapter, therefore, we will examine pathways to change for cities and look at two main strands of thinking for understanding systemic change within cities: socioecological systems (SESs) and sociotechnical transitions (STTs). We will focus particularly on STTs to show how transition theory (comprising the multi-level perspective) and transition management can be used as analytical and conceptual frameworks for understanding, shaping and guiding urban transitions. In doing this, we will focus on examples from our own research and other work. The chapter concludes by providing key lessons from this body of work and what we can learn by using transitions theory in an urban context.

Cities: pathways for change

As we saw earlier in this book, complexity is an inherent characteristic of cities. This complexity is related to the many and various networks and connections between people, businesses, flows and outputs in cities, and a science of cities has developed to understand how this complexity can be understood and modelled. Cities also mirror and represent society in that they have evolved into complex structures with interrelated sectors (for example, energy, water and waste) and socioeconomic and technological trends such as the internet of things and big data have all added to this complexity at a variety of scales.

The built environment, as a major part of the fabric of our cities and urban areas, is complex, involving a variety of stakeholders and actors, from property owners and investors through to occupiers, tenants, residents, businesses, policy-makers and others, often with competing interests. The built environment essentially represents the product of human activities through buildings, roads and infrastructure and the places in between. Based on Health Canada (2002; quoted in Srinivasan et al, 2003), the built environment is defined as encompassing:

> ... our homes, schools, workplaces, parks/recreation areas, businesses and roads. It extends overhead in the form of electric transmission lines, underground in the form of waste disposal sites and subway trains, and across the country in the form of highways. The built environment encompasses all buildings, spaces and products that are created or modified by people.

As the built environment forms a large part of the fabric of our cities, we can think of inherent urban complexity operating at building, neighbourhood and city levels, for example. This complexity also makes it difficult to address what are called 'wicked and persistent' problems at an urban level, which have consequences for the built environment and the natural environment, or the world involving living things and organisms beyond that influenced directly by humans. An example of a wicked and persistent problem is climate change (see Box 6.1). It is wicked and persistent because human impacts are entrenched in societal norms and values and it involves multiple and conflicting inputs and multiple possible outcomes, all of which play out over time against, or occasionally with, each other, and can even create new problems. This understanding is certainly true of Rittel and Webber's (1973) account of city planning and its inherent wicked problems – for example, building more roads to solve congestion not only treats the city as a black-box system, but also fails to understand that unless a properly focused transport policy deals with modal shift, car use would simply continue to be encouraged. Rotmans (2005) suggests that persistent problems are in fact a superlative view of wicked problems, in that they are not only complex, involving multiple causes and consequences and affecting different sectors and different scales, but they are also uncertain without ready-made solutions, difficult to manage and often hard to grasp.

Box 6.1: Climate change: a wicked and persistent problem

Addressing climate change is a global challenge with local impacts, which require immediate and transformative action.

- Data from the World Meteorological Organization indicates that atmospheric carbon dioxide (CO^2) concentrations may have exceeded 410 parts per million by the end of 2019, which is unprecedented over the past three million years.
- By the end of 2017, approximately 2,200 gigatonnes of anthropogenic carbon dioxide ($GtCO^2$) (± 320 $GtCO^2$) were already emitted – leaving only an estimated 580 GtCO2 required for a 50 per cent chance of limiting the global temperature rise to 1.5°C by 2100. This means that global warming is likely to reach 1.5°C between 2030 and 2052 at current rates.
- The risks associated with a 2°C warmer world include species extinction, global and regional food insecurity, severe impacts on human and economic activities and limited potential for adaptation such as in certain low-lying Pacific nation states, where migration may be the only solution.
- To lessen these risks and retain a 50 per cent chance of limiting the global temperature increase to 1.5°C, mitigation efforts would need to secure carbon neutrality – net-zero greenhouse gas emissions – in about 30 years.

Meanwhile, the direct impacts of climate change can already be felt: glaciers have shrunk, the polar ice caps are melting rapidly, ice on rivers and lakes is breaking up earlier, heatwaves are longer and more intense (as evidenced by the recent bushfires in Australia and the United States in 2020), plant and animal ranges have moved and sea-level rise is accelerating.

Data source: Matsumoto et al (2019: 5–6)

Certainly, many of the urban challenges outlined in Chapter 2 are what might be termed wicked and persistent and, in many ways, reflect the unsustainability of society. By the same token, the 'urban paradox' means that while cities are part of the problem, they are also a very important part of the solution to climate change and other socioeconomic issues that countries and the world as a whole face today.

The ultimate goal of urban sustainability (through the path of sustainable development) for cities is closely linked with the ambition of many cities to now target zero carbon rather than simply move to a low-carbon future. Globally, climate activism, through the work of

Extinction Rebellion, Greta Thunberg and others, has certainly played an important role in influencing cities and municipal governments to set ambitious net-zero targets for 2030. A concerted move to declare 'climate emergencies' (which was word of the year in 2019 in the *Oxford English Dictionary*) began in October 2017 with the 'City by City' programme by the Climate Mobilization initiative (Rode, 2019). As at April 2020, 1,490 jurisdictions in 29 countries, and 274 out of 408 (67 per cent) district, county, unitary and metropolitan councils in England and Wales had declared a climate emergency (together with eight combined authorities/city regions).[1] Many of these local authorities have also set net-zero carbon targets for 2030, as against the UK government's greenhouse gas emissions target of net zero by 2050. Globally, this includes cities such as New York and Sydney, which have set challenging targets: New York has set a net-zero carbon economy target for 2050 (and a net-zero energy target for 2040) and Sydney a net-zero target by 2050.

These targets mean that cities must move away from simply gradualist or piecemeal actions, towards more systemic (or system-wide) change. For example, a recent report by the Committee on Climate Change (CCC) (2019) for the UK government, suggested that, while the foundations are in place to meet the 2050 national target, it will be (perhaps not surprisingly) highly challenging and involve, for example, substantial energy efficiency and retrofitting measures in the built environment, further decarbonisation of the national grid, carbon capture and storage measures and electric vehicle infrastructure, underpinned by a low-carbon hydrogen economy and more energy-efficient farming. To meet the same targets by 2030 for cities will therefore be even more challenging.

Yet cities are in a unique position to help tackle climate change. For example, across 30 countries of the Organisation for Economic Co-operation and Development (OECD), regions and cities were responsible for 55 per cent of total climate- and environment-related public spending, and 64 per cent of such investment, in 2000–16 (Matsumoto et al, 2019), and it is often the case that cities (as in the UK) have more ambitious targets than their national initiatives. Yet it is important to recognise that cities should be seen within the wider multi-level governance systems and political contexts in which they are embedded and enmeshed (Bulkeley et al, 2011). Cities are also multi-sectoral and involve different actors and stakeholders (public, private and civil society) often working across spatial boundaries – Santiago in Chile, for example, has 34 municipalities, each with its own mayor and administration (van der Heijden et al, 2019).

If cities are to realise their ambitions as agents for change, then not only do the complexity and often fragmented nature of internal politics need to be recognised, but also the alternative pathways that stakeholders might adopt to move to a sustainable future. Such pathways can be characterised as *adaptive* (or resilient), *transitioning* or *transformative*, which represent how ambitious they are in challenging the status quo. This characterisation is based on work by Pelling (2010) and has been used in an urban context, for example by Pearson et al (2014) and Hordijk et al (2014). Pearson et al (2014) highlight the three pathways to urban change:

- *Adaptive or resilient change* is characterised by improving existing practices without questioning the underlying assumptions or power structure. These marginal changes focus on technology; management and power structures are usually not affected.
- *Transitioning* generally implies incremental changes in governance systems but with norms, principles and the sociopolitical regime unchanged, although regulations and decision-making will need to be adjusted.
- *Transformation* requires regime change and a shift in our worldview and our place within it. This means changing the city and its wider political and societal context and developing a new system and city within a different kind of society. Here, recognition of radical change to existing conventions (including the conventional economic growth model) is required.

The term 'transition' has been used in the 'transitions town' movement to much effect globally (Hoppe and van Beuren, 2015) and there is a growing movement for a 'just transition' to a zero-carbon future, which promotes social equity and inclusion by ensuring economic and environmental justice for everyone who is impacted by climate change (Robins et al, 2018). Ultimately, the three pathways are all alternatives to simply coping (or even doing nothing and therefore ensuring societal collapse), and certainly it is fair to say that transitioning and transformative pathways could both potentially lead to more sustainable ways of living in urban areas; and so, to that extent, they are not entirely mutually exclusive choices.

The concept of a pathway to change for cities invites the question: how can we best plan and develop a strategy for change in a city so that it can achieve a sustainable future? This in turn means we need to think about how a city should be viewed in theoretical terms to understand this ambition, and how best to frame the theoretical understanding of the question itself. There has been previous work that has attempted to use developmental or stage models to show how cities might move through various evolutionary stages. For example, Bai (2000) shows how environmental problems in cities can be divided into three groups – poverty-related issues, production-related issues and consumption-related issues – each of which presents different behaviour over the course of economic development. From this, Bai suggests that in East Asia (China, Japan and Korea), cities are passing through the first two to three of four stages of urban environmental evolution:

- stage 1: poverty stage
- stage 2: industrial pollution stage
- stage 3 consumption stage
- stage 4: sustainable eco-city stage

As things stand, there are enormous challenges to cities in these countries (and indeed many others globally) if they are to achieve the fourth stage of enlightened development. This is especially important when some of the governance and political challenges are identified: for example, there are often inherent temporal ('not during my term of office'), spatial ('not in my patch') and institutional ('not in my organisation') barriers to tackling long-term change, particularly when planning horizons are relatively short (Bai et al, 2010a, 2010b). There is, therefore, a disconnection between the short-term political expediency of 'business as usual' and longer-term wicked and persistent environmental and socioeconomic challenges.

This kind of developmental model is, however, a normative view of the world in that it reflects value judgements, and there is, of course, a place for this kind of thinking to develop new ideas and concepts. We also need to try to offer improved understanding of why things are the way they are, and how we might change them. Complexity science (or a science of cities) offers us real insights, but we need to think about how, in practical terms, it could be possible to understand how, for example, our planning, regulatory and governance structures should be adapted and changed, and how a planned management of urban transition and transformation could be facilitated. This calls for a social science perspective to be set out alongside complexity science. Ultimately, this means focusing on sustainability science or sustainability transition studies, which is a primary focus in this book.

Two main ontological strands (or the foundational assumptions about the world and its causal relationships) for understanding systemic change within cities can be distinguished (Wolfram and Frantzeskaki, 2016; Mendizabal et al, 2018; Moore et al, 2018).

The first strand of socioecological system (SES) frameworks includes institutional analysis and development (Ostrom, 2009) and resilience thinking (Folke et al, 2010). The second strand of sociotechnical transition (STT) studies, includes a number of elements, but the best known is the multi-level perspective (MLP) (see, for example, Geels, 2010). Broadly speaking, the climate change research community has frequently focused on SESs while the transition studies community has focused on sociotechnical systems, which comprise the interactions and resultant structures in the nexus between society and technology (Mendizabal et al, 2018).

The SES strand has often been used to explore the interaction of social and ecological systems and the concept of 'resilience' (or the ability to bounce back from systemic shocks). This complex interdependency has been especially important in the study of the place-based impact of climate change (Moore et al, 2018). All systems (and particularly SESs) exist and function across multiple spatial, temporal, organisational and social scales, and the interactions across scales are crucially important in determining the dynamics of the system at any particular scale. This interacting set of hierarchically structured scales has been termed a 'panarchy' (Gunderson and Holling, 2002), and this has given rise to the concept of 'adaptive governance', which aims to deal with long-term change and to respond to and bounce back from events such as major flooding, earthquakes, other natural hazards or, as we have witnessed all too painfully recently, pandemics. SESs therefore focus on the capacity to maintain conditions under changing circumstances throughout what is referred to as the 'adaptive cycle' – which may be the result of natural or socioeconomic responses. SESs have grown and developed through the combination of natural resource management (see, for example, Gunderson and Holling, 2002) and self-governing institutional theory (Ostrom, 2009), and the framework also enables a view of system dynamics to be analysed over time. This adaptation action cycle comprises:

- growth and exploitation (when resources are freely available);
- conservation (slow capital accumulation);
- collapse or release (peaking after a low-flexibility phase is reached when resources are susceptible to shocks); and
- reorganisation, which may be rapid or slow and during which new opportunities for increased efficiency may arise. (Mendizabal et al, 2018)

In contrast to the SES strand, the STT strand emerged in the Netherlands in the late 1990s (especially in the science policy debate leading up to its fourth National Environmental Policy Plan – NMP4 – in 2001) (Loorbach et al, 2016), with a strong focus on energy studies and technological innovation, and has grown in importance since the mid-2000s in other sectors and at a variety of scales. Within what can be broadly described as 'transitions theory', the main STT frameworks are the multi-level perspective (MLP), which is often used as an analytical framework for understanding past transitions, and transition management (TM), which focuses on the governance systems required in the transition towards the goal of sustainability (Grin et al, 2010). In the MLP, there is a process of successive stages:

- *a pre-development stage*, where experimentation occurs at a project level;
- *a take-off stage*, where innovation emerges, creating structural change and destabilisation in the existing regime;
- *an acceleration stage*, when sociocultural, economic, ecological and institutional factors combine to create structural transformation; and
- *a stabilisation phase*, when the system reaches a new state of equilibrium. (Geels, 2004, 2010)

In contrast, the TM approach envisages a more managed and planned transition to a wider societal challenge (rather than a technological innovation), based on the following elements (Kemp and Loorbach, 2006):

- systems thinking across multiple domains, actors and scales;
- long-term thinking (or visioning) as a frame for short-term policy;
- backcasting and forecasting;
- a focus on learning about and experimenting with a variety of options;
- stakeholder participation and management.

Both the SES and STT strands emphasise the need to take into account the interactions between technical innovations, the structure and type of socioeconomic system, and system functions and services at multiple levels. Both also use a form of temporal logic to examine how systems can adapt over time. Table 6.1 summarises the main similarities and differences between these two approaches.

In this book, we focus on setting city foresight methods within the context of transitions theory, but with a particular emphasis on TM thinking and visioning. Given the practical nature and application of

Table 6.1: Comparison of sociotechnical transition (STT) and socioecological system (SES) approaches to transitions

Characteristic	STT	SES
System	• Sociotechnical (society and technical systems evolve)	• Socioecological (resilience)
Governance	• Transition management (governance)	• Adaptive management (governance)
Complexity	• Yes – recognised	• Yes – recognised (and uses the term 'panarchy')
Stages	• Pre-development • Take-off • Acceleration • Stabilisation	• Reorganisation • Growth • Conservation • Collapse
Steps	• Analyse the system/set the scene, frame the challenge • Create a vision, explore pathways, engage and anchor • Actions/experiments	• Structure the problem and establish the adaptation arena • Create a vision • Define an agenda and develop a pathway • Implement the pathway • Evaluate, monitor and learn
Approach	• Sociotechnical transition theory	• Incremental adaptation • Transformative adaptation • Reformist adaptation
Methods and tools	• Multi-level perspective • Backcasting • Urban transition labs (or living labs) • Transition pathway	• Adaptive policy setting • Adaptation pathway • Dynamic adaptive policy pathway

Source: Based on Mendizabal et al (2018)

TM, our work also emphasises the importance of a sequential and planned approach to city visioning, setting this in the context of spatial urban planning. That is not to say that visioning is not important in SESs – for example, as McPhearson et al (2016) argue, there is a clear role for positive visions for cities in a variety of contexts. In the remainder of this chapter, however, we will focus on STTs with a particular focus on MLP TM, highlighting some recent examples of their application in an urban context.

Urban transition and transformation – the role of transitions theory

As an important part of transitions theory, the MLP is designed to analyse transitions based on the implementation of a particular technology or innovation. The MLP recognises the co-evolutionary development of technologies, institutions and social and economic subsystems. As in the SES model, the MLP envisages nested levels of change, but instead focuses on the interactions between three interrelated scales:

- the sociotechnical *landscape* (that is, the overall sociotechnical setting of cultural, political, economic and environmental factors);
- the *regime* (that is, the structures representing current practices and routines and the dominant rules and technologies that maintain the existing sociotechnical system); and
- *niches* (that is, the level for experiments and radical experiments) (see Figure 6.1).

In this perspective, lock-in to an existing system is overcome as a result of break-throughs in niche experiments as new sociotechnical configurations (innovations) occur within protected niches. As a result, transitions can occur and these factors, combined with landscape or policy pressures, destabilise and transform the existing regime (Rip and Kemp, 1998; Geels, 2010; Eames et al, 2013).

The MLP has been applied in a variety of sectors, including energy, water and hydrogen transportation (Eames et al, 2013; Twomey and Gaziulusoy, 2014). Cities have also been shown to be important contributors to technological transition at the national scale: first, through being primary actors that can help enact the transition; and second, as seedbeds and locations for radical innovations in the early phases of transitions (Geels, 2011). For example, Geels (2011) uses the MLP to show how cities played a vital role in the historical transition from wells to piped water in the Netherlands between 1870 and 1930. Nonetheless, it is often the case that the notion of 'spatial scale' remains underdeveloped within MLP studies; many studies have focused on national-level technology implementation rather than the subnational level, including cities (Hodson and Marvin, 2010; Truffer and Coenen, 2012; Huxley et al, 2019). Naess and Vogel (2012) summarise some of the key challenges in applying the MLP to urban areas:

- Cities are complex and vary in size, sectoral composition, wealth and so on, and so sociospatial structures also vary between cities so that cities are shaped and moulded in very different context-dependent ways.
- Cities include many different interacting sectors where technological innovation may occur (for example, housing, transport and energy),

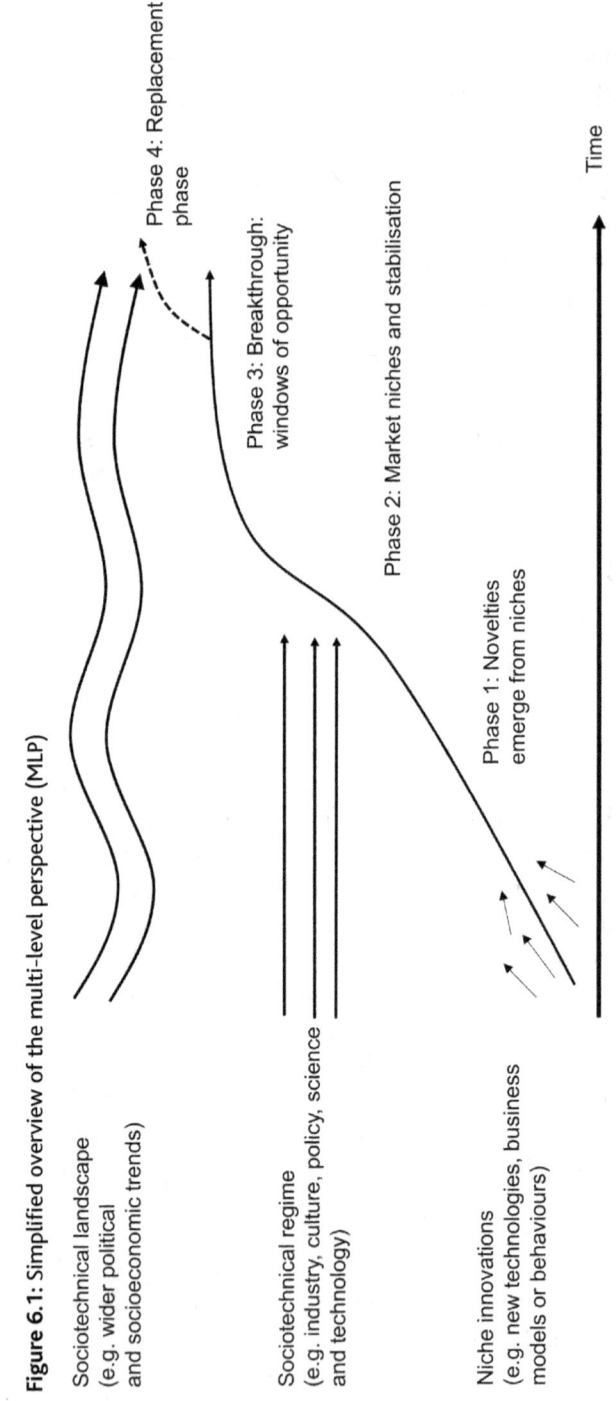

Figure 6.1: Simplified overview of the multi-level perspective (MLP)

Source: Geels (2002)

Figure 6.2: Transition management (TM); governance framework for transitions

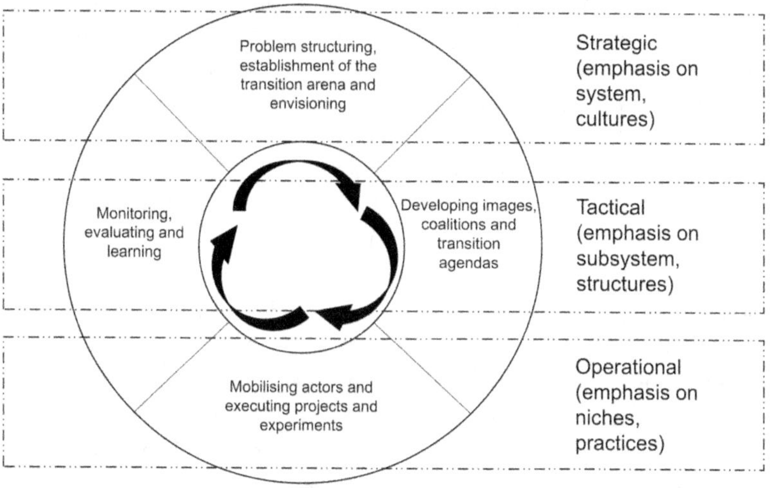

- Problem structuring, establishment of the transition arena and envisioning — Strategic (emphasis on system, cultures)
- Developing images, coalitions and transition agendas — Tactical (emphasis on subsystem, structures)
- Mobilising actors and executing projects and experiments — Operational (emphasis on niches, practices)
- Monitoring, evaluating and learning

Source: Loorbach (2009)

and so applying the MLP at the city level in a multi-modal context is difficult.
- In cities, often so-called 'new' technologies may in fact be existing technologies, so it may be difficult to isolate and identify regime change when these technologies (for example, petrol/diesel cars) continue to be promoted alongside new technologies (for example, electric vehicles).
- Cities have a track record on inertia in the built environment, with existing building stock and infrastructure often creating lock-in through sunk investments, so diffusion of technology may take some time.

Despite the problems with the MLP at the city level, the basic concepts of the framework have been adapted and developed to promote the use of TM, which is designed to help actors influence transitions through governance structures (Wittmayer et al, 2014; Frantzeskaki et al, 2018). TM is primarily concerned with the dynamics of structural societal change and how and when such transformation can be initiated, developed and shaped (see Figure 6.2). At the heart of TM in a city context is the fundamental idea that transition or systemic change can be promoted to deal with wicked and persistent urban challenges. As Grin et al (2010: 108–9) suggest:

> Transition management ... is the attempt to influence the societal system into a more sustainable direction, ultimately resolving the persistent problem(s) involved. But

because there are no ready-made solutions for persistent problems, we can only explore promising future options and directions. Managing transitions therefore implies searching, learning and experimenting. As such, transition management is a quest, not a recipe for robust solutions.

There is, therefore, a distinction between TM and strategic urban planning. In contrast to planning, TM (Frantzeskaki et al, 2018):

- focuses on transformative change;
- facilitates co-creation processes to provide pathways to visionary futures; and
- links long-term visions to medium- and short-term actions, using experimentation as the foundation for reflexive planning, and at the same time emphasising the importance of transformation of the existing system through system innovation.

These differences have repercussions for urban planning. Urban planning is a deeply institutionalised and globally practised form of state-led action and regulation to direct and guide urban development, whereas TM represents an academia-led conceptual framework for guiding and shaping sociotechnical innovations (Wolfram, 2018). Wolfram (2018) also outlines the implications of using TM in a city context to help complement and strengthen urban planning. TM, as a 'governance niche', is characterised by a focus on long-term envisioning, and is founded on societal initiation and leadership, which promotes bottom-up processes, leading to experiments and innovative projects. It actively involves innovators and institutes and helps promote a vital role for local science and academia in facilitating and contributing expertise. These roles cannot be performed ordinarily by planning authorities in municipal governments and may also challenge existing assumptions about a place. In practical terms, it often makes more sense for academia and business to lead on TM in a city because of the high resource demands (for example, human resources, time, capacity and skills/knowledge), since many local planning authorities may be pressured by budgetary constraints and multiple legal responsibilities.

The TM perspective perceives cities as complex adaptive systems; in other words, cities are seen as self-organising systems with emergent properties and adaptive capabilities, which can not only add to existing sustainability problems, but also offer solutions. This means they can defy tightly structured top-down control, and so the problems that conventional policies and regulations try to solve, such as pollution, emissions and congestion, are often the result of underlying systemic issues (Loorbach et al, 2016; Frantzeskaki et al, 2018). TM can be used as a heuristic device for understanding the nature of urban transitions and how to guide them, and also as a practice-based process for real-world operational applications.

For example, the Dutch Research Institute for Transitions (DRIFT) suggested that TM for cities should include the following five stages (Roorda and Wittmayer, 2014):

1. Preparation and exploration, including formation of the transition team, process design and stakeholder analysis (and the formation of the transition arena).
2. Problem structuring and envisioning, including participatory visioning.
3. Backcasting, pathways and agenda-building.
4. Experimenting and implementing, including dissemination of visions, pathways and the transition narrative, and broader coalition-building.
5. Monitoring and evaluation, through participatory approaches, reflection on the vision and strategy, learning and process feedback.

This process has some synergy with foresight processes, which can also be participatory and use visioning and backcasting techniques. For example, backcasting is a technique for visioning that starts with defining a desirable future and then works backwards to identify policies, programmes and pathways that will connect the present with the specified future.

TM (and the MLP, as we saw earlier) is not without its critics, however. These critical contributions often identify the role of power relations as being a crucial issue and a real challenge for TM in terms of who is governing, whose perspectives are important (in terms of the initial framing of the system, problems, goals and sustainability) and what the relationship with institutions, incumbent regime actors and dominant discourses is. Others question the narrow focus of desired (versus undesired) transitions, technical systems and the identification of key actors (Shove and Walker, 2007; Loorbach et al, 2016). Furthermore, as Loorbach et al (2016) suggest, TM in cities should not be considered a tool box or silver bullet, but rather as an 'exploration of a new city governance approach for the co-creation of innovative pathways and processes in a strongly reflexive manner' (Nevens et al, 2013: 121). Seen in these terms, and in the context of urban sustainability problems, TM offers cities and urban areas the opportunity to provide:

- a sense of direction (or vision) for the city;
- a catalyst for local change; and
- collective empowerment because it potentially enables actors to address challenges and seize opportunities. (Roorda et al, 2014)

In the next section, we will look at how TM-related work has been applied in a number of urban contexts internationally.

Applying transition theory to cities: pathways and visions

When TM is applied within an urban context, there can be beneficial outcomes, which include the following (according to Wittmayer et al, 2014):

- A shared and valuable narrative or understanding of the past, present and future of a city can be created.
- New networks and constellations can arise, particularly through the connection of top-down visioning and strategic planning approaches and bottom-up project-based or urban experiment approaches.
- New roles and relations may be developed as a result of a common learning journey to develop the vision as institutional barriers and preconceived ideas are overcome.
- Participatory-based approaches enable the co-production of societal knowledge and new long-term structures, cultures and practices.
- Participants in the process gain a better understanding of the complexity of the societal challenges involved in urban sustainability.

TM has been used in an urban context by a variety of actors and stakeholders, including municipalities, local authorities and universities (Wittmayer et al, 2014; Loorbach et al, 2016). In many instances, these groups will work together in tandem and with other change agents in the transition arena, which provides a shared space for societal learning, where the group challenges preconceived ideas and the status quo, existing power interests and routine and institutionalised tasks and activities. The group helps to shape the process of creating new dynamics between government, civil society, business and academia (or what is known as the 'quadruple helix' in other innovation and foresight-related literature; Dixon et al, 2018).

TM (and related city foresight) activities have played a role in helping to shape city visions within three main city contexts:

Table 6.2: Comparison of urban sustainability transition programmes

Programme	Geographical focus	Cities	Primary focus	Website
Retrofit 2050	UK	Cardiff and Manchester	Urban retrofitting	www.retrofit2050.org.uk
VP2040	Australia	Adelaide, Melbourne, Perth and Sydney	Urban systems and carbon emission reductions	http://www.ecoacupuncture.com/visions-and-pathways-2040
MUSIC	EU	Aberdeen, Ghent, Ludwigsburg, Montreuil and Rotterdam	Urban carbon and energy reductions	https://drift.eur.nl/projects/music/

- national 'future city' programmes – for example, 'Cities of the Future' in Norway (2008–14) and 'Future of Cities' in the UK (2013–16);
- academic-led research programmes – for example, EPSRC Retrofit 2050 (UK), Visions and Pathways 2040 (Australia) and MUSIC (European Union [EU]);
- city-specific vision programmes (for example, Reading 2050 and Newcastle City Futures 2065 in the UK).

In this section, we will examine the second group to highlight key principles and findings. Other futures-based city academic-led research programmes in addition to those we have just listed include Visions 2030 (UK), CRISP (EU), SPREAD (EU) and Post-Car(d) Urbanism (EU) (Ryan et al, 2015). However, in this chapter, we will focus on the three we have listed here because they all involve strong TM and city foresight elements. In Chapters 7 and 8 we will look in more detail at the links between city foresight and TM and how city visions in individual places can be shaped and translated into practice. We also present only an overview of each of these three academic-led projects; more information on each of the projects is available through the project websites and the relevant key references in this chapter. Table 6.2 provides a comparison of the three programmes.

Retrofit 2050

The Retrofit 2050 programme of work, which ran from 2010 to 2014, was funded by the Engineering and Physical Sciences Research Council (EPSRC) in the UK. It brought together Cardiff University, the University of Durham, the University of Salford, the University of

Reading, the University of Cambridge and Oxford Brookes University, with non-academic industrial, non-governmental organisation and local government partners. It aimed to deliver a step change in current knowledge and the capacity to deliver urban sustainability, by examining challenging but realistic social and technical pathways for the systemic retrofitting of UK city-regions. Focusing on the retrofitting of primarily residential, non-residential buildings and city infrastructure, the programme drew on transition theory as an analytical framework to examine city retrofit futures (Eames et al, 2013, 2018; Dixon et al, 2014a, 2014b). The programme focused on overcoming the current separation between what is needed (that is, technical knowledge, targets, technology options and costs) and how urban-scale retrofitting can be delivered (that is, through institutions, capacity, public engagement and governance structures), in order to develop a managed approach to sociotechnical transition in the built environment and urban infrastructure.

The programme adopted a normative definition of retrofitting: 'the directed alteration of the fabric, form or systems which comprise the built environment in order to improve energy, water or waste efficiencies' (Eames, 2011: 2). This definition included primarily existing buildings and the 1–2 per cent of additional building stock added on average each year to existing cities. The research started from the premise that new forms of interdisciplinary working are needed to address the gaps in understanding about urban-scale retrofitting, building on the notion that urban retrofit transitions are complex, co-evolutionary and non-linear processes involving many actors, and different spatial scales and dimensions over time (Geels et al, 2008; Eames et al, 2014a, 2014b). The research viewed the city as a 'complex adaptive system', with urban retrofitting as an interlocking system of innovation challenges. The MLP was used in the research, therefore, to conceptualise a more systemic approach (rather than the conventional fragmented and piecemeal approach), and the work also drew on TM frameworks and the performative roles of visions. To help frame the visions whichthat were ultimately developed, three broad regimes were identified and developed: (a) housing; (b) non-domestic buildings (that is, commercial and public); and (c) urban infrastructure and land use.

The generic visions, which were ultimately developed from backcasting and visioning, comprised (Dixon et al, 2014a):

- A *smart-networked city* – the city is seen as a hub in a highly mobile and competitive, global networked society and technology provides the impetus for a market-oriented focus on retrofitting.

- A *compact city* – the city is a location for intensive and efficient urban living, and urban land use, the built environment and infrastructure are used to create densified settlements that are resource-efficient.
- A *self-reliant green city* – the city is a self-reliant bioregion based on circular metabolic thinking and it lives within its limits.

Focusing on Cardiff and Greater Manchester as city-region case studies, the research compared approaches to urban retrofitting in the two local and regional contexts and also applied city-specific visions to Cardiff through workshop and interview work – for example, 'Connected Cardiff', 'Compact Cardiff' and 'Orchard Cardiff' (de Laurentis et al, 2018).

Visions and Pathways 2040

The Visions and Pathways 2040 (VP2040) project was an investigation of possible and plausible pathways for the transformation of the southern capital cities of Australia, aiming for an 80 per cent reduction of their greenhouse gas contributions by 2040 (Ryan et al, 2015, 2019). The project, which ran from 2013 to 2017, was designed as an interlinked research and engagement process to develop, analyse and communicate visions, scenarios and pathways for this transformation. VP2040 involved three universities (the University of Melbourne, the University of New South Wales and Swinburne University of Technology) and a range of government and industry partners, including the cities of Adelaide, Melbourne, Perth and Sydney. Its research objectives included: tracking international research and coordinating with related international projects; identifying emerging technological and social innovations that could disrupt current trajectories of development; and developing and refining a set of pathways, visions and scenarios for low-carbon resilient cities.

Using the MLP and TM as a loose reference, VP2040 focused on eight inter-related urban systems of provision: energy, water, food, transport, buildings and open space, waste disposal, information, and products and services (Ryan et al, 2015). The research used a scenario-building approach to examine plausible and desirable futures and used visualised images of the future as part of the visioning and backcasting process. The methodology for VP2040 was underpinned by a 'drivers for change' analysis, which scoped out social, technological, economic, environmental and political drivers for the scenarios.

This work and the foresight elements were led by the Victorian Eco-Innovation Lab (VEIL), and four scenarios were developed for the cities (Candy et al, 2017):

- *Community balanced living* – a city of low consumption promoting a socially and meaningful life with enhanced wellbeing and liveability.
- *Network entrepreneurial living* – a city where major corporate and government power is diminished but where economic growth is based on self-organised entrepreneurial activity.
- *Planned regulated living* – a city where environmental challenges are tackled through stronger government, planning and tighter regulations.
- *Clean-tech corporate living* – a city with clean and efficient production driven by the market, with a strong emphasis on innovation.

Ultimately, these were streamlined into two overarching scenarios: a 'commons' transition based on rapid consumption reduction; and a 'green growth' scenario, based on an economic growth model for decarbonisation. The research used quantitative modelling to test these scenarios against emissions targets by utilising the Australian Stocks and Flows Framework (ASFF). This framework is a scenario modelling platform for integrated analysis of the physical economy of Australia. It is a process-based simulation model of all sectors of the Australian economy, tracking the dynamics of major capital and resource pools, and the flows associated with these stocks such as productive output, resource inputs and changes in capital and carbon emissions (Ryan et al, 2019).

Ultimately, the VP2040 research showed that, although a radical urban decarbonisation is possible in Australian cities, a performance target does not best meet the conditions of its realisation. This is particularly pertinent as it runs counter to the widely held notion that achieving low-carbon futures is essentially a technological challenge, with the outcome more or less technologically determined.

Mitigation in Urban Areas: Solutions for Innovative Cities (MUSIC)

The MUSIC project ran from 2010 to 2015 and was funded through the European Regional Development Fund (ERDF). The work was supported by two research institutes – the Dutch Research Institute for Transitions (DRIFT, the Netherlands) and the Public Research Centre Henri Tudor (Luxembourg) – in partnership with cities and stakeholders. The five cities involved in the MUSIC project (Aberdeen, Scotland; Ghent, Belgium; Ludwigsburg, Germany; Montreuil, France;

and Rotterdam, the Netherlands) all used a common TM approach as a methodological basis, although this was grounded in distinctive local urban contexts (Roorda and Wittmayer, 2014).

In Ghent and Ludwigsburg, the approach was seen as an innovative way of bringing together local actors to help develop a future vision for the city. In Rotterdam, the TM approach was more limited as a way of involving local stakeholders in drafting a policy agenda as part of a larger visioning exercise. In Aberdeen and Montreuil, the approach was driven by the need to develop new governance structures for climate change and energy, and here the TM element was initiated as a separate project. The initial focus also varied in each city, from a 'climate neutral' city (Ghent) to the 'future of energy' in a city (Aberdeen, Ludwigsburg and Montreuil) and 'greening and densification' of the inner city (Rotterdam) (Roorda and Wittmayer, 2014; Loorbach et al, 2016).

In the city of Aberdeen, the transition arena group identified two time horizons that related to the vision and possible transition pathways: 2030 as a medium-term target for achieving feasible options; and 2050 as a longer-term target for a post-oil future for Aberdeen (Frantzeskaki and Tefrati, 2016). The transition group agreed on five guiding principles: Aberdeen as an 'opportunity city'; Aberdeen as an 'attractive city' to visit and live in; Aberdeen as a 'learning city'; Aberdeen as an 'accessible city'; and Aberdeen as an 'energy-efficient and resilient city'. For each guiding principle, a vision image was created from a synthesis of statements, ideas and arguments from the group, which embodied a vision that described the practices, lifestyle and characteristics of a sustainable Aberdeen in 2050.

The MUSIC research showed that local authorities driving transition management may struggle to create the space and resources to develop this specialist role or indeed to develop further roles, so that effective leadership may be more viable when it comes from a research institute. There also needs to be a balance within the stakeholders selected for the transition arena, for example between more radical and moderate actors, and thinkers and doers. Cities differ as to the pace with which they want to engage with TM. Moreover, TM, as we saw earlier in this chapter, is not, in itself, a silver bullet for achieving what are often urban sustainability objectives, and the approach needs to be underpinned by and founded on complementary practice and policy solutions and interventions. The MUSIC project was focused on northern European cities where context, culture and institutional frameworks may be very different from those in other cities. Nonetheless, as a result of the work in Aberdeen and the other MUSIC cities, DRIFT produced a guidance manual on TM in an urban context (Roorda et al, 2014).

Summary

In this chapter, we have seen how urban pathways can provide a trajectory to transformative change, and that transitions theory has an important role to play in helping to show how cities can guide and shape the nature and direction of their urban futures. Doing this presents cities and their governing institutions with substantial challenges. As we saw, applying transitions theory at the city scale faces difficulties because of the complex and multifaceted nature of cities. The use of TM techniques also throws into focus its position in relation to existing urban planning and whether visioning supplants or complements existing urban planning practice.

Moreover, the ability of city stakeholders to influence some of the most important sectoral aspects of urban sustainability may be constrained in certain respects; for example, there is less ability at the city level to influence energy supply compared with water, buildings, waste and transport. As the Coalition for Urban Transitions (CUT, 2019) notes, local governments have direct power over less than a third of the emissions reduction potential in their cities. National and state governments have power over a further third and about a third depends on different levels of government working together to cut emissions. Emissions targets at national and subnational levels may also differ in their underlying basis and extent.

Although TM and city visioning offer real opportunities to help plan and manage long-term change at the city level, their use also raises the issue of power relations in a city. This translates into important questions such as, whatever the vision, who is constructing the vision for a city and for what purpose? Again, to what extent are participatory techniques used in the visioning and is a partnership approach to vision development being adopted? What is clear, however, is the importance of city visioning and city foresight in constructing viable and pragmatic urban futures. In the next chapter, we will examine city foresight methods in more detail, illustrating them through the use of practical examples.

7

Using city foresight methods to develop city visions

Think well to the end and consider the end first.
Leonardo da Vinci

Introduction and background

In the previous chapters of this book, we have seen, in an increasingly urbanised world, how our perspectives of cities and the narratives we deploy to explain them have shifted, morphed and evolved over time. Cities are hugely important today and have through many centuries led to diverse and rich explorations of idealised futures through art, literature and film. This has led to visionaries in planning and architecture framing new futures for our cities and, as climate change and environmental issues become important in a pervasive digitised and globalised world, the concepts of 'smart cities' and 'sustainable cities' have found growing interest across the world.

However, if cities and the people who live, work and play in them are to have a say in both how the urban future unfolds and what our real-world cities should look like in 2050 and beyond, then we need to understand the processes by which this could be achieved. The next two chapters are designed to offer a practical guide on how city visions can be developed through participatory-based foresight methods, and how new projects and experiments can help to transform cities and lead to a sustainable (and smart) future. This is a fundamental part of what we term 'urban futures' and recognises complexity and the need to manage a transition to a shared and desirable future.

In this chapter, we will look in more detail therefore at what city foresight really means in practice, how we define a 'city vision' and how such a vision can be developed with a range of techniques, including visioning and backcasting. To do this, we draw on our own research, working on Reading 2050 and Newcastle 2065 city visioning projects, but we also examine other examples of how foresight activities can help frame city visions in different contexts internationally.

What is city foresight?

As we saw in the earlier part of this book (Chapters 1 and 3), futures thinking is a way of identifying the long-term issues and challenges affecting and shaping the future development of a policy area and enabling the exploration of the implications for policy development (GOfS, 2016a). Foresight is an important part of a more general futures studies, and it is believed the term 'foresight' was first used in a BBC broadcast by H.G. Wells who called for the establishment of 'Departments and Professors of Foresight' in 1932 (Kuosa, 2011). Usually, foresight is concerned with longer-term futures of more than 20 years (or at least 10–15 years) away, and with concerns with alternative futures and how to get there. Such futures may be:

- *possible futures*, relating to imagination and the creation of interpretive alternative futures;
- *preferred futures*, relating to critical and desired or normative futures; and
- *prospective futures*, which incorporate the capacity and readiness to act to change the future. (Gidley et al, 2009; Gidley, 2017a, 2017b)

Interestingly, Poli (2017) distinguishes between three facets of futures studies: forecasting, foresight and anticipation. For Poli, forecasting is the predictive component of futures studies, with a very short (for example, econometric models) or very long (for example, climate change models) temporal perspective. Such an approach is often quantitative, based on past trends and founded on future extrapolation. In contrast, a foresight approach is usually qualitative, and not predictive, and often explores a range of possible (explorative) or desirable (normative) futures. In the former case, the starting point is a forward-looking view from the present to the future to explore a range of futures, while the latter takes a perspective that works backwards from the future to the present (backcasting), often focusing on a more limited number of (desirable) future(s). The third and increasingly important element of futures studies is anticipation (which Poli also refers to as 'foresight 2.0' or design-based foresight): this refers to an approach that, although grounded in the outcomes of foresight and forecasting, aims at implementing the results into decisions and actions. There is then an inherent sense in which anticipation can be used to acknowledge complexity and to create new policies and institutions to help shape the future. This also makes it important to think about different kinds of anticipatory futures. For example, *contingency futures* imply planning for unanticipated surprises from external forces such as a pandemic or natural disaster; *optimisation futures* are things that we believe can be helped to happen in the future through premeditation and planning (that is, to impose our will on the future and 'colonise' it); and *exploratory* or *novelty futures* are unpredictable and generally unknowable futures (Miller, 2011). Anticipation therefore builds in reflexivity to the process of foresight and explicitly acknowledges the presence of decision-makers in the process of imagining and creating the future (Minkkinen, 2019).

From its origins in the government and business sectors, the growth of futures studies has in recent years focused increasingly on environmental issues and related socioeconomic impacts. International organisations, such as the World Economic Forum (WEF), the World Social Forum (WSF), the German Advisory Council on Global Change (GACGC) and science-based organisations, such as the Intergovernmental Panel on Climate Change (IPCC) and the International Resource Panel (IRP), have undertaken a growing role in developing futures studies, which have sometimes used forecasting and foresight-based techniques to reimagine alternative futures (Swilling, 2020). Some of these studies have also taken an urban or cities perspective: for example the GACGC (2016) report *(Humanity On The Move: Unlocking the transformative power of cities)* looks in detail at the future of cities in a global context, as have other reports by organisations such as the United Nations (UN) (UN-Habitat, 2016). Aside from international or global studies, we have seen a focus on the future of cities in the developing world as well – for example, the *African Agenda 2063* programme takes a long-term view of the African continent, where the future of cities is an important focus (Ndizera and Muzee, 2018; Karuri-Sebina, 2019).

Perhaps the most important programme to focus on the future of cities using a foresight approach was the UK Government Office for Science's (GOfS) 'Future of Cities' (FoC) programme (2013–2016) (see Chapter 1). This placed city foresight at the heart of a programme of research that was designed to provide an evidence base on the future of UK cities to inform decision-makers. The programme defined city foresight as 'the science of thinking about the future of cities. It draws on diverse methods to give decision-makers comprehensive evidence about anticipated and possible future change' (GOfS, 2016a: 7). This perspective was based on the view that the UK had rarely looked very

Figure 7.1: City foresight

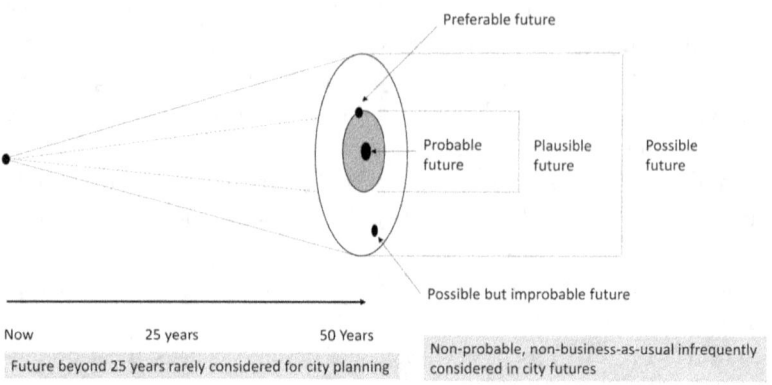

Source: GOfS (2016a)

far into the future of its cities. Although longer-term thinking was more common in the post-war period (for example, in Abercrombie's London Plan and the masterplans for new towns), more recently, most cities generally looked no more than 15–20 years (at most) into the future (in England and Wales through a statutory local plan, for example), whereas a perspective of more than 20 years, and up to 40–50 years ahead, opens up a possibility space to explore and influence a wider range of creative and imagined futures. As shown in Figure 7.1, therefore, city foresight can consider different kinds of future besides simply business as usual or probable views of the future.

As GOfS (2016a) suggested, in practice city foresight involves exercises to:

- uncover new ideas;
- challenge existing assumptions about the future; and
- explore the interactions between future trends and the forces driving change.

This requires the bringing together of government (local and central), businesses, civil society, academia and other organisations, which is also a feature of the transitions management – TM – framework we looked at in Chapter 6. The benefits of this approach were seen as both tangible (for example, the generation of new ideas; insights into policy inter-relationships; strong narratives to underpin city branding; and early risk identification) and intangible (for example, new relationships, capacity-building and trust; greater buy-in for decisions about the future; external confidence in long-term prospects; and facilitated learning).

The FoC programme highlighted five main types of thinking involved in city foresight. These were:

- *Visioning activities* to provide intelligence for setting the direction of future change, based on identifying aspirations and developing city visions, through exploratory or normative techniques.
- *Analysing activities* to build a knowledge base of assets, constraints and opportunities.
- *Designing activities* to create new possibilities and future options and develop scenarios or new designs for the future.
- *Testing* these options to see if they work and can cope with a range of future outcomes.
- *Assembling activities*, which can identify the new policy and practice required for change and to implement and evaluate the changes required.

These different ways of thinking about the future are complementary and imply a degree of iteration, with links between the five elements: a focus on a city's long-term objectives using visioning could inform and influence future land-use development options, with a range of urban design scenarios for example, which could then offer new insights into the city's aspirations for the future. Certainly, understanding the past and the present of a city, to understand its future, is a key attribute to this perspective, and which was also highlighted in the *Farrell Review of Architecture and the Built Environment* (Farrell, 2014) as part of a place-based understanding of cities.

The FoC programme also highlighted some of the key techniques that could be used for city foresight, including: creative visioning, or using dialogue, fiction or craft in a participatory way; and analytical aspiration mapping, to explore longer-term goals for a city. During the course of its work, the programme brought together and developed a network of UK cities, both large and small, a number of which developed long-term visions partly as a result of the programme. The FoC network (which comprised 22 cities) incorporated four major UK cities (Cardiff, Liverpool, Manchester and Newcastle), additional city pilots (Bristol, Milton Keynes and Rochdale) and a city vision community of other cities including Belfast, Birmingham, Cambridge and Reading (Cowie et al, 2016; Ravetz and Miles, 2016). Further work by Forum for the Future (2016) also built on this work by investigating urban system integration in the UK through the use of scenarios.

Although not directly focusing on foresight, two other recent programmes are noteworthy. First, there was the Urban Living Partnership programme (2016–18), funded by UK Research and Innovation, which funded further work in Birmingham, Bristol, Cardiff, Leeds, Liverpool, Newcastle-Gateshead and York to tackle specific place-based challenges (for example, health, wellbeing and environment) for each city, with a strong focus on co-designing solutions with people living in these cities (UKRI, 2018) (see Chapter 9). Second, a UK 2070 programme was established to foster cross-cutting thinking and solutions to tackle the UK's spatial inequalities (UK2070 Commission, 2018).

The UK has not been alone in developing large-scale programmes to develop detailed insights into future cities (Moir et al, 2014b; Swilling, 2020). Other large programmes that have included elements of futures thinking include the following:

- Norway: The *Cities of the Future* project (2008–14) was a collaborative project between the Norwegian government and 13 of the largest Norwegian cities (representing half of Norway's total population), with a strong focus on reducing greenhouse gas emissions and making the cities more liveable. Each of the cities developed action plans and worked with other stakeholders to specify binding agreements to commitments on land use and transportation, consumption and waste, energy in buildings, climate adaptation and improving the quality of the urban environment (Ministry of Local Government and Modernisation, 2014).
- Saudi Arabia: The *Saudi Future Cities* programme (2016–18) was designed to provide advisory services and logistical support to the national government in implementing the goals of the programme in collaboration with UN-Habitat. There was a strong focus on linking the programme with the *Saudi Vision 2030*, which embraced an ambitious target of having three Saudi cities being recognised among the top-ranked 100 cities in the world (UN, 2016).
- Africa: *Future Cities Africa* is a partnership initiative that was launched by Cities Alliance and the UK Department of International Development (DFID) in November 2014. The programme is designed to support African cities to be 'inclusive and resilient and have growing economies with better services, opportunities and quality of life' (Cities Alliance, 2016: 4). There is a strong focus on promoting environmental resilience, and two analytical tools (a

normative framework and an environmental risk framework) have been developed to underpin futures thinking in Ethiopia, Ghana, Mozambique and Uganda.

Other countries such as Brazil, Sri Lanka, Australia (Moir et al, 2014b) and Canada (Future Cities Canada, 2018) have developed futures-oriented thinking about cities, and more recently India's smart city programme, designed to develop more than 100 smart cities, has received considerable attention, much of it critical (Das, 2020). There is a strong focus on future cities thinking in the European Union (EU) through such programmes as the Joint Programming Initiative, URBACT and also more recent reports by the European Commission on urban futures (European Commission, 2019). Furthermore, the EU has a strong focus on what is termed 'regional' or 'territorial' foresight (EU, 2011; ESPON, 2018).

Besides national programmes for future cities, in Chapter 6 we saw how a number of academic-led research programmes had used city foresight to help shape city visions in Australia, the EU and the UK. However, we should remember that the focus on foresight within these national programmes is not new. There is, as we saw earlier in this book, a strong and longstanding utopian tradition in urban and regional planning, which has been previously traced and reviewed by the academic Robert Shipley (see, for example, Shipley, 2000, 2004). For example, during the 1980s and 1990s, there were attempts to create city visions in some cities in the United States such as Atlanta and Portland. John et al (2015) describe other examples, ranging from Gothenburg 2050, to York (Canada) 2051 and Sydney 2030.

Where foresight principles have been adopted in city visions, a particular feature is the concept of 'participatory futures'. This has been framed as 'visioning as participatory community planning' by Shipley and Michela (2006: 225), and as Shipley and Newkirk (1999) note, visioning in this sense involves three main elements:

- working with key groups of stakeholders to identify issues of concern in the city;
- motivating participants to think in new ways about existing problems and galvanise action to solve them through team-building; and
- providing solutions to those problems.

This differs from standard planning because the process of constructing the vision is designed to be open to all and the end goals are defined in concrete terms rather than more abstract or scientific terms.

This idea of participatory futures in foresight is fundamental to thinking about sustainable futures. Given the focus on intergenerational equity in social, economic and environmental terms, a substantial academic literature has recently focused on visioning in sustainable urban contexts (Dixon et al, 2018b; Swilling, 2020). As McPhearson et al (2016: 6) note: 'Positive visioning processes are an opportunity to dig deeply into the key tensions and challenges to bring communities together to create shared visions, or even create pluralistic visions within which to reveal underlying conflicts, trade-offs, and tensions.' Indeed, the concept of 'participatory futures' has found growing interest among those favouring a more democratic and transparent approach to decisions affecting the long-term future: some countries such as Brazil and Portugal use participatory budgets to allocate scare resources (Guimarães, 2019). NESTA's (2019) recent report, *Our Futures: By the people, for the people*, shows that beyond citizen assemblies and conventional public engagement, art and creative processes, such as immersive experiences and digital technology, can all play a role in enriching public participation, which can democratise and encourage long-term thinking, including visioning processes. The growing momentum for visioning has also been driven by increasing localism in England, with the emergence of neighbourhood planning.

What is a city vision and how can it be developed?

City visions

A vision can be thought of, in general terms, as a shared view of a desirable future. Different visions have been conjured up for cities over many hundreds of years, as we saw earlier in this book, and much of the thinking in science, art and literature has reflected and been reflected in the cities we see around us today and will see in the future. However, in a more formal sense, visions can be thought of as a subgroup of scenarios (possible future states) and clearly distinguished from predictions or likely future states (Wiek and Iwaniec, 2014). Visions should also be distinguished from the pathways that lead to them, and visioning is therefore the process of creating the vision.

In the context of cities, we see city visioning as an important technique in city foresight, which, in turn, is part of what we call the study of urban futures (see Chapter 1). The concept of 'urban futures' is used to describe the process of imagining what cities and urban areas will be like, beyond the short to medium term and into the long term (that is, more than 20 years from the present day), how they will operate, what infrastructure and governance systems will underpin and coordinate them, and how they are best shaped and influenced by their primary stakeholders. Such thinking should be analytical, investigative, diagnostic and participatory in its ambition, by exploring the future through city foresight techniques, including visioning.

Community-led planning created some impetus towards city visioning in the United States (for example, Chattanooga in Tennessee) and elsewhere (Gaffikin and Sterrett, 2006), and visioning was also seen as an important part of 'city development strategies' (CDSs), which were strongly supported by the UN (2012) and other organisations, such as the Cities Alliance (2017), particularly in the developing world, and elsewhere – for example rebuilding war-torn Kosovo's cities (UN-Habitat, 2012). A CDS, which includes a vision and a strategy for a city, is defined as 'a tool that helps a city harness the potential of urbanization through strategic planning. As an action-oriented process, it is developed and sustained through participation. It seeks to promote equitable growth in cities and their surrounding regions to improve the quality of life for all citizens' (Cities Alliance, 2017: 7).

This underpinned a growing call for strategic urban planning by academics, such as Albrechts (2010), founded on visioning and participatory-based approaches. More recently, the growing use of foresight and futures thinking has led to a growing interest in developing city visions particularly focusing on smart and sustainable cities (Dixon et al, 2018a). For example, Ingerborgrud (2018b) sees the visioning process of sustainable cities as a sociotechnical effort combining both social and technical elements. Visions can therefore be seen as offering the opportunity either to create consensus-building tools that enable actors from different fields and areas of expertise to collaborate, or to create 'trading zones', where different interests and expectations can be negotiated and traded off between different actors and stakeholders.

What specifically, though, is a city vision as referred to in this book? Jennings (2008: 1) suggested that a long-term vision for a city 'is the starting point for catalyzing positive change leading to sustainability. The vision needs to reflect the distinctive nature and characteristics of the city.' Yet as Shipley and Michela (2006) note, there is no universally agreed definition for the terms 'vision' or 'visioning' in the context of urban planning. Building on Jennings' work, in its purest form (or in a normative sense) we see a city vision as follows:

> A city vision is a long-term shared and desirable view of the city (or city-region), developed through the use of participatory-based visioning and related foresight methods.

> Place-focused, underpinned by appropriate policy, and aspirational in content and context, the vision should reflect the distinctive nature of the city and its key characteristics, and be based on the shared aspirations of the people who live, work and play in the city. The city vision should incorporate core principles of sustainability, equity and individuality, and integrate and connect with existing and relevant strategies and visions.

This is very much an ideal, or normative, view of a city vision, but we can also think of other strategic plans or visions (including masterplans) that have been developed or are being developed that do not necessarily meet all the requirements of our definition (see Chapter 8). We are careful to exclude the more generic, non-specific visions of ideal cities developed by urban planners and architects from what we refer to as a specific city vision for a place (city or city-region) (see Chapter 3 for example). In this sense, a city vision is linked to a wider group of spatial visions (or a set of imaginary and material views of a territory's future, structured in a materially coherent way) and which have often provided a general framework for strategic urban planning (Ek and Santamaria, 2009; Albrechts, 2010). Put in a looser and less formal way, there have been other instances where specific cities have, over the past decade, developed longer-term climate change strategies and plans for actions, and this is set to increase with the growing number of climate emergency declarations (Rode, 2019) (see Chapter 6).

Despite this, it is clear that cities are often generally very poor at taking a long-term strategic view when it comes to both sustainable and smart thinking, often because of political constraints and a focus on short-term thinking (Bai et al, 2010a, 2010b). For example, in recent research, it was found that 33 per cent of 885 urban areas in the EU-28 still did not have a local climate plan (Reckien et al, 2018) and, in another study of 401 global cities with more than a million inhabitants, only 18 per cent of cities had adaptation plans (Olazabal, 2019). Similarly, in a survey of local authorities in the UK, it was found that only 22 per cent of UK cities claiming to be a smart city had a smart city action plan or strategy in place (Dixon et al, 2017). Nonetheless, there have been other attempts at what might be broadly termed long-term visioning' For example, Moir et al (2014b) point to other types of future city vision with a long-term viewpoint, often focused on strategic planning: examples here include the London Infrastructure Plan 2050 and the Metro Vancouver 2040 regional growth strategy. However, such visions often lack the deep participatory insights that would have been provided by a wider engagement with the people and communities in those cities.

City foresight methods

To explain how city foresight methods can be used to help construct city visions, we need first to look at how foresight works in practice. As we saw in Chapter 1, foresight is a systematic and participatory way of gathering intelligence and building a vision of a long-term future so that we can plan and mobilise joint action for the future. Foresight can be seen as a way of enabling policy planners and decision-makers to think about the future and plan for it in order to influence the future more effectively. The complexity of present-day development challenges, volatility and uncertainty in the policy environment, and the changing nature of the role between the state and citizens, all play their role in creating difficulties for national and subnational governments to respond to growing environmental and socioeconomic challenges in our cities (UNDP, 2018). Yet, foresight does offer real opportunities for democratising the development of shared visions for our cities. This means understanding the future, its unpredictability and its complexity (see Box 7.1).

Box 7.1: Ten things we need to know about the future

1. The future cannot be fully predicted.
2. There are multiple possible futures, with some more probable or plausible than others. Normative or preferable futures are those that stakeholders really do want to create.
3. We create the future as we experience it, so we need to think about the future in terms of different group and individual perspectives.
4. Business-as-usual thinking should always be challenged.
5. Technology is not the future – how we use it now and how we develop new technologies will determine how they are used in the future.
6. The future belongs to the curious and those who see beyond existing thinking.
7. The future is a process, not a destination, as the future is a moving target.
8. Expect the unexpected and learn how to be sceptical.
9. For every future that will happen, there are many others that will not happen, so we always need alternative plans.
10. The worst thing is to live someone else's past, thinking it is your future.

Source: Adapted from UNDP (2018)

Using what might be termed 'fully fledged' foresight requires our thinking to be: prospective (gathering genuine knowledge and information about future realities); policy-related (using anticipatory and adaptive capacity to deal with uncertainty, disruption and innovation); and participative (where the process is focused on collective intelligence and many different perspectives to avoid groupthink) (UNDP, 2018). The UK GOfS (2017) has developed a *Futures Toolkit*, which outlines four sequential stages of futures and foresight:

1. Gathering intelligence about the future.
2. Exploring the dynamics of change.
3. Describing what the future may be like.
4. Developing and testing policy and strategy responses.

There are a variety of foresight tools that can be used in a city context. Table 7.1 summarises the main tools mapped against these four basic stages. Clearly, when a city vision is being developed, visioning will be at the heart of that process. Wiek and Iwaniec (2014) suggest that the process of city visioning adopts the following process:

1. Framing the visionary process.
2. Creating initial vision material.
3. Decomposing and analysing the material.
4. Revising and recomposing the material.

Visioning essentially identifies, develops and enriches a compelling preferred future (UNDP, 2018). Sometimes, in foresight, visioning is referred to as 'incasting' because it goes into depth into one particular future, rather than the often 'shallower' vision statement of conventional strategic planning. Visioning should capture people's imagination and provide challenges and new opportunities to think outside existing mindsets (Bibri and Krogstie, 2017; Bibri, 2019). Visioning exercises usually involve workshops, the use and development of visual material (Pollastri et al, 2017) and other forms of participation from key stakeholders (including different demographics), and forms an important part of transition management thinking – see Chapter 6.

In addition, backcasting is a helpful and valuable technique for city vision development. The method was originally developed for thinking about transport futures, and the process starts by developing a normative preferred future and then working backwards from that point to identify major events and points in time that will help

Table 7.1: Futures toolkit

Intelligence gathering about the future	
Horizon scanning	This is the process of looking for early warning signs of change in policy and strategy, often with a wide group of stakeholders and undertaking data gathering.
Seven questions	Seven questions is an interview technique for gathering strategic insights from a range of stakeholders.
Issues paper	This presents the findings from the seven questions interviews as a report to illustrate and define important strategic issues.
Delphi survey	This is a consultation process that gathers opinions from a group of experts to gather information about the future and prioritise strategic issues.
Tools for exploring the dynamics of change	
Driver mapping	This is used to identify the political, economic, societal, technological, legislative and environmental (PESTLE) drivers that shape the future policy environment.
Axes of uncertainty	These are used to define critical uncertainties that define future policy areas and to frame scenarios (see the next part of the table).
Tools for describing what the future might be like	
Scenarios	These are stories or narratives that describe alternative views of the future and explore how different outcomes influence or are influenced by policy and strategic decisions.
Visioning	This is used to create a shared view of the future, underpinned by a common set of aims and objectives.
SWOT analysis	This is an analysis of the strengths, weaknesses, opportunities and threats. Strengths and weaknesses are internal factors that need to be taken account of in developing policy and strategy. Opportunities and threats are external factors that need to be considered.
Tools for developing and testing policy and strategy	
Policy stress-testing	This is a method for testing strategic objectives against a set of scenarios to see how well they stand up to changing external conditions.
Backcasting	This is an analysis of the steps that need to be taken to deliver a preferred future.
Roadmapping	This shows how a range of inputs, research, trends and policy interventions can combine over time to help shape policy and strategic outcomes.

Source: Adapted from GOfS (2017)

Figure 7.2: Backcasting

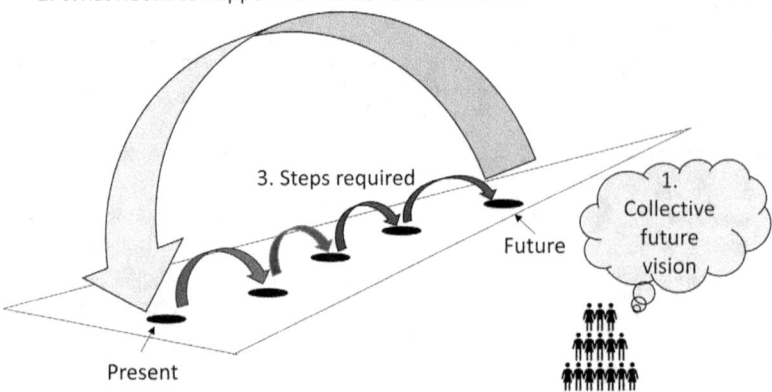

1. Start with the 'end' in mind.
2. Go backwards from the preferred future to the present.
3. Move step by step to the future.

Source: Adapted from Natural Step Canada (nd)

generate that future. This provides a potential trajectory of how the future could happen, and what policies are needed to make it happen (see Figure 7.2).

It may also be that visioning is helped and assisted by thinking about time horizons in a city. The 'three horizons' model, for example (see Figure 7.3), can help us think about urban sustainability transitions and the innovations that underpin them (see, for example, Newton, 2008). Horizon 1 (H1) innovations are strategically important now (over, say, the next 5–10 years) and are visible and well understood and become less important over time. Horizon 2 (H2) may overtake H1 trends in the medium term (say 10–20 years) and although it may not be clear how H2 innovations develop in the future, the drivers for change that define them are already in play. In the longer term, H2 gives way to more radical disruptive innovations – Horizon 3 (H3) – (more than 20 years) and a new set of policy and strategy challenges emerges.

Scenarios can also be helpful in city visioning work. These enable us to develop different stories about the future. For example, three well-used and adapted global scenarios from the Stockholm Environment Institute were developed to understand sustainability transitions (see, for example, Raskin et al, 2002): 'Conventional Worlds' are governed by the forces that have dominated globalisation to date; alternatively,

Figure 7.3: Three horizons

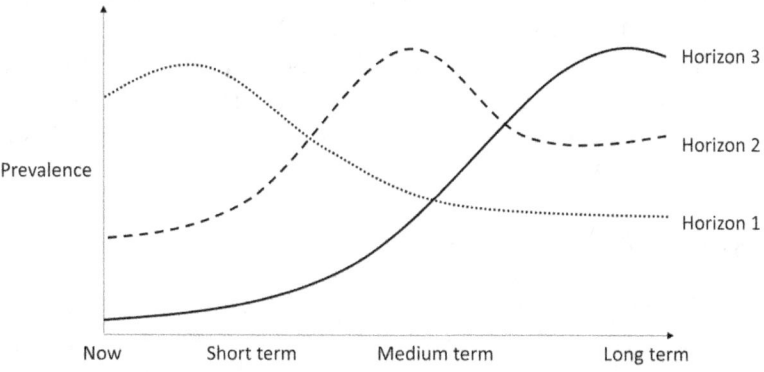

'Barbarisation' might emerge from the wreckage of Conventional Worlds (with an authoritarian world and harsh environmental mandates); or there might be 'Great Transitions', with a fundamental shift in the model of development towards sustainable living. Rogers (2018) helpfully describes the possible use of long-term scenarios in an urban context to 2065, for example: as extreme-yet-plausible outcomes that challenge existing thinking; as aspirational outcomes, which meet a set of criteria that are considered essential or desirable; or as morphological analysis, where two cross-cutting axes describe the issue, and the four quadrants created form the basis of four scenarios.

Roadmapping can play an important role in helping to develop a city vision. The roadmaps used in futures studies essentially replicate the characteristics of a spatial roadmap, which is designed to set out paths or routes in a geographical space (Saritas and Aylen, 2010; Dixon, 2011). Roadmapping has therefore been frequently used as a metaphor in technology management, strategic decision-making and action planning since the early introduction of the technique by Motorola in the 1970s (Phaal and Probert, 2009). Galvin (2008: 803), the chief executive of Motorola, suggested that a roadmap is '[a]n extended look at the future of a chosen field of inquiry composed from the collective knowledge and imagination of the brightest drivers of change in that field'. Roadmaps have been used in developing, supporting and shaping the city visions used in some of the previous academic-based visioning studies (see Chapter 6). For example, roadmapping was used in the EPSRC Retrofit 2050 project to identify disruptive and sustaining retrofit technologies (Dixon et al, 2014b).

Finally, 'experiential futures' are an additional and growing area of foresight work, which makes use of experiences and immersing stakeholders in specific future situations. A recent example in an urban context is the use of future design, which was developed in Japan and involves role-playing by today's generation as future generations. Municipalities in Japan have begun crafting development plans using this method, where residents wear ceremonial outfits and pretend to be future residents from 45 years in the future (Peach, 2019; Saijo, 2019).

City visioning: examples

In the context of the bigger picture, GOfS (2016a) outlines the steps for using city foresight in a specific city. This is seen as comprising six sequential stages:

1. Exploring aspirations and visions (visioning and aspirations mapping).
2. Understanding the history of a city and its individual characteristics.
3. Exploring future trends (including trends and projections, drivers of change and Delphi surveys).
4. Considering future options (using axes of uncertainty).
5. Testing future options (which might use 'what if' scenarios).
6. Connecting with roadmaps using backcasting and roadmapping techniques.

This process recognises the inherent differences between cities and their unique characteristics – a reference also alluded to in the GACGC report on cities as 'eigenart' (GACGC, 2016), or in other work as 'resonance' (Simone and Pieterse, 2017; Swilling, 2020). In this section, we will look at how city foresight methods (including visioning) have been used to develop city visions in specific cities in the UK. We draw on our own research to do this by focusing on Reading and Newcastle, and we also reference other visioning work in developing countries as examples of the processes and activities underpinning co-created city visions.

Reading 2050

Although Reading is not (yet) officially a city, it forms part of one of the most economically vibrant and connected small urban areas in the UK. Reading, 41 miles (66 kilometres) west of London, is part of a wider functional urban area (including part of West Berkshire and Wokingham) and has a population of 318,000 (2011 figure); this is set to grow to 362,000 by 2037 (Dixon and Cohen, 2015). Drawing on urban foresight methodology used by Eames et al (2013, 2014a, 2014b) in both Cardiff and Manchester (EPSRC Retrofit 2050 – see Chapter 6), the Reading 2050 project used a 'participatory backcasting' approach to develop the vision, supported by 'visual conversations' during the workshops. A participatory backcasting approach was used not only because of its successful implementation in previous urban foresight research, but also because the technique: (a) incorporates a high degree of stakeholder engagement; and (b) enables a transparent set of realistic and coherent urban futures to be developed by identifying possible urban futures(s) and the conditions, processes and pathways needed for their realisation (Eames et al, 2018).

Building on this previous research, the Reading 2050 project brought together the University of Reading (School of the Built Environment), Barton Willmore (a major planning and design consultancy) and Reading UK (the economic development unit for Reading) to lead the development of the vision. The programme was initiated in 2013 and used an initial participatory framing for stakeholder engagement, which was designed to combine elements of a smart city with those of a sustainable city (Dixon et al, 2018a). This was because there was, at that time, a strategic long-term aspiration for Reading to be low carbon by 2050 (through the Reading Climate Change Strategy) and because Reading has a strong technology focus in its existing economy. Moreover, a 2050 time horizon not only provides space to think beyond today's immediate problems, but also facilitates a greater sense of strategic thinking by identifying desirable as well as undesirable outcomes, in line with the UK's climate change target date. The starting point for the development of the vision was therefore a smart and sustainable city, which was based on the International Telecommunication Union (ITU) definition (ITU, 2014: 12–13; see also Chapter 6) as one that:

> ... leverages the ICT infrastructure to:
> a) Improve the quality of life of its citizens.
> b) Ensure tangible economic growth for its citizens.
> c) Improve the well-being of its citizens.
> d) Establish an environmentally responsible and sustainable approach to development.
> e) Streamline and improve physical infrastructure.
> f) Reinforce resilience to natural and man-made disasters.
> g) Underpin effective and well-balanced regulatory, compliance and governance mechanisms.

Throughout the process, all elements of the vision were tested and validated against these core principles for developing Reading as a smart and sustainable city by 2050. All workshops were run under Chatham House rules, with a set of protocols for courteous engagement. The process of developing the vision is summarised in Figure 7.4.

Invitees to the workshops were grouped into four broad categories: business/industry; government (primarily local); university/ academia (University of Reading); and civil society groups (non-governmental organisations). Invitations were made to pre-selected individuals in existing local and regional networks developed by the Reading 2050 partner organisations, and participants were chosen on the basis of their individual knowledge and expertise within these groups.

During the first workshop, which was designed to scope out the initial ideas for a Reading 2050 vision, three sessions were developed to help think about Reading's long-term future to 2050, in the context of: place and environment; people and lifestyle; and economy and employment. The three sessions were as follows:

- What should a smart and sustainable Reading look like in 2050? (Developing the vision): What should Reading look like in 2050,

Figure 7.4: Reading 2050: visioning process

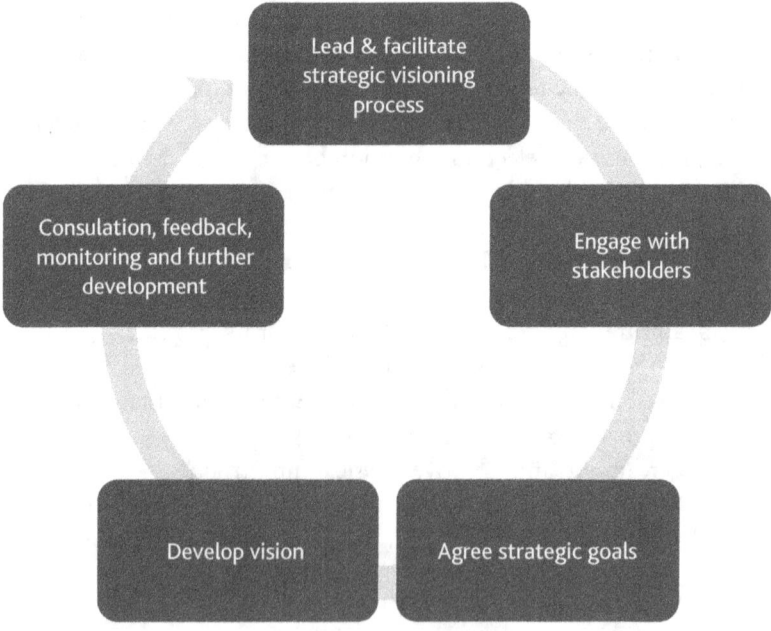

how will it feel, and what will it be like living there? How do we join smart technologies with sustainable thinking in Reading to set it apart, building on the strengths Reading already has? This part of the workshop used group working to focus on: place and environment; people and lifestyle; and economy and employment.

- How do we achieve a smart and sustainable Reading by 2050? (Developing the roadmaps or pathways to the future). What do we need to do, and by when, to achieve the smart and sustainable vision for Reading? Structured roadmaps and matrices were used to identify: challenges and opportunities, based on governance structures; behavioural changes; key technologies; and other factors.
- Physical infrastructure, growth and development. This session focused on integrating the thinking from the earlier sessions into the fabric of Reading. This focused on scoping out the physical changes that could support the smart and sustainable vision, in the short, medium and long term. Group work examined, through base maps at large and smaller scales, how specific key developments might emerge and what infrastructure changes were needed. 'Postcards from the future' (imagining what the city would be like in 2050) were used to summarise the thinking of groups in the first two sessions, and these were at the heart of developing the urban design futures for the final session (see Figure 7.5).

As a result of this workshop, three interlinked themes for Reading emerged: a 'city of rivers and parks'; a 'city of festivals and culture'; and a 'green tech city'. This was then fed back to Reading Borough Council councillors to generate further discussion and feedback, through the direct links Reading UK has with Reading Borough Council.

These themes were then examined in more detail in the second workshop in December 2015. This workshop again used backcasting techniques as a focus for examining the following:

- What are the strengths and weaknesses of Reading as a place? What are Reading's achievements, how could it do better and what needs to change over the longer term to 2050? This session used breakout group discussions to populate matrices and identify the challenges.
- What would a smart and sustainable Reading look like for each of the three urban futures (in terms of: place and environment; people and lifestyle; and economy and employment)? This session

Figure 7.5: Reading 2050 workshop activities

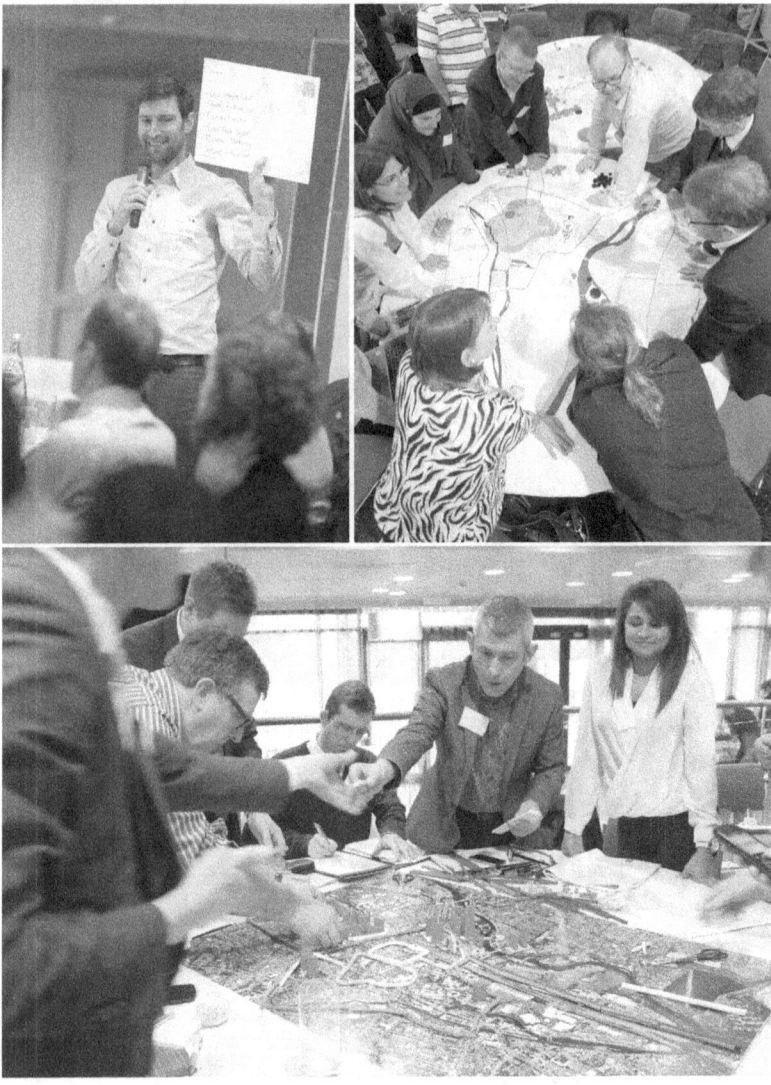

Source: Images of Reading 2050 are courtesy of Reading 2050, a collaborative initiative, jointly led by Barton Willmore, Reading UK and the University of Reading

used groupwork and narrative descriptions to help identify what the three futures would be like.
- What needs to happen and by when for each of the urban futures? This session used roadmapping techniques to help identify what changes would be needed in Reading to fulfil the alternative futures, in terms of infrastructure, governance and technological development.

The urban design workshop, which was held in January 2016, examined visualisations for each of the three scenarios, based on specific locations in Reading. This workshop brought together urban design experts to help visualise what the three urban futures could look like.

In March 2016, the project also ran a major public engagement event through an exhibition and display on a bus operated by Reading Buses in the town centre. This public engagement activity was supplemented by further activities, including engaging with young people through workshops and an art and design competition, and linking with Reading Museum's *Where's Reading heading? Happy Museums Project*,[1] which was designed to imagine how Reading's future could be more sustainable.

Finally, during March 2016 to June 2017, the research team engaged in further detailed discussions with Reading Borough Council councillors and the council's planning team to consult on the vision contents and ensure that it could be integrated with the local plan (which was in consultation during April to June 2017) before the vision was launched in October 2017. Ultimately, the Local Plan (Reading Borough Council, 2019a) and Corporate Plan (Reading Borough Council, 2019b) both include a detailed statement of the vision and link their content to the overarching vision. In November 2019, a further workshop was run to refresh the vision in the light of the moves to a net-zero Reading by 2030 (declared by Reading Borough Council). During the course of its work, which is still continuing, the Reading 2050 programme has engaged with 21,000 people and more than 400 businesses with some 15 linked events.

Newcastle City Futures 2065

Located on the River Tyne, Newcastle and Gateshead is the geographic and economic hub of the North East region of England, and is the main focus of economic growth within the region. The population of the city of Newcastle upon Tyne rose from 266,200 in 2001 to 280,200 in 2011. In 2012, Newcastle's population was 282,400, an increase of 5.7 per cent since 2001. The city is growing still and relatively vibrant economically, but within a wider region whose neighbouring towns and cities are not fairing so well. Newcastle and Gateshead's combined population is 381,100 (2011), within a Tyneside population of 879,996. In general, the region performs below average on a number of socioeconomic indicators – economic activity, educational attainment and health – whereas it has significant attributes in life sciences, biomedicine, digital technology, engineering and connectivity.

The Newcastle City Futures 2065 (NCF2065) project was funded by the UK GOfS as part of the Future of Cities project (GOfS, 2016a), and was led and progressed by Newcastle University as a collaborative engagement project. It aimed to pilot a foresight methodology that would be capable of being applied within a city-region, by mobilising the intellectual resources of regional universities and local stakeholders, and trialled to see whether it could be adapted elsewhere.

The project had three goals:

- to work with local partners and national bodies in establishing a review of key research applicable to the city-region;
- to establish a transferable methodology through which expertise in the local universities could be mobilised on a sustainable basis and focused on the long-term future of a city-region; and
- to develop long-term thinking capacity in the partnership around key future challenges such as environmental sustainability, long-term economic development, the healthy and ageing city, urban to urban relationships and urban and rural dynamics.

Although the title of the project specifically identified Newcastle, any study on the future of the city cannot ignore the wider urban region within which Newcastle is situated. Accordingly, the project team took the space and flows of the metropolitan area – equivalent to Newcastle, Gateshead and Tyneside – as the basis for analysing the city. The project was launched in December 2013. A Lead Expert Group (LEG) was established with representation from key partner organisations: Newcastle University, Northumbria University, Newcastle City Council, Gateshead Council and the North East Local Enterprise Partnership. In addition to this, an expert panel of stakeholders was established, drawing on a broad spectrum of interests and sectors within the regional economy and society. These two bodies provided the oversight and knowledge base vital to the project. After January 2015, the LEG was merged into a new Newcastle City Council-initiated City Futures Development Group (CFDG), a new committee comprising representatives of higher education, the local authority, enterprise, business and the voluntary sector, to forge stronger relationships and to boost research–policy links.

A detailed work programme was then developed, which had a number of phases:

- Phase 1: To develop a baseline of evidence about the city-region and the challenges and opportunities it faces. A stakeholder workshop was held to assist this phase of the project.
- Phase 2: To develop a more detailed understanding of the key themes and how expert stakeholders understood the relationship between the themes.
- Phase 3: To embed foresight thinking in the policy-making process within Newcastle and Gateshead to assist in the creation of new processes and networks to enable closer relationships between academic research and the policy community around long-term issues.
- Phase 4: Iterative discussions with insights from the national GOfS Future of Cities programme and the development of a network of universities/cities interested in city futures.

Foresight methods were used to form a multidisciplinary, multi-perspective approach to understand Newcastle as a city past, present and future, and to explore the effect of economic, social and environmental change in an integrated way. This included a range of engagement tools within the foresight approach to create five inter-related elements:

- Consulting with a range of stakeholders in the North East of England – more than 100 academics, policy-makers, non-governmental organisations, agencies, businesses and individuals were consulted between May 2014 and May 2015. This work provided a rounded picture of the major challenges for the future of Newcastle.
- Receiving the opinions of approximately 2,500 members of the public at a specially convened futures' facing city pop-up exhibition and events series located in Newcastle city centre in May and June 2014, which also generated more than 100 comment cards and ideas on a range of topics. Citizens gave detailed comments and feedback at each of the 24 public forum events organised within the exhibition arena.
- Collecting the intelligence from approximately 100 evidence-based academic and policy papers on a broad range of topics relating to Newcastle and the North East from leading academics and library

sources. These papers were not commissioned specially for the Newcastle City Futures 2065 project but covered recent relevant thinking and trends. Some of this work speculated on possible futures for the subject in question.
- Informal backcasting by providing an historical perspective – the lead team considered the historical development of the city in its region to gain an understanding of change and trends in the city since the early 20th century.
- Drawing on national and international evidence to analyse how other cities around the UK and the globe have tackled the future of cities. This work focused on issues and responses that were more relevant and/or transferable to Newcastle and informed the approach to the project.

The NCF2065 project progressed through these phases and employed a range of methodologies, while the project team were at the forefront of establishing new research–policy relationships. The project became embedded within Newcastle University as an anchor around which a dialogue emerged on a number of tangential but nevertheless important issues that focused on: the future long-term direction of Newcastle; the role of the university in its civic responsibility towards the city in which it is located; and the new ways in which the city and the university could precipitate more innovative forms of public engagement about the future.

The project therefore sought to build on the academic knowledge and experience developed over the past few decades within Newcastle University, as well as the knowledge and practice developed by the national foresight project, to test and evaluate a series of methodologies capable of engaging on a regional basis the full spectrum of stakeholders in producing a long-term vision for the region, which could, in turn, allow principal partners to form their own strategies. The project therefore used seven methods over the research period:

- baseline evidence;
- a public visual exhibition and discussion forum, named Newcastle City Futures;
- a research and literature database focusing on the city-region;
- stakeholder workshops;
- Delphi surveys;
- scenario building; and
- systems thinking.

The combination of methods, in addition to being a means to an end, also sought to be an end in itself at a time in England when strategic long-term planning and policy have been largely abolished in the largest cities (Shaw and Tewdwr-Jones, 2017). It is into this void in strategic planning and governance that Newcastle University decided it had the potential to fulfil the role of the civic university (Goddard and Vallance, 2013) and provide the necessary space for deliberation and debate to inform such strategic planning. The series of methods therefore sought to establish a community of interest about places that would have the necessary capacity and leadership to deliver plans and projects once developed and matured.

The first of the methods used by the project team was a desk-based evidence-gathering process, which sought to understand the present situation facing the region. These data were benchmarked against national and other regional data to show the relative strengths and weaknesses of the region. A second important method that dovetailed with the initial scoping study for the project was the establishment of a temporary city futures exhibition and events space, which looked at how Newcastle and Gateshead had always looked forward, and covered the period of the city's history since 1945. The intention here was to informally backcast and use imagery to initiate public conversations about change, to identify what had been built and what had not been built, and why, and to stimulate a conversation about future developments.

Both method 1 (baseline evidence) and method 2 (the city futures exhibition) aimed to situate the discussion and provide a framework for thinking about the future. This is particularly important when considering the time horizons used within the foresight project. It is often difficult for individuals to imagine their own lives in 50 years' time, never mind what the world will look like. There is often recourse to science fiction or other narratives to provide the basis for futures thinking. Taking stock of the present and looking back at previous plans for the future helps ground people's expectations and hopefully provides a more positive and realistic set of future scenarios. As these methods progressed, the baseline evidence base was constructed.

A stakeholder workshop also took place in May 2014 with representatives from the public, private, voluntary and academic sectors. The aim of the workshop was to get an understanding of the current opportunities and challenges facing the city-region and start to develop the key themes that would inform the development of future scenarios

Table 7.2: Themes identified in the NCF2065 stakeholder workshop

---
Education and skills
Health and ageing
The built environment of the city-region
The natural environment of the city-region
The social networks within the city-region
The national and international institutional and political networks
The governance structures within the city-region
The economy of the city-region
Technology
Public transport
Other infrastructure
Housing
Cultural institutions and assets
Newcastle City-Region's place in the UK/world
Climate change

---

and systems later in the project. Following a review of the knowledge produced during the workshop, a set of 15 key themes was produced. These are highlighted in Table 7.2.

A Delphi survey was chosen to develop a deeper understanding of the themes generated by the stakeholder workshop. The Delphi results generated a series of themes and inter-relationships between the themes. As a result, four overarching but multifaceted themes were identified to take forward. These were identifying Newcastle and its region as: An Age-Friendly City; A Sustainable City; A Creative City; and A Science City.

The final method centred around the development of scenarios. These were not intended to be predictions about the future but provided a prompt for discussion about the choices and decisions that would need to be made to generate ideas or visions of the future for a specific place and, simultaneously, avoid 'unpalatable' future outcomes. The project team developed three scenarios primarily using the information gathered through the Delphi survey and the stakeholder workshop, but also incorporating the material produced by the national foresight project in areas such as demographics and employment. The three scenarios were intended to construct an alternative narrative of the development of Newcastle over the following 50 years to 2065: 'continuation of present socioeconomic trends'; 'London implodes'; and 'Newcastle finds its niche as a test-bed city' (see Chapter 8).

The final report from the project was published in July 2015 (Tewdwr-Jones et al, 2015). Five thousand printed copies of the report were published by Newcastle University and distributed to regional organisations free of charge; a website[2] was also created to enable download versions. Over the following 18 months, the report findings were disseminated to specialist and lay audiences in more than 50 events. The key organisations – Newcastle City Council, Gateshead Council and the North East Local Enterprise Partnership – utilised the report in various official policy documents and strategies in the aftermath, particularly around seeing the city as a smart and sustainable place, a hotbed of digital creativity, and for economic and skills development.

Other city visioning examples

These two case studies are based in the UK in a global north context. However, there are other examples of city visions that have been produced through visioning activities and a participatory process in the UK and elsewhere, and this is further discussed in Chapter 8 (see also the Appendix). Not all of these cities have deployed formal foresight methods for producing visions; however, and in other instances the work has been academically led without necessarily coming to fruition or resulting in the implementation of the vision(s) created.

Interestingly, Pereira et al (2018) used participatory futures methods as part of the *Seeds of a Good Anthropocene (SOGA)* project, to create scenarios ('Rhiz(h)ome', 'Radical Translocal', 'Post Exodus' and 'Demos 42 Ubuntunse') for South Africa, including its urban future. The *Imagine Durban* initiative (2007–09) (Corporate Policy Unit, 2009) included some interesting participatory visioning work to develop a long-term plan for Durban in South Africa. In contrast, Swilling (2020) points to the clear differences and distinctions between urban visions and imaginaries in the global north and global south where culture and context are very different, and other writers point to the principles of 'vision and division' in top-down, imposed strategic plans in many developing world cities. Marom (2019), for example, provides a critical review of strategic planning visions in Mumbai and Cape Town. In terms of ensuring a right to their city, people in unregulated settlements also may well have no reason to buy into a vision that for them carries no meaning in their everyday lives, for example. This resonates with those theorising about the existence of 'shadow cities' in the global south outside the conventional circuit of international policy-making and boosterism (Neuwirth, 2006; Caprotti, 2018).

This critique is also implicit in other work. For example, Simone and Pieterse (2017) point out that it is often futile in many cities in the global south to agree consensus in a highly complex, informalised and unregulated environment: what is more important is to anchor 'visioning' in urban experimentation and innovation (involving, for example, social innovation or sustainable technologies) and build consensus around projects at grassroots level that make a difference in people's lives. This point is made by Karuri-Sebina (2019) through the concept of 'urban tinkering'. In this sense, experimentation rather than 'deterministic masterplanning' is advocated. Nonetheless, it can also be argued that without a sense of vision or purpose it is difficult even to develop such experiments. We would argue that there is still space for both city visioning and experimentation to co-exist and create synergies, provided they are built on sound and fully participatory methods. We will return to this point in more detail in the next chapter.

Summary

In this chapter, we have seen how real-world city visions can be developed using city foresight methods, including visioning and mapping. This is fundamentally important to what we define as 'urban futures' (see Chapter 1). However, it means that participatory methods that do engage with people (civil society), businesses, government, academia and other groups are crucial to successful visioning. The use of imaginative techniques, immersive experiences and experiential futures can all play a part in helping people develop shared and desirable futures. This presents challenges as well as opportunities – too often city visions are narrow or rely on business-as-usual trajectories, or they may be based on top-down imposed and highly technical views of the future, often through an economic lens (Caprotti, 2018). Furthermore, simply promoting legitimacy through consultation on preconceived ideas rather than being truly participatory and generating new ideas runs the risk of accusations of exercising power and dominance and closing down discussion (Kornberger and Clegg, 2011).

Moreover, visions need to be set in the context of the unique characteristics of each city. Understanding this, or what might be termed 'eigenart', is fundamental to our shared understanding of the past and present of a place to understand its future. City visions need to respect their national culture and context and need to be carefully shaped and acknowledge the differences in urban challenges between the global north and the global south. In the next chapter we will look in detail at the outcomes of the Reading 2050 and Newcastle

City Futures 2065 visioning process and compare and contrast other city visions from around the world to develop important principles of visioning and to highlight the real opportunities and challenges for city vision development.

8

Shaping the future: city vision case studies

> Vision is the art of seeing what is invisible to others.
> Jonathan Swift, 1667–1745

Introduction

Visions provide us with the means to see the critical issues and challenges that lie ahead, to help fight complacency and to see how things might be different. As Louis Albrechts (2010: 1123) wrote: 'Visions provide actors with views of the future that can be shared: a clear sense of direction, a mobilisation of energy, and a sense of being engaged in something important'. This is important in the context of transformative change in cities and how we manage and plan for future change. However, visions need to be a shared view of the future and rely on participatory methods to underpin them.

In the last chapter, we saw how the process of city visioning (as part of city foresight) can help us to develop meaningful city visions. In this chapter, we look at some key outputs from these visioning processes. To do this we begin by tracing the evolution of city visions, and the distinctions we should draw between them, and masterplans. We also examine the evolution of city visions over time and look at some specific examples highlighting the linkages between the process of visioning and the development of strategic urban planning. Finally, we look at two very different examples of city visions where foresight has played a major role (Reading 2050 and Newcastle City Futures 2065), and examine what makes a good vision and the opportunities and challenges surrounding the development of city visions.

From masterplans to city visions

As we saw earlier in this book, urban planning's roots lie in a strong tradition of utopic, visionary thinkers who were focused on imagining the ideal city. Even before these thinkers, there had been periods in history when real-world cities had been reimagined – for example Christopher Wren and John Nash in London during the 16th and 17th centuries.[1] These early seeds of thinking spawned the development of large-scale plans, or grand designs, in the 19th and early 20th centuries for large cities around the world, including those for Paris (1853) by Georges-Eugène Haussmann, Barcelona (1855) by Illdefons Cerdà, Chicago (1909) by Daniel Burnham and Vienna (1911) by Otto Koloman Wagner. These so-called 'big plans' included not only impressive graphics, but also illustrations of what was termed in the United States the 'city beautiful' (Schubert, 2019) (see Figure 8.1).

The plans were developed with the altruistic and noble aims of improving society but were essentially top-down in nature. As Burnham was quoted as imploring (Moore, 1921: 72–3):

> Make no little plans; they have no magic to stir men's blood and probably themselves will not be realized. Make big plans; aim high in hope and work, remembering that a noble, logical diagram once recorded will never die, but long after we are gone be a living thing, asserting itself with ever-growing insistency. Remember that our sons and our grandsons are going to do things that would stagger us. Let your watchword be order and your beacon beauty.

The 'big plan' was at that time seen as almost an end in itself and, despite the reformist and utopian ideals behind much of the thinking, the accusation of paternalism and authoritarianism is perhaps too easy to make. The concepts of large-scale planning for a city ultimately became more formalised in the urban planning and land-use control systems developed in the Netherlands, the UK and the United States in the early 20th century (Firley and Groen, 2013). In turn, this provided the foundation for 'masterplans', particularly through the work of Edward M. Bassett in the United States in the 1930s, the 'father of zoning'. Masterplans came to represent formal planning frameworks for city or, indeed, 'sub-city' scales. As Firley and Groen (2013: 17) suggest, a masterplan is 'a framework that provides more or less detailed design prescriptions for a specific development area'.

However, by the 1960s, the concept of 'masterplan' had become even more of a metaphor for inflexible, top-down urban planning. Writers such as Rowe and Koetter (1978), who were architects, instead conceived the notion of urban 'bricoleur', working in cities on the basis of what already existed and rebelling against the conception of scientific rules in an authoritarian society, where there is no singular

Figure 8.1: Images from Burnham's Chicago Plan (1909) and Cerdàs Barcelona Plan (1855)

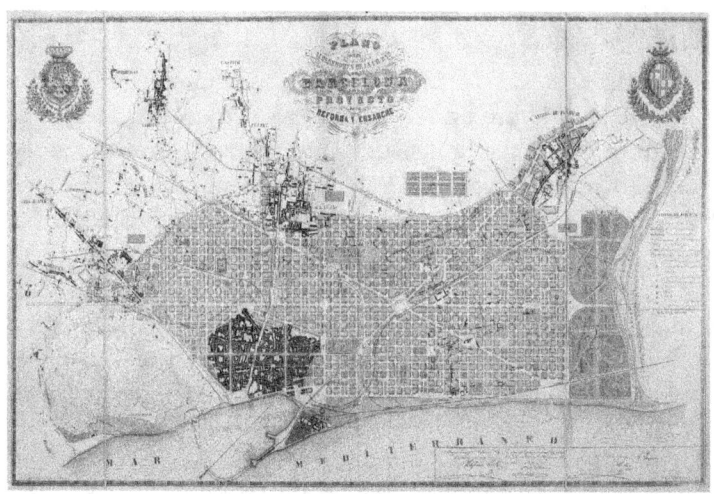

Source: Wikimedia Commons

plan or story, but many stories. This represented something of a backlash against order and large-scale planning.

It is fair to say, however, that since the 1960s we have subsequently moved and swung away from master planning as an inflexible and static process. As Bullivant (2012) argues, the best masterplans for places today are more flexible and more grounded in citizen participation or consultation. Indeed, Bullivant goes so far as to suggest that, in many respects, the term 'masterplan' is interchangeable with the word 'vision'.

Nonetheless, there is, in our view, a clear set of distinctions between the present-day use of the terms 'masterplan' and 'vision' at a city level. Table 8.1 highlights what we believe are the most important differences. These revolve around the earlier definition of city vision that we set out in Chapter 7. The traditional and conventional masterplan is very much top-down in its approach, often with public consultation *ex-post* the plan development. In contrast, a foresight approach, based on formal futures thinking, and with the public and other stakeholders involved in its co-production or co-creation, offers a more flexible approach, which recognises complexity in a city. Even in more recent and more dynamic masterplans, we therefore argue that the unique characteristics of participatory foresight-based thinking made explicit in a city vision does make for an important and crucial distinction.

The terms 'co-production' and 'co-creation 'are important to understand and define in the context of city visions. Co-production is anchored in scholarly studies on the public sector and represents the direct involvement of users (or people) in the production of a service (Brandsen and Honingh, 2018). For many, co-creation is used interchangeably with co-production, but Brandsen and Honingh argue that co-creation involves the shaping of the service at an earlier

Table 8.1: Key differences between a city masterplan and a city vision

'Traditional' city masterplan	'Foresight-based' city vision
Spatial planning focus with large-scale urban design and infrastructure	Integrated focus (including place-based and sectoral focus) on physical and non-physical characteristics ('eigenart')
Often 'top-down' with little recognition of existing plans, visions or strategies	Connects high-level vision with 'bottom-up' projects and experiments across scales
Frequently static in nature and lacking in responsiveness	Flexible and responsive to changing conditions
Rarely explores costs or the financing of development	Can explore different futures and different scenarios with different parameters
Often a low degree of public participation	High degree of public participation and a focus on 'co-production' and 'co-creation'
Timelines vary from short to longer term	Long term (15–20+ years) but with roadmaps of how to get there, including the short to medium term
Simplifies and compartmentalises	Recognises and embraces complexity

stage, with perhaps even users taking the initiative. In this sense, a city vision is co-produced when, for example, those developing the vision, perhaps the local municipality, involve people and communities from the outset, but a city vision is co-created when it is the people themselves or the community as a whole that may start the process. In another sense, co-production can be seen not only as 'a cooperative ethos of enquiry and set of practices' (Perry and Atherton, 2017: 2), but also part of a wider process, which is an holistic approach, 'beginning with the conception of individual projects, and continuing through to adoption, communication and publication of findings' (MISTRA, 2018). In other words, in an urban visioning context, co-creation could even be seen as the combination of co-design, co-production and co-implementation (MISTRA, 2015). These important defining characteristics have not been as important in underpinning masterplanning as they have in visioning. Indeed, using Arnstein's (1969) ladder of citizen participation, co-production and co-creation are equivalent to at least partnership, with some acknowledgement of delegated power, perhaps with masterplanning anchored further down the ladder in consultation (see Figure 8.2).

However, when did the concept of 'city visioning' develop? Shipley and Michela (2006) see the origins of what they call 'vision planning' in the management leadership literature of the 1970s to 1990s (for example, from authors such as Tom Peters). As they suggest (Shipley and Michela, 2006: 226): 'Beginning in places like Chattanooga, Tennessee, taking root in communities like Hamilton, Ontario and prospering as far away as Sydney, Australia, visioning exercises, where whole communities were invited to participate in the creation of a vision that would inspire future planning, were in full swing by the mid-1990s.'

These activities led to the publication of seminal works on visioning in planning such as *A Guide to Community Visioning* (Green et al, 2000) and the *Community Visioning and Strategic Planning Handbook* (National Civic League, 2000). As Gaffikin and Sterett (2006) note, there was a significant move towards city visioning exercises in North America during the 1990s and 2000s as part of a growing focus on strategic urban planning. As we saw in Chapter 7, the promotion of city development strategies (CDSs) (and their accompanying toolkits, which placed the development of an urban vision centre-stage) drove the development of visions, especially in the developing world (Robinson, 2008; UN, 2012; Cities Alliance, 2017). Indeed, Landry (2012) in the *Creative City* suggests that visions have been developed by cities for three main reasons: first, cities wanting to stay competitive and ahead of

Figure 8.2: Arnstein's ladder of citizen participation

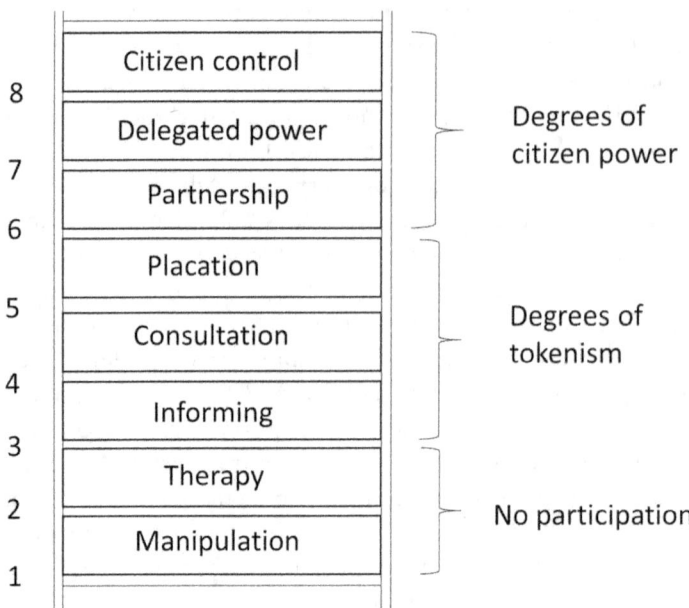

Source: Adapted from Arnstein (1969), via Wikimedia Commons (https://commons.wikimedia.org/wiki/File:Ladder_of_citizen_participation,_Sheey_Arnstein.tif)

the game (for example Barcelona); second, cities wanting to resolve urban crises (for example Detroit); and third, cities wanting to create opportunities (for example Dubai). In summary, Figure 8.3[2] shows the evolution over time of city visions from the early planning-led or community-based visions to the more recent participatory and foresight-based visions (see the Appendix for further details).

There is some debate as to whether some of these early visions offered anything more than broad options for debate, but the Atlanta Vision 2020 project is often highlighted as a leading example from this period. This project was very much based on a strong participatory focus, with collaboration training and what was described as the largest community collaborative planning effort ever conducted. In reality, however, as Helling (1998) suggests, the promises in the vision (which cost $4.4 million to produce) fell some way short because process-related rather than outcome-related objectives were specified, and the visioning process not only limited the potential for planning and action without stimulating compromise and change, but also played down the role of planning expertise. Other authors such as Iwaniec and Wiek (2014) highlighted how sustainability visioning could play an important role in updating general plans (in the case of Phoenix in Arizona, for

Figure 8.3: The evolution of city visioning

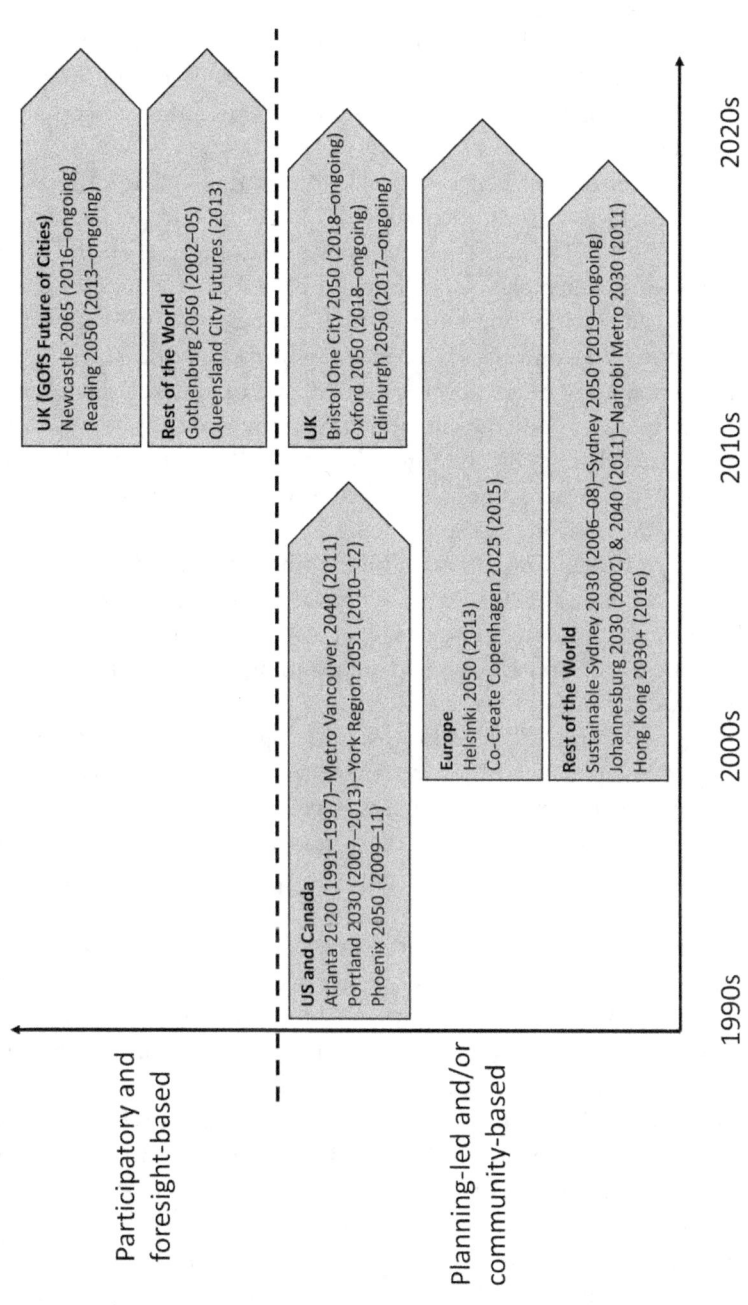

example). In Portland, Oregon, the mayor led a major community visioning exercise from 2005 to 2007 with more than 21,000 pages of comments collected; a survey was carried out asking residents what they most valued about their community, what changes they would like to see and their visions for Portland in 20 years and how to get there (Pettibone, 2016). This work underpinned the subsequent city plan development.

We saw the emergence of city visions with a strong sustainability focus emerging during the 2000s and 2010s in Europe and the Rest of the World. These included visions for major cities in the Nordic countries (for example, Copenhagen and Helsinki). Often, the visioning here was driven by other factors such as: the growing need to foster competitiveness and attractiveness in a globalised world; the increasing fragmentation of urban governance and growth in stakeholders making partnership and cooperation more important; and the growing impact of climate change and resource depletion (Krawczyk and Ratcliffe, 2006). Similar motivations drove cities elsewhere to develop visions such as Hong Kong, Johannesburg, Nairobi and Sydney, and in the UK, cities including Bristol, Edinburgh and Oxford. Some of the visions we have included here as typical of the genre are what might be termed 'visionary' strategic spatial plans (for example, Hong Kong, Johannesburg and Nairobi) and are planning-led with differing levels of consultation (Watson, 2013, 2016).

Figure 8.4 shows three examples of images from vision documents for Sydney, Bristol and Johannesburg. The Sustainable Sydney 2030 programme, for example, aimed to make the city as 'green, global and connected as possible by 2030'. To do this, the vision looked beyond the boundaries of Sydney and was a response to what the city administration saw as a growing set of complex issues, including climate change, rising oil prices, increasing economic competition from other cities and the promotion of a city branding agenda (Kornberger and Clegg, 2011; City of Sydney, 2019). More recently, further consultation was being progressed to help develop a new Sydney 2050 vision. In the case of Bristol, the development of the 'One City Plan' grew from the strong environmental and green thinking that has characterised Bristol since the 1990s. The election of Marvin Rees as mayor of the city in 2016 built on the foundations set by his predecessor, George Ferguson, and the One City Plan, launched in 2019 (and which looks to 2050), aims 'to make Bristol a fair, healthy and sustainable city. A city of hope and aspiration, where everyone can share in its success' (Bristol One City/Bristol City Council, 2020: 5). Turning to the third city, in 2011 the Johannesburg 2040 vision extended and replaced the initial

Johannesburg 2030 vision from 2002. The original Johannesburg 2040 vision focused on growth and development and aimed towards creating a vibrant, equitable, diverse, 'World Class African City of the Future'. It consolidated various other city strategies and included a wide-reaching engagement and feedback process. The vision was a response to two primary issues: (a) the continued transformation of the inherited Apartheid City; and (b) the uncertainties of present and future challenges, such as migration, globalisation, climate change, natural resource scarcity and financial markets. In 2016, the Spatial Development Vision 2040 (see Figure 8.4) built on the 2011 vision to identify the main challenges and opportunities in the city, setting a spatial vision for the future city and outlining a set of strategies to realise that vision. The core objective of the 2040 vision was to 'create a spatially just world-class African city' and was developed through a participatory process, gathering opinions from a wide range of stakeholders. The 2030 and 2040 vision documents must also be seen in the context of the National Development Plan for South Africa to 2030, which seeks to promote and enhance economic growth (Robinson, 2008: Rogerson and Rogerson, 2015).

Finally, during the UK Government Office for Science's (GOfS) Future of Cities programme (see Chapter 7), a number of cities developed participatory, foresight-based visions. In Figure 8.4 we highlight Milton Keynes, Reading and Newcastle, but there were other visions of varying descriptions created as well, including those for larger cities (see Chapter 7). For example, in Newcastle, the vision process was initiated by Newcastle University and drew on the private sector, the public sector and civic society (Tewdwr-Jones et al, 2015; Goddard and Tewdwr-Jones, 2016). There has been some broader reflection on the lessons of the Future of Cities programme (Cowie et al, 2016; Ravetz and Miles, 2016): for example, Cowie et al (2016) noted the wider importance of capacity and leadership in city visions, while Ravetz and Miles (2016) highlighted the importance of the relative power and influence of stakeholder groups in relation to the development of the visions. However, to date, with the exception of Newcastle (Urban Foresight, 2018; Vallance et al, 2019, 2020), there has been little or no in-depth analysis and critical reflection on individual case studies that were part of this programme and the ensuing implications for other cities.

A fundamental distinction of the Future of Cities programme from much of previous city visioning was its focus on participatory-based foresight thinking. Although not all the visions developed in the programme came to be embedded in practice within their cities, in

Figure 8.4: Examples of city visions

Source: Bristol One City/Bristol City Council (2020), City of Johannesburg (2016), City of Sydney (2019)

Note: The examples are Bristol One City Plan 2050, Johannesburg 2040 Spatial Development Framework and Sydney 2030

some instances, such as Reading, they were. In some other cities, such as Milton Keynes, which were part of the Future of Cities programme, city visions were developed and embedded but were not formally focused on participatory foresight-based methods. The development of participatory foresight-based studies was not restricted to the UK, however. In South East Queensland, Australia, four cities/urban areas developed visions using similar techniques and futures thinking (Russo, 2015, 2016a, 2016b). These comprised: Maroochy 2025 ('A Visioning Journey'); Logan 2026 ('City Directions'); Gold Coast 2037 ('Our Bold Future Initiative'); and Our Shared Brisbane ('Living in Brisbane 2026'). All the Queensland cities carried out extensive public participation exercises in developing their visions, with a strong emphasis on futures thinking. Finally, in Sweden, the Gothenburg 2050 vision was developed with input from Chalmers University, with backcasting playing a key role (Ramnero, 2005; John et al, 2015).

It is noticeable that city foresight methods have been relatively rare: a survey of 225 cities and 400 sustainability initiatives found that foresight was used in only 8.5 per cent (34) of the initiatives, mainly in housing and land use (Castan Broto et al, 2019). The Cities Alliance toolkit (Cities Alliance, 2017) does not use the term 'foresight', although there is a strong emphasis on city visioning. In the next section of this chapter, we will look in further detail at two of the Future of Cities foresight-led city visions (Reading 2050 and Newcastle City Futures 2065) by examining the basis of the visions and their contents (see Chapter 7 for a description of the processes by which these visions were developed).

Case studies: participatory foresight-based city visions in the UK

Reading 2050

At the heart of the Reading 2050 project was the concept of a 'co-produced' vision. This concept of collaboration is linked directly with the development of a 'quadruple helix' conceptualisation of the innovation process, which has emerged from a European Commission policy focus on civic engagement and open innovation (Arnkil et al, 2011; Goddard and Tewdwr-Jones, 2016; Kimatu, 2016; Tewdwr-Jones, 2017; Vallance et al, 2020) (see Figure 8.5).

This new innovation model sees the triple helix perspective (university, government and business) as limiting, and lacking a civil society (or citizen) focus (Arnkil et al, 2011; Goddard et al, 2014).

Figure 8.5: The quadruple helix

Critics, for example, have questioned the effectiveness of the model as expected levels of innovation and economic growth have often failed to materialise (McAdam and Debackere, 2017). In the new quadruple helix model there is therefore an emphasis not on three, but on four groups working together to drive innovation and structural change: civil society is therefore an additional source of knowledge, which is required to shape and test university research (Arnkil et al, 2011; Goddard and Tewdwr-Jones, 2016; Tewdwr-Jones, 2017.) The fourth element of the helix is, however, far from being well-established in innovation research, and there is often disagreement over its precise constitution: for example, the extent to which it includes innovation 'users' as well as civil society (Hogland and Linton, 2017). Nonetheless, recent work has highlighted the usefulness of the quadruple helix as a way of conceptualising the participatory approach to vision development in smart cities (van Waart et al, 2015; Mora et al,

2018). For example, van Waart et al (2015) see vision development as a collaborative process that helps shape the participatory domain (or the city visioning element at the centre of Figure 8.5). This views the innovation process not as linear, but as layered, shaped and influenced by the relationships between the primary stakeholder groups (Carayannis and Campbell, 2010). In other words, the quadruple helix model represents a matrix model where society and citizens can drive research priorities as well as react to research findings (Goddard and Tewdwr-Jones, 2016).

As a result of the participatory processes conducted (see Chapter 7), the Reading 2050 vision was launched in October 2017. The vision is described in more detail in Box 8.1 and the images connected with the three elements of the vision are shown in Figure 8.6. A website was launched with videos covering the three main elements and other supplementary and supporting material (see the Appendix).

Box 8.1: Reading 2050 vision

The overall vision statement that emerged from the series of workshops and participatory engagement was that:

By 2050, we believe a strong vision will help us to establish Reading as an internationally recognised and economically successful city region. A city where low carbon[3] living is the norm, and the built environment, technology and innovation have combined to create a dynamic, smart and sustainable city with a high quality of life and equal opportunities for all.

By 2050, Reading will therefore be:

- a cosmopolitan city celebrating and supporting its cultural diversity;
- retrofitted and developed to create a smart, sustainable, high-quality built environment;
- a leading destination offering a vibrant city of arts, culture, architecture and the public realm;
- supported by a comprehensive sustainable transport system that accommodates walking and cycling, as well as rapid transport and zero-emission vehicles;
- a city of equal opportunities for all and decreasing levels of poverty and deprivation;
- a dynamic, resilient and confident city, attracting new businesses and entrepreneurs operating sector-wide;
- a leader in smart and green technology and sustainable living solutions;

- a city that has rediscovered and embraced its heritage and landscape;
- a city that generate a large proportion of its own energy from renewables.

Within this vision, three interrelated urban futures were developed, as follows.

Green Tech City – a city that builds on its established technology focus. It celebrates and encourages diversity through business incubation units, 'ideas factories' and a city-centre university campus through which to exhibit and test cutting-edge ideas and approaches, no matter what discipline they are emerging from.

City of Rivers and Parks – a city that recognises how water has shaped much of Reading would celebrate its waterways, opening them up to offer recreational spaces such as animated parks, a lido, food production opportunities and city-centre waterside living.

City of Culture and Diversity – a city that builds on the success of the iconic Reading Festival to deliver arts and culture to people of all ages and ethnicities. Reading would facilitate community interaction and opportunity. The city would integrate, enhance and celebrate it heritage, bringing it to life through modern interpretations and uses of space as well as preservation.

Source: livingreading.co.uk/reading-2050/

Through the workshops, the research also focused on examining how Reading could achieve the vision and ensure that it was a smart and sustainable city by 2050. To do this, the intention was to consider a range of factors including leadership and infrastructure issues (particularly Crossrail) over the period from 2020 to 2050 (see Table 8.2). Reading's three unsuccessful attempts to achieve city status were highlighted and that, in a new era of city devolution in England, perhaps city status would be of positive benefit. Certainly, this was seen as a longer-term objective, with the development of new types of finance in the city being important to help deliver bold carbon reduction targets. For example, during the workshops, a strong feeling was expressed that Reading should be able to 'administer its own destiny', and have the powers to bring about change, as well as a structure that allows for planning of a wider area through integrated decision-making with areas that are currently neighbours.

City vision case studies

Figure 8.6: Three main elements from the Reading 2050 vision

Source: Images of Reading 2050 are courtesy of Reading 2050, a collaborative initiative, jointly led by Barton Willmore, Reading UK and the University of Reading

Note: From top to bottom the elements are 'green tech city', 'city of rivers and parks' and 'city of culture and diversity'

Newcastle City Futures 2065

As we set out in Chapter 7, a foresight project entitled Newcastle City Futures 2065 (NCF2065) had been undertaken in 2013–15, led by Newcastle University but partnered with local government, business and the community sector. The approach here was similar to that

Table 8.2: How can Reading deliver its vision? A roadmap to 2050

2020	2050
Develop the vision. Review how leadership can respond to the challenges. Market the vision widely and encourage 'buy-in' by government and private sector investors. Undertake social, economic and environmental assessments. Develop a flexible futures framework for short-, medium- and long-term development. Complete Crossrail, and consider opportunities for rapid transit, a third river crossing and further improvements to the walking and cycling network. Establish and drive a programme for big data broadband delivery. Review self-sufficiency in energy production options and establish key waste and water enhancements required. Begin retrofitting programme and consider means to drive for high-quality, sustainable architecture. Achieve city status. Assess cultural opportunities, the potential for growth and the requirements to support this. Explore financing opportunities at government, LEP and local authority levels.	Support the ongoing vision evolution and promotion of Reading City. Have strong collaborative leadership in place and facilitate joined-up thinking across 'Greater Reading'. Consider flexible futures framework successes and continue to evolve. Deliver sustainable low-carbon building as the norm. Explore and utilise financing opportunities such as carbon bonds, social impact bonds, crowd funding and local investment funds. Progress plans for rapid transit and deliver a third river crossing and free public transport. Enhance cycle ways and footpaths and ensure road pricing is driving changes in behaviour. Establish a thriving cultural calendar with enhanced facilities and promotion. Deliver a business hub and flexible commercial space opportunities.

in Reading, in developing a quadruple helix approach across higher education, city (or local) government, industry and communities. However, unlike Reading, the project was not co-owned by local government and there was no direct obligation on the part of local government to endorse or adopt outcomes of the project as a single vision. Council officials did, nevertheless, participate in workshops and worked in partnership with other sectoral representatives to utilise foresight methods to diagnose problems and finalise future city narratives. The reasons why local government was not fully committed to the project are multifaceted, and relate to three key factors: the delicate political context in the North East region; a preference on the part of the political leadership not to commit to any long-term vision or plan when more immediate issues such as austerity and public service funding crises occupied their days; and, at the time, protracted negotiations between the region and central government in Whitehall to progress a devolution deal (Shaw and Tewdwr-Jones, 2017).

As a consequence, the university-led team was always conscious that, by bringing a range of actors into discussions about the future of the city, it would merely assist the local authority and other strategic actors to inform their roadmap for determining policy and decisions for the future. This point was reiterated to participants throughout the project, in order not to raise false expectations but, equally, it did not cause any major setback; after all, most of the participating agencies, being based in and of the city, were well aware of the political context and political barriers to carving out alternative strategic visons, especially if some involved possible policy directions that were at variance with the prevailing political leadership direction.

What we saw with the NCF2065 project was, therefore, a city vision exercise that sought to develop support politically and collaboratively in an incremental way over time. With some city and national governments across the globe regarding strategic planning as too long-winded and top-down, we may well see a need in future for city visions to develop in more agile ways, rather than as a 'big bang', especially if those visions are co-produced by non-governmental actors and undertaken as a challenge to existing politically elected state preferences.

The issues identified in the NCF2065 Delphi surveys undertaken with a range of stakeholders in the region formed the basis of scenario work to develop three alternative *narratives* (rather than visions) of where Newcastle and its region might be heading to over a 50-year timescale. This time period was essential to avoid getting bogged down in immediate political policy concerns and to enable local government officials' participation that could be described as being more 'blue-skies' thinking compared with day-to day activities. The issues covered: education and skills; the North East economy; public transport; social networks; housing; cultural institutions; governance structures; the built environment; health and ageing; Newcastle's place in the UK/world; national and international networks; climate change; and the natural environment. Ideas in respect of these issues were then extended into three alternative scenarios (the narratives):

- *Continuation of present socioeconomic trends.* This portrays a city that develops in much the same way as it has over time. The city is affected by global and national decisions taken elsewhere, and intra-regional politics is often conflict-ridden, leading to ongoing uncertainty for businesses and citizens. The economy struggles to compete with London's continued domination. Newcastle's geographical position,

too far from the 'northern powerhouse' focused on Manchester and the central belt of Scotland, becomes a disadvantage.
- *London implodes* as it is unable to cope with demographic and environmental pressure. Rebalancing the national economy portrays Newcastle as a confident place that has recognised its assets, generates a successful economic transition, and has implemented a range of infrastructure projects to boost its presence internationally and nationally. The city's quality of life leads to a rush of development activities, a programme of urban renewal and a thriving arts and cultural scene. Although successful, the city also has to deal with a property bubble and increasing unaffordability for citizens.
- *Newcastle finds its niche as a test-bed city.* This portrays the city as a demonstrator platform for a range of scientific and technological future-facing public/private projects and programmes that are socially inclusive. The city has developed confidently, and opens up strong relationships with northern Europe. The city becomes a test bed for an engineering powerhouse, with the result that Newcastle achieves international prominence as a forward-thinking science city. Social and cultural developments and consumer services support this platform role.

These developed in narrative form, assisted by the production of computerised imagery and visualisations, to act as prompts during workshop sessions (see Figure 8.7). These visualisations, created by Northumbria University working as part of the NCF2065 team, were accompanied by the use of older photographs of Newcastle and Gateshead from the period 1945 to 1980, and all were intended through backcasting techniques to encourage people to remember how things used to be, what had changed and why, and whether the future would be the same or different.

These scenarios did not form, nor were they meant to provide, a single vision for the city. As the project team developed the NCF2065 project and embarked on the various foresight methods to underpin and inform the work, a concerted effort was made to develop lasting collaborative partnerships. So the emphasis was very much on not expecting a vision to be driven by and adopted into a single strategy document of the city council, but rather seeing the vision as a looser frame that allowed multiple actors to operate, and within which the partnerships and projects aligned with particular scenarios could be developed further. These partnerships were intended to be forged with various academic experts across Newcastle University, and between the university and outside

City vision case studies

Figure 8.7: An example of computerised visualisation

Source: Northumbria University VRV for Newcastle City Futures, reproduced with permission

Note: This visualisation was developed by Northumbria University in 2015 to support the NCF2065 project, intended to generate discussion about high-speed rail and the high-rise development of the city centre in Newcastle upon Tyne

organisations representing government, business and civil society, and to become a series of ambitious projects that were short, medium and long term in roll-out. Over time, the projects appeared to align much more with one of the scenarios, *Newcastle finds its niche as a test-bed city*, than the others. So it was only some years later after the publication of NCF2065 in 2015, that the city council started referring to the NCF2065 document and using the phrase 'test-bed city' in its own documentation.

This commitment of the university-led team to work with and for the city was very much in the spirit of Newcastle University being seen as a civic university (Goddard and Vallance, 2013), working with multiple partners in the city in which it is located, and finding new opportunities for engagement, collaboration and research. The additional benefit of aligning multiple common interest agencies to work in partnership on projects of mutual interest was that it avoided the possibility of a single agency (such as the city council) either reneging on carrying out a commitment or even abandoning more ambitious future narratives of the city.

The NCF project team did not set out to develop a new model of cross-disciplinary or cross-organisation collaboration with NCF at the centre. However, as time passed, it became clear that the various partners involved in the project were starting to identify with the aims and objectives of NCF. Some of those organisations relied on the project and project team as a neutral broker or facilitator in a much larger conversation relating to city-wide issues. This occurred at a time when many city services and city governance processes were under scrutiny both within and beyond Newcastle.

The city council did play an active role, and found outlets for the co-produced ideas within its existing governmental structures and initiatives. This included, for example, the work of *Newcastle 2020*, a consortium city board led by the chief executive of Newcastle City Council, comprising senior representatives of the public sector organisations in the region, discussing the implications of public cutbacks and austerity, and finding new ways to meet public service delivery. More significantly, the city council also set up a new governance vehicle specially to address the long-term futures of the city. The *City Futures Development Group* was formed in January 2015 as a quasi-council committee. This group comprised experts from across two universities, two local authorities, the Local Enterprise Partnership and business interests. The group performed two roles: to engage with policy officers on discussion of long-term trends affecting the city; and to discuss and disseminate ongoing and emerging research work undertaken at the universities that may have implications for the future of the city (see Box 8.2). Finally, a *Newcastle Policy Cabinet* futures group was formed in September 2014 by the city council, to advise the leader of the council on possible future long-term trends affecting the city and to provide intelligence to the city council's public-facing policy cabinets on specific themes, including community development, education and skills, youth employment and mental health.

Box 8.2: City Futures Development Group, Newcastle

Aims

The City Futures Development Group is a collaborative arrangement between universities and Newcastle City Council, the North East Local Enterprise Partnership (LEP) and other policy organisations.

The purpose is to provide a one-stop shop for the universities, the council, the LEP and industry to discuss emerging and new areas of research that could be of benefit to the city, to identify ongoing research being undertaken at the universities and colleges that could be disseminated to a policy audience, and to hear of city intelligence needs to inform future research project bids.

Vision statement

To ensure the economic growth of Newcastle and the North East where all people in the city equally enjoy positive wellbeing and good health irrespective of age. Newcastle is a post-industrial city at the heart of the region with two million people. It has a long and illustrious history of scientific and technological innovation that it is using to address 21st century challenges: supporting the city's population, harnessing digital platforms and encouraging broad civic engagement and business development, leading to improvements in quality of life and new models of governance.

The group is committed to:

- improving services, quality of life and economic growth, utilising existing academic and industry excellence;
- creating opportunities for research and product development by facilitating access to infrastructure and residents;
- ensuring that Newcastle is seen as a test bed for innovation, providing further chances for research, investment and business growth;
- developing partnership and joint working between academia, industry and the public sector.

Working practices

- identifying potential projects that focus on ageing, digital, infrastructure and those not in employment, education or training (NEETs);
- developing new collaborative arrangements across experts and organisations;
- sharing intelligence, data and ideas in brainstorming conversations;
- disseminating work and initiating conversations;
- utilising visualisations to inform and educate citizens of developments and change.

Operationalising the civic university in Newcastle was achieved through four inter-related tasks by researchers:

- developing engagement and facilitation techniques for other sectors across the city;
- using systems thinking and long-term scenarios as methods to think critically about options for the future;

- aligning research work devoted to understanding change in the city with policy-makers' needs from government; and
- exploring, within the university, ways to join together science, medicine and technology with social sciences and the arts and humanities, and outside the university, between researchers and all other sectors.

Although a city vision as a single all-encompassing strategy was not the intention of the exercise, in many ways the initiative did have the effect of drawing together a diverse group of organisations to develop a critical mass of experts and intelligence to begin to address some of the big societal challenges associated with cities in the 21st century.

What makes a 'good' city vision?

Despite a growing number of real-world examples, there is still a paucity of evidence available as to the success or otherwise of city visioning. However, as Van Dijk and Weitkamp (2017) note, a powerful and successful vision is one that is supported by all the relevant actors and for which support begins when the stakeholders interact to construct the vision. A good vision therefore needs broad representation from stakeholders, active participation and clarity about the terms of engagement: in this sense, everybody should be able to contribute ideas, and everyone should benefit from the results. Shipley (2002) suggests that to be successful, visions need to be challenging – setting high, but realistic, goals will result in high performance, and a vision also needs to set specific goals with specific tasks allocated to stakeholders in order to overcome fragmented responsibility. Clear strategies for action are also required rather than the construction of utopias (Helling, 1998), and people should be part of the co-production process (or co-creation) early on before any solutions are provided (Shipley, 2004); in this sense, preconceived ideas and thoughts can often drown out creativity. However, while it is true that participation by diverse groups is a positive element, John et al (2015) point out that, structurally, such a process does not necessarily need to have a large number of participants to be successful. Their analysis of a range of city visions suggested that highly diversified teams supported by certain project partners but with relatively lower participation by citizens can often lead to better results in terms of good governance practices, planning and assessment because of the more agile and responsive structures in place. In addition, having a small dedicated and diverse group of people over a long timescale can often lead to clearer and more productive dialogue and exchange.

The leadership model for city visioning varies. As Landry (2012) notes, some cities develop city visions with strong and charismatic leadership (for example Vancouver); others with municipal leadership; others with business leadership; and others with a partnership model. Landry sees these as examples of civic creativity. The role of experts in city visioning is important, as Helling (1998) notes in her analysis of the Atlanta 2020 vision process – they can provide important missing information, but care must be taken to embrace all voices and build support among all stakeholders. Fundamentally, there must be a shared sense of urgency in the goal of the city vision and a compelling image of the future (Helling, 1998; Van Dijk and Weitkamp, 2017). This means having a story that is consistent and specified in a direct and specific timeline, and with a narrative that is embedded and shaped by the vision's target groups and integrates their multiple interests. Van Dijk and Weitkamp (2017: 354) summarise these elements as:

- setting high goals that are appealing and consistent;
- creating a roadmap with steps and assigned tasks to reach those goals and break them down into concrete, realistic projects;
- building on early participation;
- including the right amount of expert knowledge;
- maintaining a sense of urgency; and
- connecting multiple mutually benefiting interests.

In a pragmatic sense, guidance from the Cities Alliance (2017) suggests that city visions should contain the following unique elements of the city or city region:

- comparative and competitive advantages;
- the values and preferences of its residents;
- the relationship of the city to the global, domestic, and subnational economies (especially its hinterland and competitor cities);
- its history and culture; and
- its physical characteristics, for example its location, climate, terrain, water supply and scenic attributes.

This was based on the notion of a four-step process for city development strategies (CDSs): Where are we now? Where are we going? How are we getting there? And how do we benchmark and monitor? (Cities Alliance, 2017).

Quality criteria for assessing a good city vision are outlined by Wiek and Iwaniec (2014) and shown in Table 8.3. Their focus is very much

Table 8.3: Quality criteria for a good vision

Quality criterion	Key features
Normative	
Visionary	Desirable future state; with elements of 'aspirational' surprise, utopian thought, far-sightedness and holistic perspective
Sustainable	In compliance with sustainability principles, featuring radically transformed structures and processes
Construct	
Systemic	Holistic representation; linkages between vision elements; complex structure
Coherent	Composed of compatible goals (free of irreconcilable contradictions)
Plausible	Evidence-based, informed by empirical examples, theoretical models and pilot projects
Tangible	Composed of clearly articulated and detailed goals
Transformational	
Relevant	Composed of salient goals that focus on people, their roles and responsibilities
Nuanced	Detailed priorities (desirability)
Motivational	Inspire and motivate towards the envisioned change.
Shared	Display a critical degree of convergence, agreement and support by relevant stakeholders

Source: Wiek and Ivaniec (2014)

on sustainability-based visions, which today are increasingly relevant for city visioning activities. Certainly, the classification of criteria helps in terms of understanding how we need to think about city visioning in a holistic way. The key features of systemic thinking and shared visions are also key touch points for foresight-based thinking and transition management (see Chapter 6).

However, foresight-based thinking is also about thinking about the future in ways that recognise the complexity of cities, represented by their physical and non-physical structures and through their governance and overarching socioeconomic systems. This raises some other important practical considerations that we need to think about in planning any city visioning exercise. These include:

- *Framing the problem.* A key issue to address in a city vision project is how the problem is framed from the outset and what comprises the overall ambition(s) or goal(s) of the city vision (Ravetz and Miles, 2016). This raises the question of whose vision is represented and how such visions are developed. For example: Who is part of the initial scoping/framing? For whom does the visioning process contribute to capacity-building and empowerment? How is the vision disseminated to people and the wider community? (McPhearson et al, 2016). It is therefore important to recognise the starting point for such research early on before the visioning starts.

- *Co-production and leadership.* Finding the right balance within the quadruple helix model is important – is the vision being led by local government, or by business/academia or by the community/ civil society? For example, in the case of Reading 2050, the vision was primarily business/academia-led. Newcastle City Futures 2065 (NCF2065) was university-led but had to operate in the middle of the quadruple helix at arm's length to the university. During the course of the development of the vision, the project partners sought input from community groups to help develop the vision. Nonetheless, because the vision was academic and industry-led, the vision inherently reflected the interests of those leading the vision.
- *Understanding the past, present and future of a city.* This is vital if we are to set the city vision in context. How has the history of a city given it its unique characteristics? How has the city changed over time and what forces have shaped it? These are all important to understand and should be an underpinning foundation of the city vision. Building up a solid empirical evidence base of the city and its environmental and socioeconomic character is also vital to undertake and is directly linked with this. Furthermore, any new vision for a city must connect and acknowledge other relevant visions and strategies for the same city – see our definition of a city vision in Chapter 6. The concept of an 'urban room' as a physical place to bring these elements together is also an important element in this thinking (Dixon and Farrelly, 2019) (see Chapter 9).
- *City visioning as a continuing and dynamic process.* Once a city vision is developed, that is not the end of the process. Visioning is a dynamic process and monitoring, assessment and refinement are key elements of the process of continuing the visioning process (Tuiskunen et al, 2015).

An imperfect world? The opportunities and challenges for city visions

As we saw earlier in this book, the development of city visions presents potential opportunities for developing a planned transformation for a desirable and shared view of the future. This is at the heart of transition management (TM), and recognises the inherent complexity of cities. Good visions help us provide a framework for understanding how to plan and change our cities, and the development of new technologies and digital platforms provides further opportunities to develop participatory approaches to planning and envisioning the future.

Despite this, key challenges remain over the development of city visions. These revolve around: (a) the process of visioning; (b) the quality of outputs; and (c) the differences and distinctions between visions in the global north and those in the global south. First, in terms of the process of visioning, although urban foresight tools offer a useful way of developing a city vision, there are critical questions to resolve, including: Who is the vision for and who leads (and owns) the vision? The 'participatory domain' at the centre of the quadruple helix model (see Figure 8.5) is not necessarily one of equivalence, therefore. Although visions tend to reflect dominant power relations, in the case of the Reading 2050 vision, the partners sought to engage inclusively with a variety of groups to develop the vision (adopting a co-produced approach that tried to incorporate reflexivity in research and practice), and the support of Reading Borough Council has been crucial in this respect. Moreover, as we saw earlier in this chapter, looser assemblages of partners and a less-specific drive for a single vision can produce transformational capacity within a city (Newcastle City Futures, 2065).

The quadruple helix model also raises the issue of the role of universities in their local and regional contexts because of their substantial economic weight and influence (Goddard and Vallance, 2013; RSA, 2014). For example, as Goddard and Kempton (2016) highlight, there may be tensions between the expansion of a university's estate and student housing and the needs of the city in which the university is located, or indeed the desire not only to partner with larger successful multinationals rather than smaller local enterprises, but also to focus on international research rather than more local and regional-scale city research. Despite these tensions, the 'quadruple helix' concept is founded on a growing recognition that, as trusted anchor institutions, universities can play important civic, economic and 'place leadership' roles within the cities in which they are located (Goddard and Vallance, 2013; Hambleton, 2014; Goddard and Tewdwr-Jones, 2016). These roles can be potentially fulfilled through fostering networks across the public and private sectors, by identifying gaps in city intelligence and data gathering, and by becoming more actively involved in city visioning processes.

Second, previous research has shown that the quality of outputs from city visioning exercises is variable (see, for example, Helling,

1998). There is a danger that cities produce 'vision-wash' and that visions are anodyne and sterile in their thinking if they also promote business-as-usual outcomes. John et al (2015) suggest that visions do not always consider the city as being anchored within its hinterland and so synergistic thinking may not be created. In the case of Reading 2050, for example, the focus was on 'Greater Reading' because Reading was considered an 'under-bounded' urban area where its administrative boundary is smaller than its wider functional area and urban footprint (Dixon and Cohen, 2015). Yet the term 'Greater Reading' itself needed careful explanation because geographically it included other local authorities such as Wokingham Borough Council and parts of West Berkshire. It is also the case that some visions may too narrowly focus on limited aspects of the city (for example, the built environment and physical infrastructure); the best visions treat all the relevant dimensions of sustainability with equal respect.

Third, city visioning needs to recognise the very different contexts of cities in the global north and those in the global south (see Chapter 7). Critics have observed that a globalised urban built environment network (founded on a hegemonic neoliberal agenda) has often sought to apply eco-city, sustainable and/or smart city visions in cities across the world, without acknowledgement of the very different circumstances in the developing world and creating 'visions of divisions' (Marom, 2019) (see Chapter 4 on the related 'global discourse network'). This planning monoculture (Watson, 2016) has often been driven by the imperative to reimagine cities as world-class cities, or 'worldling cities' (Roy and Ong, 2011) where 'urban fantasies' may create not only enchantment for people living in the city but also a sense that they can never attain the levels of living that the city vision is conjuring up (Watson, 2013; Smith, 2017; Cote-Roy and Moser, 2019). This approach, which is often part of the application of strategic spatial planning (and master planning) in both new and existing cities in the global south, may also ignore the rights of informal settlement dwellers (and other informal homes) unless community engagement and participation are undertaken carefully (Robinson, 2008). Gender balance and socioeconomic diversity are therefore vital issues in ensuring inclusive participation in a city vision.

Summary

In this chapter we have seen how city visions have evolved and can be developed using city foresight methods. Good-quality city visions that are truly participatory require clear ambitions and goals, co-production (or co-creation) and good leadership. Understanding the past, present and future of a city is very important, and it should be stressed that city visioning is a dynamic process. The quadruple helix model is useful for helping us understand the balance of power relations in constructing a city vision and the role of universities in the process of city visioning is also important to highlight. As we saw in the cases of Reading and Newcastle, different but still beneficial outcomes can be produced by contrasting and distinctive visioning processes that are underpinned by city foresight. As always, however, we need to consider the important differences in context and culture between cities in different parts of the globe. In the next chapter we will look at how different projects and experiments have been developed in cities to link with the development of city visions.

9

The innovative and experimental city

He that will not apply new remedies must expect new evils; for time is the greatest innovator.
Francis Bacon, 1625

The difficulty lies, not in the new ideas, but in escaping from the old ones, which ramify, for those brought up as most of us have been, into every corner of our minds.
John Maynard Keynes, 1936

Introduction

Cities play a vital role in the process and ultimate outcomes of innovation. By their very nature they can acts as hubs of creativity and new ideas, brought about by the concentration of people, businesses and sources of capital to fund innovation. The agglomeration of these crucial elements of urban innovation can create opportunities for key stakeholders in the city, not only for working together collaboratively to develop a participatory-based vision for the city, but also for co-producing projects and experiments that potentially create jobs and economic growth for the city.

Innovation and experimentation are at the heart of how a managed transition to a sustainable future can be influenced and shaped by a series of planned and strategic projects, which can, for example, also underpin a vision of the city as smart and sustainable (Dixon et al, 2018a). The role of a university in the city and its engagement in a civic role has been highlighted as fundamentally important not only in economic growth theory and innovation theory, but also in city visioning literature.

In this chapter, we will examine the importance of cities as centres for urban innovation and urban experiments, before looking at some of the most important spaces that have developed in cities for those activities, including innovation districts, living labs, urban rooms and science shops. We then look at the concept of 'place-based leadership' and the role of the university in visioning, experimentation and innovation, before examining a detailed case study of urban innovation and civic engagement at Newcastle University.

Cities, urban innovation and urban experiments

Throughout history, cities have been at the heart of new and transformative ideas and innovations, in both the technological and social spheres. During the renaissance, city states such as Delft, Florence and Venice were very successful, acting as hubs of innovative thinking, which led to these cities outcompeting even nation states in terms of economic growth (Kattel et al, 2011). In the 16th and 17th centuries, writers such as Giovanni Botero and Antonio Serra were the first to highlight how the diversity of a city's industries, trades and crafts provided the basis for the growth of wealth and power (Johnson, 2014). Since then, many books and papers have been written about the connections and relationships between innovation and city growth (see, for example, Athey et al, 2007; Shearmur, 2012). At the heart of this is the concept that cities, through their power of agglomeration, provide crucially important environments to nurture interactions and relationships, often between creative and innovative industries, which also take advantage of the economies of location to help develop new tools, products, innovations, policies, processes and services (Concilio et al, 2019). Moreover, there has been a growing emphasis on seeing cities not just as the vehicles for innovation but as active generators for new ideas, creative thinking and new forms of enterprise and organisational form (Florida, 2002; European Commission, 2016). In a nutshell, cities provide an ideal environment for innovation and creativity because of what they offer in terms of proximity, density and variety (Athey et al, 2007).

More recently, the growing importance of cities as focal points for tackling climate change and resource depletion and acting as hubs of innovation to transition to a sustainable future has become a dominant theme in policy, practice and academic discourses (McPhearson et al, 2016). The idea of a city as, for example, a 'marketplace' for funding innovation, a 'problems lab' for testing solutions to urban challenges or an 'idearium' for bringing together skilled workers to generate solutions to urban problems, have become common features in these discourses (Concilio et al, 2019). Certainly, the concept of 'innovation' has been fundamentally important in theories of economic growth and economic geography – the theory of innovation and growth that was core to Schumpeter's waves of economic growth had its roots in Marxian analysis (Florida et al, 2016).

What do we mean by innovation though? The answer to this question depends very much on the viewpoint or sectoral focus that is taken, and so definitions are many and varied. In its broadest sense, however, innovation is a process that leads to some sort of novel outcome, where the novelty relates to the fact that it is doing something different from what happened previously (Godin, 2008; Shearmur, 2012). For Crowley (2011: 9), innovation is 'the successful exploitation of new ideas', which takes the concept beyond a focus on simply invention to place an emphasis on successful exploitation or commercial value. Moreover, whereas innovation was once viewed as a relatively simple, linear process beginning with research and invention and ending in commercial exploitation, today the process is considered to be more complex and non-linear, involving different collections of assets and interactions between many stakeholders such as business, universities, research bodies, funders, business support bodies and infrastructure bodies, which generate ideas and knowledge within and between the various groups (Crowley, 2011; BIS, 2015).

Innovation is important in policy and practice for a number of reasons, and this is true of the UK and internationally. First, it is seen as being crucial to long-term economic growth as it can create new products, new markets and new jobs and lead to improved productivity. Second, there has been a large body of research that has shown that innovation can enhance urban resilience, or the ability of cities to withstand socioeconomic and other types of external shocks. The juxtaposition of innovative milieu (or the innovative environment in a regional context), close collaboration between the four groups in the quadruple helix model (see Chapter 8) and the concept of 'open innovation platforms and networks to share ideas', are all important elements in this because they encourage knowledge transfer and bring ideas, innovations and markets closer together. Successful innovations have been found to be influenced not just by the creation of new products and processes but also by their effective diffusion and the capacity of firms to absorb and adopt them. Third, in cities the drive towards innovation (or urban innovation) helps cities improve their economic performance, creates new markets and helps drive up the productivity and competitiveness of firms, which can support income and employment growth (Athey et al, 2007). In the UK, however, research has shown that rates of innovation are uneven, with places such as London and the South East outperforming other areas. This is compounded by disparities in research & development (R&D) spending rates. As an example of this, just three subregions of the UK – Oxford and its environs, Cambridge and its subregion and inner

West London – account for 31 per cent of all R&D spending in the UK (Jones, 2019c).

More specifically, then, urban innovation is broadly innovation that occurs within cities and urban areas. In this sense, it can refer not only to new technologies and novel processes, but also to new and novel governance systems and social innovation (see, for example, Dixon et al, 2015; Nguyen and Moehrle, 2019). As the United Nations (UN) (UN, 2013b: 12) suggests:

> Innovation in the urban context refers to any new method, business model, policy, institutional design or regulation that meets the needs of urban populations in a more efficient, effective and sustainable way. It may refer to improved rules or legislation as well as improved institutions, models of stakeholder participation or new means of delivering services.

In this sense, cities are the vehicles for innovation by promoting connections, face-to-face contact, the agglomeration of consumption and transport connectivity, all of which produce crucial benefits for businesses partnering and collaborating with others seeking to innovate.

Drawing on a variety of innovation theory from urban studies, economic geography and innovation systems approaches, Athey et al (2007) highlight the interaction of urban hubs and local links as being crucial to the success of urban innovation in cities. Urban hubs, which emphasise urban assets, market size and business networks, are based on urban economies that offer scale and choice for firms seeking to innovate. Cities provide access to skilled workers and venture capital, and finance markets and knowledge spillovers, as Jane Jacobs (2019) noted, are promoted in cities. By the same token, while some cities act as hubs, others have the advantage of strong local links. This concept is drawn from 'localisation economies' literature (Storper, 1997), which suggests that specialist connections and networks enhance faster innovation and the development of specialist clusters or concentrations of small, networked companies (Porter, 1998). Together, as is shown in Figure 9.1, these comprise what is termed an 'urban innovation system' by Athey et al (2007). For example, Reading and the Thames Valley information and communications technology (ICT) industry, often referred to as the UK's 'Silicon Valley' (with more than 8,000 technology-led companies), is an important example of a successful urban hub, which includes a mix of excellent transport connectivity, land availability and the presence of a large skilled labour force.

Figure 9.1: Urban innovation system

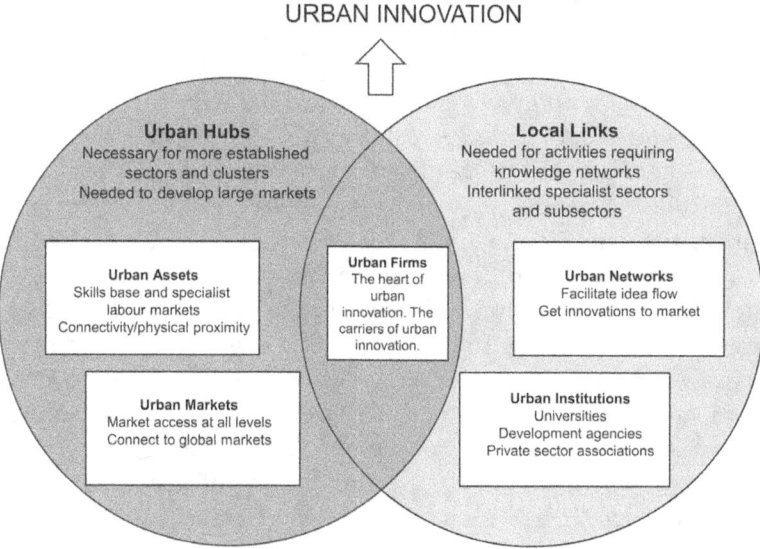

Source: Athey et al (2007)

Although this model is a helpful way to conceptualise an urban innovation system, it does not place an emphasis on civil society engagement, in contrast to the quadruple helix model that we discussed in previous chapters. It is, perhaps, more closely related to a triple helix worldview (that is, government, business/non-governmental organisations – NGOs – and academia) whereas we know that people are vital to the success of innovations as users and adopters of new technologies and practices. This has certainly been a growing emphasis on smart and sustainable city agendas in recent years, given that urban innovation is a crucial element in such cities (Dixon et al, 2015). This idea of urban innovation projects and experiments has also given rise to a new conceptualisation of the 'experimental city' (Evans et al, 2016).

Previous research has identified key factors that might influence a city's ability to innovate. These include: entrepreneurial culture; institutional capacity; cultural value; environmental awareness; and social activism and integration (Concilio et al, 2019). The concept of 'experimentation' is closely related to the way in which stakeholders in a particular city might decide to develop innovative projects and experiments to underpin the transition to a smart and sustainable future. Urban experimentation can take a variety of forms, from the development of specific projects attempting to tackle climate change (perhaps by installing environmental monitors city-wide), through to the development of 'urban living labs' (described later in this chapter). In this sense, urban experimentation offers a framework within which to arrange instruments, materials and people to induce change in a controlled way and to evaluate and learn from those changes so that successful innovation projects can be rolled out elsewhere (Karvonen and van Heur, 2014; Evans et al, 2016).

The literature on urban experiments is also closely related to sociotechnical transitions, which we discussed earlier in this book, particularly in relation to sustainability transitions (see Chapters 6 and 7) (Sengers et al, 2016). For example, experiments at the city scale provide the seeds for change that can lead to societal shifts in energy, water and waste use or mobility use. The focus on strategic niche management in the multi-level perspective (MLP) therefore focuses on practical experiments as a way of developing a transition pathway to a sustainable future, in contrast to the transition management approach, which highlights the importance of visioning before city-level experiments are developed. Sengers et al (2016: 21), for example, define an experiment in the context of a sustainability transition as '[a]n inclusive, practice-based and challenge-led initiative designed to promote system innovation through social learning under conditions of uncertainty and ambiguity'. It is not surprising, therefore, that many cities have developed city visions that incorporate direct acknowledgement of urban innovation and experimentation. Table 9.1 gives some examples of the vision statements associated with UK cities.

Although the notion of urban experimentation at a variety of scales has been criticised as an 'empty signifier' by some (see, for example, Caprotti and Cowley, 2017), cities have increasingly been influenced by funding and by policy initiatives focusing on innovation projects and experiments. This is not surprising when evidence suggests that successful cities are those places that have developed innovation ecosystems to create new products and services (Crowley, 2011; Walt et al, 2014). This 'success', measured by key indicators relating to jobs growth and wealth creation, tends to coalesce around 'institutional thickness', which helps to bring together a powerful mix of local, social and cultural conditions conducive to economic growth (Amin and Thrift, 1995). During a decade of lost growth and austerity in the UK during the 2010s, cities have increasingly focused on city visions that seek to highlight their innovative potential, and which can help to provide a framework for seeking R&D and innovation funding opportunities in an increasingly competitive landscape.

Table 9.1: Examples of UK city vision statements: urban innovation and experimentation

City	Vision	Example statement	Reference
Belfast	2035	Belfast will be a city re-imagined ... It will be a producer of and magnet for talent, investment, innovation and creativity – a compassionate place where people create value and are valued.	Belfast City Council (2017)
Edinburgh	2050	In 2050, Edinburgh will be a place of opportunity and ambition, where innovators and entrepreneurs can achieve prosperity and success.	Edinburgh City Council (2017)
Bristol	2050	Increase the sustainability and scalability of innovations by supporting them with a new model of city partnership, with the City Office taking on a role as a key enabling hub to support and coordinate city resources and assets through shared agendas and common city goals.	Bristol One City/ Bristol City Council (2020)
Reading	2050	Reading in 2050: an internationally recognised and economically successful city region where low carbon living is the norm and the built environment, technology and innovation have combined to create a dynamic, smart and sustainable city with a high quality of life and equal opportunities for all.	Reading 2050 (2020)

Innovation, experimental and engagement 'spaces'

The emphasis on urban innovation and experimentation has focused attention on what might be termed the spatial representation of projects and experiments and new ways of thinking about a place, which also implies a level of engagement with the public and other stakeholders in a city. This has led to the development of physical (and sometimes virtual) spaces, represented by the emergence of 'innovation districts', 'living labs', 'urban rooms' and 'science shops'.

Innovation districts (IDs), for example, have emerged as spatial representations of clusters of firms at a district level within a city. These have grown in number since the 1990s and, although varying in nature globally, can be defined as 'geographic areas where leading-edge anchor institutions and companies cluster and connect with start-ups, business incubators, and accelerators. They are physically compact, transit-accessible and technically-wired, and offer mixed-use housing, office and retail' (Katz and Wagner, 2014: 1).

Globally, we have seen districts emerging in, for example, Barcelona, Berlin, Boston, London, Medellin, Montreal, San Francisco, Seattle, Seoul, Stockholm and Toronto, sometimes characterised by their location in 'anchor plus' sites (central areas of cities), in reimagined urban areas (for example, brownfield sites) or in an urbanised science park, for example in suburban areas or outside the main urban area. In each of these contexts, companies in innovation sectors see the benefits of co-location and agglomeration where the proximity and density of firms, skilled workers and research and knowledge institutions make it easier to collaborate and innovate (Clark et al, 2016). Innovation districts are characterised by their scale and can act as hosts to a wider ecosystem of innovation across the city-region or even nationally and internationally. They have been a particularly important phenomenon in the United States, where they drew on the success of the 22@ Barcelona Innovation District (ID) project, which was developed in 2000 (Drucker et al, 2019).

The Barcelona ID was developed on a former industrial area within the Poblenou neighbourhood, which had formed the focus for the 1992 Olympics. In 2000, the city created a private legal entity, 22@BCN, with specific management, financing and investment powers, which led to the regeneration of 115 city blocks into a hub for innovative economic activity in five industrial sectors: media, ICT, medical technology, energy and design. Ten universities and nine research and design centres are located in the ID, and the area has attracted many start-ups and created high economic growth for the city (Drucker et al, 2019).

Urban living labs (ULLs) can be seen as another spatial representation of urban innovation and experimentation. They represent a form of experimental governance where stakeholders develop and test new technologies and new ways of living to tackle climate change and urban sustainability problems and challenges (Marvin et al, 2018). They enable cities to highlight their credentials in moving to a sustainable transition and can act as supporting statements of high-level intent in order to secure funding. The origins of the term 'urban living lab' can be found in the writing of William J. Mitchell of MIT MediLab in the late 1990s, who suggested that a living lab (with its basis in buildings, institutions or cities) would be an interesting concept to study people and their interaction with new technologies in a living (*in vivo*) environment. Indeed, what lies behind the term is the concept of 'open space for experimental learning', or user-driven open laboratories, where knowledge spills over by collision among all the individuals involved (Bertolin, 2014). Although there is no single agreed definition as to what a ULL means, the concept has been considered to be an arena (within a geographically or institutionally bounded space) and as an approach for intentional collaborative experimentation involving researchers, people, companies and governments (Marvin et al, 2018). To give an example of one definition (ENoLL, 2016): 'Living labs are user-centred, open innovation eco-systems based on a systematic user co-creation approach integrating research and innovation process in real life and communities.'

Since the early 2000s, the ULL concept has received endorsement from the European Commission and has been embedded within the organisational structure of various businesses. In 2006, for example, the European Network of Living Labs (ENoLL) was founded to bring together living labs across 26 European countries and eight other countries globally. Broadly, these covered the following themes in 400 active labs: assisted living; e-health and sports; energy; buildings; and transport. Universities such as Harvard, Yale and Cambridge have used the concept in making campuses the test beds for sustainability innovation. There are a variety of ULLs internationally, stretching from strategic funding models, such as Mistra Urban Futures and Fraunhofer Institutes, to civic embedded agencies such as those in Newcastle in the UK (explained in detail later in this chapter) and Boston in the United States (Keith and Headlam, 2017). For example, the Mayor's Office of New Urban Mechanics (MONUM) in Boston was set up in 2010 to encourage wider civic engagement in the city through the use of innovation and experimentation because the mayor (Thomas Menino) felt the city was too bureaucratic and lacked a human face (Jordan, 2019). MONUM has tackled innovation projects involving housing, education and the future of Boston. Before a project is chosen, it is researched and evaluated through Boston's social network incubator, based in a cross-departmental group of 15–20 city employees. Led by a public agency, MONUM represents a good example of public sector innovation bringing together business and civil society (Bevilacqua et al, 2020).

Turning to 'urban rooms', the UK's Farrell Review of Architecture and the Built Environment, influenced by the thinking of Patrick Geddes (Tewdwr-Jones et al, 2020), highlighted that there needs to be a physical space in a city where everyone can reflect on how a place – a town or city – has evolved, what sort of a place it is now and how it could, and should, develop in the future (Farrell, 2014). This concept of an urban room is an important building block in making a city vision 'real' for the people who live there. An urban room can act as an exhibition space, a community space and a learning space, and also provide an exciting way of engaging with people and giving them opportunities to help redesign and reimagine a city's future. When the Farrell Review was completed, the final report highlighted the importance of urban rooms, where the public could directly engage within a physical space dedicated to understanding the origins of the city in which they were located. This is not a new concept, and there are, as Farrell acknowledged, plenty of international examples of urban rooms, urban planning museums or city galleries. Many of these spaces not only incorporate very large physical models of the city (for example, Beijing, Hanoi, Hong Kong, Shanghai and Singapore), but also have space dedicated to understanding the urban planning narratives and future paths of these cities. The use of a physical model is a useful tool to help the public visualise key public spaces and the impact new design proposals will have on the existing cityscape. For example, Singapore's city mega-model is located in the Singapore city gallery and first opened in 1999 to tell the story of the nation's planning efforts (Dixon and Farrelly, 2019). In the UK, a network of urban rooms now exists across the country, facilitated by Place Alliance. This brings together places as diverse as Bristol, Hereford, London, Newcastle and Weymouth, with each urban room creating:

> a physical space where people can go to understand, debate and get involved in the past, present and future of where they live, work and play. The purpose of these Urban Rooms is to foster meaningful connections between people and place, using creative methods of engagement to encourage active participation in the future of our buildings, streets and neighbourhoods. (Place Alliance, 2020)

Finally, in terms of university engagement with innovation and experimentation, 'science shops', which originated in the 1970s in the Netherlands, have become an important focus for linking citizen science and community engagement with higher education and the wider education sector. Gresle et al (2019: 60) define science shops as 'knowledge intermediary structures that jointly with civil society organisations co-create research questions, deploy participatory projects ... include students in the work and support the translation of research results'. Science shops essentially are a response to civil society's need for expertise and knowledge and are often based on university campuses: for example, 'Living Knowledge' forms a network of science shops, and the EU-funded SciShops project is a good example of how they operate in practice.

The four different approaches to urban innovation and experimentation outlined earlier have, at least, partly been driven by the fact that UK, EU and other funding has frequently been targeted towards city-level projects and experiments since the 2000s. Moreover, urban innovation was an important *raison d'être* driving both the UK and Canadian Future Cities programmes (Walt et al, 2014; Tomalty, 2017), and the Technology in Cities programme in the United States under former President Obama (Executive Office of the President, 2016). In the UK, for example, the *Urban Living Partnership (ULP)* project (UKRI, 2018) was a cross-research council initiative focused on diagnosing current problems in five different cities: Birmingham, Bristol, Leeds, Newcastle-Gateshead and York (we will discuss the Newcastle-Gateshead model later in this chapter). This programme (which ran from 2016 to 2018) brought together business, universities, civil society and government (local and national) to take 'a collaborative, integrated, "whole city" approach to problem-solving and vision-creation ... The ULP ... encouraged the partners involved ... to experiment with cross-sectoral, transdisciplinary approaches and embrace co-production' (UKRI, 2018: 4–5).

In the European Union (EU), at the end of 2017, and largely as part of its Horizon 2020 programme (which includes Lighthouse city projects), the European Commission had granted 1.7 billion euros to 612 projects on urban sustainable development, with smart cities an important part of this. This represents an increasing emphasis on smart, sustainable and inclusive growth by the EU (Engelbert et al, 2019). EU Lighthouse projects, which support the underpinning of projects and experiments in smart cities, are also an important funding stream, with cities such as Amsterdam (City-Zen project) benefiting from such schemes.

Place-based leadership and the role of the civic university

The important role of universities in such initiatives as innovation districts, living labs, urban rooms and science shops, is clearly conceptualised in the quadruple helix model we discussed earlier in this book. Universities can therefore play important civic, economic and 'place leadership' roles within the cities in which they are located (Goddard and Vallance, 2013; Hambleton, 2014). These roles can be fulfilled through fostering networks across the public and private sectors, by identifying gaps in city intelligence and data gathering, and by becoming more actively involved in city visioning processes (Goddard and Tewdwr-Jones, 2016).

To begin with, universities can be seen as leading examples of trusted anchor institutions, rooted in particular places, which can generate positive externalities and relationships and support and anchor wider economic activity within their area. Although such institutions do not have a democratic mandate, their scale, embeddedness and links with local and regional communities can play a key role in promoting local and regional development and economic growth (Goddard and Vallance, 2013). The University of Reading, for example, generates at least £800 million in gross value added and 11,550 full-time equivalent jobs for the UK economy, of which about 55 per cent is based within the Thames Valley Berkshire Local Enterprise Partnership area. Beyond this, the university supplies highly skilled graduates (with more than 20 per cent staying locally following graduation and contributing to economic growth in London and the South East) and driving business productivity through knowledge exchange and innovation, particularly for companies located on campus and in the University Science Park (Hatch Regeneris, 2019).

In the UK, universities have often taken a global perspective and, historically, there has been little focus on the role of place-based policy-making (with the recent exception of the industrial strategy and city deals) (UPP, 2019). There have therefore been increasing calls for universities to go beyond simply civic engagement and return to the notion of a civic university. This requires a clear strategy and posing three key questions (UPP, 2019: 28):

- Can people talk about our university with pride and awareness?
- Is civic activity aligned with public need?
- Are the views of local people reflected in either the formal governance or the informal and communications structures and strategies of the university?

The civic university certainly has a role to play in what are termed 'place-based university partnerships', particularly in relation to urban sustainability challenges (Withycombe Keeler et al, 2019). These partnerships, often with a focus on innovation and experimentation, are closely related to the quadruple helix model, and connect to the theoretical frameworks of transitions theory (MLP and TM). There are a number of examples globally, for example, of universities partnering with city governments to help develop and incubate R&D that addresses important challenges of climate change and urban sustainability. In a 2014 global survey of 70 such initiatives, it was found that the built environment, energy, heating and cooling, and governance and planning were the three most commonly researched themes in such partnerships, and that partnerships may be local, national or internationally based (Trencher et al, 2014). In a detailed study of two of these partnerships, based in Arizona State University and Portland State University in the United States, research identified six ways in which universities could partner with city governments to contribute to urban transformation (Withycombe Keeler et al, 2019):

- providing labour, through internships or courses for students based in the city government;
- providing expert feedback through modelling or evaluation of city plans;
- providing input into the development of specific action plans or strategies and visions;
- conducting collaborative solution-oriented research on specific problems (for example, mitigation, energy systems);
- facilitating cross-cutting collaboration across city departments; and
- facilitating capacity-building processes, ranging from in-house training to community engagement.

Through these different modes of engagement, the research found that confidence, competence and commitment for both the university and city government could be increased through co-design and co-production processes, and so help increase transformative capacity within the city in order to tackle continuing urban sustainability challenges.

The increasing role of universities within their local and regional contexts has implications for governance and place-based leadership (PBL). Leadership has been found to be an important but often overlooked factor in explaining why some cities are more successful economically and socially than other cities (Hambleton, 2014; Vallance et al, 2019). Leadership of a place, in this sense, is connected not only to individuals in a city who might be inspiring or possess special qualities of some kind, but also to the ability to mobilise and bring together different actors with either a statutory role (for example, local governments) and those with a civic interest (for example, businesses, NGOs, community groups and universities) in the overall development of the city or city-region.

In terms of governance, PBL is seen as being shared between three main groups (Hambleton and Howard, 2013): locally elected politicians; public sector managers (often based in local government); and civically minded individuals from wider society in the city. PBL can involve different kinds of power, which are based on position (institutional power), control over funding (resource power), the ability to create and develop visions for change with others (interpretive power) or personal social capital (network power) (Sotarauta, 2016). PBL therefore requires interaction across different boundaries and domains. This is particularly important given the co-produced nature of PBL, which has been associated with enabling collaboration and cooperation to promote innovation and knowledge exchange at the city level. This often increasingly involves informal partnerships and arrangements in horizontal interorganisational coalitions (Vallance et al, 2019). This implies a decentralised form of governance, with local governments partnering with private and public actors. The more inclusive nature of leadership within cities is also being driven by the need for local governments to deliver public services and fulfil policy objectives with reduced funding in an era of austerity. In the UK, this is enabling local community representatives to adopt leadership roles that were dominated previously by the state sector, although much is dependent on the time and resources available for such leaders to fulfil their role.

In terms of the development of city visions, therefore, city governments and civil society may lack the resources to fulfil a leadership role. This raises the question of who should lead the visioning process and what are the implications for PBL? The Reading 2050 vision research was led by the University of Reading (School of the Built Environment) in partnership with Barton Willmore (industry) and Reading UK CIC (the economic development company for Reading). During the course of the development of the vision, the project partners sought input from community groups, councillors and the general public to help develop the vision. Nonetheless, although co-produced, the vision was characterised as academic and business-led. The visioning research, however, brought together a diverse set of individuals from university/academia (other schools and institutes in the University of Reading), business/industry, government (primarily local) and civil society groups (NGOs) to input into the visioning process.

The main leadership role in the university was fulfilled by the School of the Built Environment and this reflects the anchor role of universities discussed in previous literature. It should be noted, however, that such literature highlights tensions between this role and the power relations created by vision leadership for the universities themselves. In the case of Reading, there was an altruistic desire to help develop the vision, and a longer-term ambition that in working with the other project partners, the development of the vision could lead to further grant applications and funding for research in the field of smart and sustainable cities (Dixon et al, 2018a). As far as industry was concerned, the main aspirations for involvement by Barton Willmore were to build on its existing capacity and knowledge base in Reading (emphasising its understanding of urban design, place-making and future-proofing) and to be seen as influential in helping to create the vision through a partnership approach. Reading UK's main aspirations in the project revolved around developing a vision that would help it promote and strengthen inward investment and economic growth for Reading. Particularly during the latter stages of the visioning process, the link with Reading Borough Council became the basis for further detailed discussions with the council planning department, and in securing high-level support from Reading Borough Council's political leadership, and support from the councillors in Reading Borough Council. This ensured that the vision became strongly linked with the development of the new Local Plan (which looks ahead to 2036) and is directly referenced within it as an important longer-term framework for Reading (Reading Borough Council, 2019a, 2019b).

The role of universities in PBL is, therefore, dynamic and complex. In the next section, we will look in more detail at the role of Newcastle University in its local and regional context.

Case study: Newcastle City Futures Urban Living Partnership

As we discussed in previous chapters, Newcastle University initiated a city foresight project for the UK Government Office for Science (2013–15). That culminated in the publication of a foresight report for the city (Tewdwr-Jones et al, 2015) and a desire on the part of the city council and other agencies to continue the spirit of the work through ongoing research, engagement and innovation. This experience proved vital in forging the early *incubator* work across the city, so that by 2016, the existing Newcastle City Futures (NCF) model could adapt and develop cohesively when it became one of the five UKRI/Innovate UK Urban Living Partnership (ULP) pilots, covering Newcastle and Gateshead (UKRI, 2018).

Broadly, the ULP approach was to fund the development of an 'experiment' for each city to be an *accelerator*, and not only to forge understanding and partnerships across the quadruple helix, between universities, local government, businesses and society, based on the needs and opportunities of each place, but also to foster co-production, and create spaces for innovation for long-term change. The geographical boundaries for a ULP were the local government boundaries for the urban area in question, and this requirement was stipulated in advance by UKRI. There was also a pre-existing requirement for multiple higher education institutions within the same urban area to work in partnership on both the bid and the project.

These pre-existing parameters did not make it easy for universities from the outset, since all required a significant amount of partnering work in advance of bid preparation. For example, the administrative boundaries of local government are often different from those of local enterprise partnerships, business improvement districts, health trusts and even water catchment areas. Requiring multiple universities from the same urban area to work together on a single project is not necessarily an easy task, when there is some rivalry, disciplinary duplication, pre-existing working arrangements and personalities all at play.

NCF was the most diverse disciplinary-wise of the five ULPs. Twenty partners were part of the original bid, spread across the quadruple helix. Over the lifetime of the ULP, that partner number grew to 196 organisations, representing government bodies, small and medium-sized enterprises, multinationals, charities and the public sector. That increase came about unilaterally from interested organisations wanting to find out more or get involved with the ULP's work. Some 60 per cent of the 196 organisations were businesses. Their stipulated reasons for involvement related to the attractiveness and potential of shaping innovation and entrepreneurialism, but some saw NCF as a unique front door of the university in an otherwise confusing array of faculties, departments, centres, buildings and so on, whose disciplinary names often in isolation bear little direct relationship to urban living issues.

Set up to become the broker between two universities, between Newcastle University and external agencies in the city region, and within Newcastle University across three faculties and 12 schools, the idea was for all sectors and disciplinary-based researchers to work together in consortia, centred around engagement for innovation projects in the city, and that these projects would develop into both capital and virtual place-based innovations.

Over the course of the three years to July 2019, a great deal was achieved, perhaps against initial low expectations (see Box 9.1).

Box 9.1: Achievements of Newcastle City Futures Urban Living Partnership, 2016–19

- £33 million levered in for the city and region, plus £120 million bids in preparation, plus a contribution of to £65 million of university initiatives.
- 78 cross-sector multi-partnered demonstrator project ideas facilitated; 30 delivered in the ULP lifetime.
- 155,000 members of the public as participants engaged in NCF/university activities.
- More than 196 organisations engaged (more than 60% are businesses).
- More than 200 one-to-one meetings with all sectors: public, private, community and higher education institutions.
- Eight 'mash-up' events organised for more than 160 organisations, bringing public, private, community and academic sectors to work together.
- Two local authority governance processes amended and permanent policy liaison established.
- Four reports commissioned on the smart city (for Newcastle City Council), strategic futures, higher education institution place innovation, and urban rooms.
- Four projects for the Great Exhibition of the North 2018 co-funded.
- Tyneside crowdfunding platform established in partnership with Newcastle and Gateshead councils.

More than 75 interdisciplinary and cross-sectoral project ideas were developed with government, business, community and university partners after 2016. Among the most successful NCF projects to date have been the following:

- *Future Homes*: digitally enabled sustainable housing for the lifecourse, with £7 million of funding levered in, and a community interest company formed with direct links to university expertise, businesses and community groups. Planning permission for 66 new housing units on a city-centre site was approved in spring 2020.
- *Metro Futures*: a digital engagement tool deployed for Nexus, asking North East residents about their design preferences for new metro trains, led by Open Lab, with 24,000 people engaged. Findings have been incorporated into the successful bid to HM Treasury/the Department for Transport (£337 million) for a new fleet of trains.

- *Northumberland Street Area*: the design and roll-out of a transformative programme for Newcastle city centre, in partnership with Newcastle City Council and NE1 (the business improvement district company for Newcastle), including engagement exercises and design charrettes, leading to the announcement of the £20 million Northumberland Street Area (NSA) project in spring 2018.
- *Gateshead Future Place*: a design and regeneration programme for the transformation of Gateshead town centre in partnership with Gateshead Council, leading to the announcement of the £90 million project in autumn 2019.
- *Big Draw at Seven Stories*: an engagement exercise developed over one weekend to encourage children to design and shape the future city using a range of digital and creative methods, with 500 participants.
- *Idea of North at the Baltic*: curating the Tyne Deck and unbuilt Newcastle exhibition with images and text supplied by NCF. A series of lectures and film screenings, during the Great Exhibition of the North, attracted 120,000 visitors over three months, including a visit by members of the UK Cabinet during their meeting in Gateshead.

Despite this success, the ULP initiative was not a straightforward process, not only because of the heady mix of organisations and researchers active in the process, and the fact that the model took a place-based rather than siloed disciplinary or institutional perspective, but also because the key parent organisations – the university and the city council – were largely ambivalent (perhaps even uncomfortable) with NCF ULP operating in 'their space'.

During its operation, NCF was seen as groundbreaking, innovative, entrepreneurial, participatory and cooperative, and was welcomed by key stakeholders. However, NCF was seen equally as disruptive, challenging, unorthodox, undemocratic, neoliberal and unwelcome by other groups. Although the majority of the agencies involved with NCF were relatively straightforward to work with, two organisations proved more challenging in their ambitions: namely the university itself and the city council.

The challenge with the ULP was always about how to operationalise the civic university not only in resource, personnel and legitimacy terms, but also in terms of the primary entity – NCF – which was outside the formal organisational structures of the university. NCF became, in many ways, an example of the civic university in operation, but it was not an example of institutional commitment; if anything, it was an example of attempting to achieve interdisciplinarity and stakeholder partnership with minimal university backing.

For the city council, NCF became a player that was, at times, seen by officials to be taking the initiative and leading the council agenda rather than reacting to it. At a time when the council was battling with the impact of austerity cuts (more than £300 million in cuts between 2010 and 2020), some officials resented NCF for embarking on an innovation agenda when it was difficult enough for the council to fund and run basic public services.

NCF was never pigeonholed into any one category and, over its longer timeframe (2013–19), it took on the role of being a facilitator for engagement, for innovation, for research, for outreach and impact, and for policy development. That it was an example of an initiative closely aligned to PBL attributes in practice there can be little doubt. It benefited from being housed in a university that had (in the formative years) committed to civic university principles and that, in turn, had created the space and agility for such a model to exist and mature over time. But NCF was, equally, vulnerable as a city intermediary that, although popular with businesses and community groups, could not endure in a somewhat fixed institutional landscape dominated by the city leadership of local government and the university, which saw it as a rival.

Summary

In this chapter we have seen how important a role that cities play in the innovation process and its outcomes. The concept of 'urban innovation' is at the heart of this, and understanding how the four main stakeholder groups in the quadruple helix model can work together to achieve positive and beneficial outcomes for the city as a whole, through a participatory approach, is crucial. Innovative cities tend to be successful cities, and the emergence of place-based initiatives, such as innovation districts, living labs, urban rooms and science shops, have increasingly focused attention on the overall role of urban innovation and experimentation and how this is best supported to create green jobs, clean economic growth and wider environmental benefits.

These developments have repercussions not only for higher education institutions seeking to highlight their credentials as civic universities, but also for the way in which place-based governance develops now and into the future. In particular, we saw how tensions between stakeholder groups can actually create a dynamic creativity and capacity for innovation and experimentation at the city level, as was the case with the NCF project. In the next chapter we will look in more detail at the implications of a continuing focus towards city foresight and city visioning for the planning and governance of our cities.

10

Visioning and planning the city in an urban age: a reality check

> For I dipped into the future, far as human eye could see,
> Saw the Vision of the world, and all the wonder that would be.
> Alfred Lord Tennyson, 1809–92, *Locksley Hall*

Introduction

In this chapter, we delve further into the idea of visioning and planning in cities. The urban has always been seen as a complex system of systems, a thriving and living organism, which constantly moves and heaves. In more modern parlance, it may also be seen as a machine of inter-related parts, each element of which works in tandem with others. Cities have developed over millennia and scholars have been continuously fascinated with this urban movement, as layers of change and development have transformed both the landscape and life within the urban arena. Cities today comprise a palimpsest, layer upon layer of history and intervention, of progress and growth, and of struggle and conflict.

Solutions to the challenges that cities face today might seem out of reach, but in reality societies and governments have always been faced with the need to respond. Having some sense of future direction, or trajectory of travel, is a significant task for any area faced with more immediate concerns. Visions are useful and valuable for their ability to contribute to democratic debate about appropriate directions forward; visions may have been much more directorial in past times than is called for today, but they do allow us to make sense of where we are and where we would like to be, even if the route to that destination is uncertain. As both city governments and urban planning powers have diminished, at least in the global north, and branded as unfashionable for the 21st century, questions remain about the usefulness of city visioning for planning, in a context where a multitude of organisations, sometimes in harmony but often fragmented, shape and reshape the city.

This will chapter examine the changing shape of cities, their complexity and transformational changes. It will set out the case for the development of city visions and for urban planning to be seen and utilised as a stock of knowledge and methods that can assist cities in both assessing and managing present-day challenges and carving out paths for the future.

The city as a thriving and complex system

Patrick Geddes (1854–1892), biologist, urban sociologist and geographer-planner, thought of cities as living organisms that are constantly changing (see Chapter 5). Cities over the world are attempting to cope with a series of inter-related issues that affect their present and future: think of the city as an ecosystem with all the constituent elements connected to each other. We can identify issues relating to housing, transport, energy, water, food, public services, government, trade, climate change and employment, which ebb and flow over time in a single city. Keeping abreast of all these changes, individually, is no mean feat. Seeing them interact and come into conflict with each other, or rather viewing them as a series of interlocking components that are shaped in part by their neighbouring components, is a skill. Yet that is exactly what a city is: a system that is alive.

When we are in a city, what do we observe? We see people being born, dying, moving in, moving out, moving around, changing their jobs, moving home, getting sick and needing health care. We see shops opening and closing, and buildings being erected, adapted or demolished. We see visitors and tourists, communicating in many different languages, trying to use transport services they may be unfamiliar with. We see hordes of people commuting from home to work and back again, every day, by train, by bus, by taxi, by bicycle and on foot and, in some cases, by plane and helicopter. We see trucks transporting goods to shops and malls, buses taking children to school, delivery riders swerving around traffic on their motorbikes and bicycles with bags full of takeaway food and parcels. We see luxuriously expensive cars with personalised number plates. We see people smartly dressed and casually dressed, walking into civic buildings, and being driven away from courts in security vans. We see people walking down the street laden with shopping bags from high-end upmarket stores, and other people holding out their hands in desperation as they lie next to the store entrances. We see thriving fruit, vegetable, fish and meat markets in full colour, noisy and bustling. We see law enforcers stopping and searching people, and paramedics speeding through the streets. We see directions to art galleries and museums, graffiti on passing metro trains and murals adorning the sides of buildings. We see cities at play, crowded parks (some even well kept) in the summer, people running, cycling, skateboarding, rollerblading, ice skating, playing games, using e-scooters and e-cycles, and taking dogs for walks. We see people waiting at the crossing, eating, drinking, spilling coffee as they walk, stepping out unthinkingly into traffic as they stare at their phones. We see people teaming out from bars onto pavements. We see people dancing, performing tai chi and lifting weights. And we see congestion, pollution, rubbish, demonstrations, homelessness, poverty and addiction (see Figure 10.1).

What we do not normally observe, though, are the utility, energy and water lines under the ground; the myriad of tunnels transporting metro systems (although we often hear and feel the rumble of the trains as they pass); the programmed sequencing of traffic lights and pedestrian crossings that change according to busyness and pollution levels; the delivery drivers rushing to make their next drop-off as one of possibly 50 sequenced deliveries they will have to make across the city that day; the taxi drivers responding to an app request for a ride from one side of the city to the other; the buses and trains working to set timetables whose frequencies change between peak and off-peak times; the logistic services ensuring the linear relationship between the manufacturing, collection, despatch and delivery of essential goods across cities and continents; the heating and air-conditioning within buildings that respond automatically to conditions internally

Figure 10.1: Seeing the city: the 'seen' and 'unseen' elements

Source: https://pixabay.com/photos/people-walking-city-urban-knapsack-1031169

and externally; the street lights getting brighter or dimmer according to time and movement; the data being transmitted through wireless technologies to and from 'the cloud', accessed by people on smart devices by the nanosecond on all manner of issues; the finance being transferred seamlessly from one bank account to another, and between consumer and provider; the electric vehicle being charged up for its next journey; the food banks providing essential supplies to those in the city in most need; the support provided by mental health workers to those finding it difficult to cope with city life, as the medics worry about how to finance their services in the future; the multi-million property deals; and the hedge fund bankers making short-term investments on the likelihood of urban collapse.

When we think of the city as a lively, thriving, healthy, sustainable and equitable urban area, we assume that the systems of the city are working effectively for our benefit. This often is our ultimate objective for a city. We rarely stop to think how that happens, and why parts of the city stop working when systems fail and faults occur. None of this city life happens by chance or, for that matter, by luck. It takes an enormous undertaking to manage all the various aspects of the city, by tens of thousands of people, in hundreds of different organisations. However, that is just to ensure that the basic levels of provision are maintained. If, on the other hand, we identify ways that city services could be improved, then proceed to envision the changes, plan for them, identify relationships between the services and the rest of the city system, and programme them, this requires some extra effort. Sometimes change is required to rectify a problem identified within the city. On other occasions, there will be a need to intervene because of changed political, economic, social, environmental or technological priorities. At other times, change happens because of activity outside the city, or at least outside the direct control of organisations within the urban region. Trade is global and dependent on ease of trading and subject to tariffs, firms are based on the other side of the world, information and communications technology (ICT) systems are designed internationally, migration and mobility in and out of the city depend on national border controls and visa availability and can be shaped sometimes by pressure points (war, famine and flooding, for example) in other parts of the world, and climate change and pandemics are not respectful of city, regional or national borders when extreme weather events or the spread of disease can affect societies so devastatingly quickly.

As we saw earlier in this book, in the context of all this inherent city complexity, the hallmark of our modern urban life, we still need to plan and manage urban regions, to make sense of the bewildering pace of change, to react and intervene when there is an overriding need, to allow people a strong voice in expressing opinions about their own city and to have some sense of direction about where we might be heading to in at least the medium term. These tasks are what urban planning, historically, has been all about (see Chapter 4). For most of the 20th century, the planning approaches we used to allow us to manage the urban system, and see us through constant urban flux, rested on a combination of elected local democracy, predetermined, boundarised masterplans spanning long time periods, a set of cross-sector organisations that required working collaboratively in cooperative relationships and a role for citizens and communities at select times who could be consulted about the future plans for places. However, a series of transformational changes since the start of the 21st century has challenged this approach.

The changing ways that cities function

Technological advancements and the onset of the digital age have disrupted cities in both positive and negative ways. Making cities smarter by joining things up digitally is only a part substitute for the skills and knowledge needed to align different urban systems, governmental and regulatory processes, and a myriad of organisations for positive benefit. Digital transformation has allowed us to create so much readily available information about ourselves, our lifestyles, our places of work and habitation, and our modes of mobility, that we are being bombarded every second by waves of data flows – sometimes directly to our smart phones and smart watches. The digital disruptive world is changing how cities function, the demand for space in urban centres, the availability and nature of employment, the modes by which we interact and make judgements about organisations and individuals, and how we visualise cities and information flows (Future Cities Catapult, 2016). Automation and, by implication, the likelihood for greater artificial intelligence, will exacerbate these trends.

Much of what we are talking about here – the functioning of the urban and our role within it – was not possible even at the turn of the millennium. The smart phone and the onset of apps have openly democratised information about city life that previously would have taken years of collection through surveys and analysis of options by urban planners. Usually, that activity would have occurred behind the closed doors of city government. Now it is instantly and mostly openly available to anyone: the data can not only be accessed by privileged political and professional actors within government, but also all those interested in seeing and interpreting urban change.

It is not only the digital revolution that has changed cities and how planners identify and respond to the challenges. Changing institutional frameworks have weakened strategic planning processes to manage metropolitan change; the availability of instantaneous intelligence and data has undermined the case for long-term strategic thinking in government, to enable the development of strategic visioning and planning to guide cities through complexity (Hambleton, 2014; Wolfram, 2018). One of the hallmarks of strategic spatial planning in this regard is to identify inter-relationships and inter-dependencies between different issues within the same city; the intention would be to examine, for example, the implications of changing transport modes for housing access and development, or the relationship between access to green space in a city and community wellbeing. Data collection across a range of agencies, coupled with the privatisation programmes of public services, and a hollowing-out of the state in some nations, has caused deep-seated fragmentation and a disjuncture for activities that either would have been more integrated across one or a handful of organisations, or at least aligned through work practices. Agencies and institutions responsible for supplying public services such as transport and utilities, or health and education, are now often separate from those responsible for formulating long-term city visions, or for regulating land and other commodities (Vallance et al, 2019). This fragmented and constantly changing governance structure during a time of economic, climate change and social upheaval is a common feature of cities and states that have witnessed declining public services, public expenditure cuts, the need to respond to critical urgent issues (such as pandemics) and a changeable uncertain framework of policy-making responsibilities.

Citizens of cities – who live with and cope with change in cities – need to play a greater role in understanding and shaping places, both in the decisions made that affect people's everyday lives, and in the design and delivery of services. The uptake of digital technologies including broadband internet, smart phones, laptop and tablet computers, and the associated 'big data' agenda has transformed the place that is cities. New digital platforms have unleashed new methods for the public to interact on urban planning issues and with government (Wilson et al, 2019). With the onset of the smart city in the 21st century, there remains an opportunity to create more representative and sustainable forms of city-wide engagement, service provision and planning responses, both within and for cities (Silva, 2020). To some sceptics of urban planning, this transformation has been viewed as an opportunity to argue for no planning. Given that the existing tools of planning were forged in 20th century forms, it is a compelling if somewhat lazy argument to make. We would argue, however, that the digital revolution, the onset of intelligence and data forms, and the willingness of citizens to engage in new ways on the issues affecting the future of their cities, are the foundations for the reassertion of urban planning albeit in a new guise to meet modern challenges and opportunities.

Urban futures: the case for a form of planning

In reality, despite the best-practice examples we have highlighted in this book, assessing the need for, agreeing on and defining an urban vision for any city can be problematic. At the outset, there is the challenge of examining the trends apparent in an urban area that themselves would have materialised over long periods of time but which are not in any way fixed, but fluid and ever changing. A backward glance to history, through the lens of backcasting, and comparisons between cities that appear to be at the same stage of development, evolution or transition, can give us some insights into what seems to be happening to a place. But that merely provides us with a mirror, which was of course focused on a different place at a different time. Deciding what is going on within and to a city also necessitates us to press the pause button, to decode the trends, and give us breathing space to think through options, before restarting play and allowing the urban to play out in different ways. However, the world does not work like that; time does not stand still for cities, even those suffering from a series of negative trends, such as population decline or economic downturn. Moreover, in an increasingly globalised world, cities are not immune and isolated from other cities across the planet and are often linked together in complex ways (Hall and Pain, 2006).

None of these contentions are new, even if some of them appear to be vastly more important today as critical issues that have to be addressed. They are, of course, the hallmark of an urban age, and they precipitate a continuous debate that revolves around notions of urban change and urban management. They include questions about the right form and extent of government, of market freedoms, of equality and opportunity, of impositions on landowners, of the extent of open democratic debate, of degrees of taxation and resourcing, of infrastructure availability and provision, of security needs and terrorism threats, of migration and demographic needs, of health provision and protection, and of border controls and freedom of movement.

Just about all the news we hear about cities relates to patterns of structural and behavioural change, how government, business, people and places cope with that change, and how different groups present different arguments of contention as to what to do and how to react, and start to come into conflict with each other about desirable or undesirable courses of action. Certainly, the COVID-19 crisis and the continuing impact of climate change have brought this sharply into focus (Batty, 2020a; Dixon, 2020).

However, the debate we are concerned with here is whether it is desirable to take a strategic and a cumulative assessment of all the activities in a single city; identify trends, including possible pathways into the near future; and examine how change in one part of a city, or in one sector, impacts on other areas or sectors or people, and which, in combination, may generate a collectively agreed desire for a particular set of actions. Historically, as we saw in Chapter 2, this has been the way that forms of urban and regional planning have sought to shape the future of cities, particularly since the late 19th century in the globalised nations of the northern hemisphere. Many of these attempts at planning the city originated from an amalgamation of various conceptual ideas about ideal urban forms, of a desire to create utopic places, or of the need to eradicate the societal and built environment externalities associated with rapid urbanisation and dense urban forms. In the 20th century, some of these urban and regional planning processes were used as a force for good (Friedmann, 1987), appropriated by governments for other ends, including coordinating responses to urban rebuilding following war and conflict, or to rejuvenate cities experiencing economic decline, or to counteract impacts on natural resources. In other cases, the desire for forms of urban and regional planning has been reflected in the expressed need for state control for political or efficiency purposes; it has even been used, shamefully, in authoritarian ways to suppress and control societal groups (Keil and Hertel, 2020).

The usefulness and appropriateness of having any form of urban and regional planning system at all remains, itself, highly contestable as we enter the third decade of the 21st century. Critics point to the negatives: to the association with dominant (and archaic 20th century) state models, to the infringement on liberties and landownership, to the notion that states can control economies in an era of globalisation, and that previous forms of urban planning have not delivered what they should have (O'Toole, 2007; Lord and Tewdwr-Jones, 2014). We must acknowledge that many of these criticisms are indeed valid to one degree or another. Nonetheless, there are proponents of urban planning that also point to the successes achieved during the same time period and include, for example, preventing the coalescence of settlements through urban sprawl, the protection of green space in urban areas, improvements to air quality, the provision of land for housing, standards of habitation for new development, coordination between new housing areas and public transport routes, ensuring that new schools and health facilities match changing population trends, the creation of new pedestrian and cycle routes, and achieving balanced sustainable development across different parts of an urban area.

The contention about using urban and regional planning to shape and manage change, and different expectations about change, do not necessarily pivot around these criticisms or successes alone. Rather, they relate to debate about degrees of governmental or state control, market and individual liberties, and the idea that it is desirable – or even possible – to include all aspects of a single city's transformation and course of action into a single, all-encompassing vision, plan or strategy. On this point, it is certainly true that the world has changed immensely over 120 years of planning's existence. What started off as single generic visions of experts, or 'planning wizards' to use Gold and Ward's (1997) terminology in the first half of the 20th century, materialised into the words, deeds and actions of the central state in the middle of that century. By the last decades of the century and more established into the 21st century, planning is no longer an activity of just well-intentioned 'experts as visionaries', or of the 'all-actionable' central state.

Today, planning may still be the function of government, locally and nationally (and regionally in some nations), but only as a broad framework of desire in shaping and controlling the urbanisation of places. The previously linear link between vision, plan and intervention has been severed over the past 40 years. Politicians still develop visions for cities, and governments can still produce desirable plans showing trends and cumulative impacts of change for individual places, but it is the market that decides whether and where to implement change on the ground. Herein lies a major problem for planning the city in the 21st century urban age: it is that national, regional or local governments' commitments to address the major challenges facing the globe, such as climate change, sustainability, balanced levelling-up economic growth, poverty and so on, can develop visions of the future, produce strategic long-term plans on how to address them, but may ultimately lack the financial means, legal requirement or even political power to intervene a plan of action. That is on the assumption, however, that those politicians and governments are in a position to be able to assemble and access the data and intelligence necessary across all sectors to create a unique total-city platform on which agreement on a vision, a strategic plan of action and selective interventions are all possible. That is why it is crucial to understand that developing a vision for a city is just the first step and can in itself present challenges, but implementing the vision and managing the transition to the future city can be even more challenging (a point we will return to in the final chapter of this book).

Developing a city vision in an uncertain urban age

Developing a vision that is expected to become a rallying call for action and what is commonly referred to these days as 'delivery on the ground' in cities, is a complex undertaking. This is not only because of the fundamental complexity of governance arrangements now to be found in cities across the globe, as we discussed earlier. It is also the consequence of competing interests and a plurality of agencies and voices calling for intervention.

In the past, it was possible to associate individual places with particular attributes that, to all intents and purposes, represented or characterised what those places appeared to be about. We referred to the city of Manchester in the UK as 'Cottonopolis', to Detroit as 'Motor City', to Las Vegas as 'Sin City' and to Rome in Italy as 'The Eternal City'. Some of these names related to fact: Cottonopolis was a reference to Manchester as home to the 19th century cotton industry and proliferation of cotton mills. Detroit was the centre of American car production throughout most of the 20th century as the location of the big three car producers – General Motors, Ford and Chrysler (Kinney, 2016). Other cities' nicknames may not be as well intentioned: 'The Windy City' of Chicago may refer to the city in the late 19th century as the home of politicians who were 'full of hot air', for example. Developing a vision for a city may not be founded on one of these characterisations, although politicians may desire to develop a vision to overcome an unpopular or unfounded characterisation. Certainly, in the case of Manchester and Detroit, there has been a need to open a new chapter in their history after both cities' industrial base collapsed and to give each city a new narrative to encourage growth, not that that has been an easy or straightforward process. Finding a new narrative and developing a new vision as a desirable future for any urban area, overcoming the profile of the past for a new era, has immense implications, however. Not least is a question about who should set about creating and owning such a vision, and whether that new vision can be shared and agreed to by a wider constituency of interests within the city.

During the last decade of the 20th century and the first two decades of the 21st century, there has also been a tendency for mayors and city governments to develop a label for a city as a form of place promotion or place branding. The idea has been to appropriate an attribute that could be utilised to support economic growth, inward investment or quality of life, which, in turn, would attempt to give a city a competitive advantage over other places. In Europe, the Spanish cities of Barcelona and Bilbao, and the German city of Berlin, became well-known examples for this branding as both started to experience rapid change compared with their previous pasts. Barcelona, after its success hosting of the Olympic Games in 1992, gained a reputation for cosmopolitanism, creativity, innovation, culture and quality of life as the foundations of its renaissance (Belloso, 2011). Bilbao, a declining industrial city in the north of the country with a range of economic, social and environmental problems, secured a home for the Guggenheim Museum. That decision, in turn, precipitated a number of other iconic projects across the city that have contributed to the transformation of the city and region, leading to the city now becoming a popular culturally infused tourist destination. Berlin, as the new capital of a unified Germany, was presented to the world through a carefully packaged branding and marketing campaign that drew attention to new architecturally crafted development projects but also used the investments as a public spectacle that would draw in further investors and tourists alike (Colomb, 2013). So successful was the Galician city of Bilbao to turn the tide, that the phrases 'the Guggenheim effect' and 'the Bilbao effect' (Gonzalez, 2010) were coined to describe cities that either were embarking on cultural-led regeneration or were striving to rebrand themselves along the lines of the Spanish growth model (Garcia, 2010). These cities were identified as possessing the same characteristics – that is, as symbols for structural change and economic development; pursuing culturally infused urban regeneration; adopting iconic architecture for new projects; and advancing local–global partnerships (Plaza and Haarich, 2013).

More recently, commentators have identified negative externalities associated with the rebranding of the three cities, with suggestions that Barcelona has become 'overtourist' to the point of suffering tourism gentrification (Lagonigro et al, 2020), that Berlin has been too selective in its presentation of itself to the detriment of its existing social movements (Hockenos, 2017) and that Bilbao's reliance on 'starchitecture' has not trickled down to those most in need (Alaily-Mattar et al, 2018).

This over-emphasis on architectural icons as a way of rebranding places and creating new visions for cities has been referred to as 'banal nationalism' (McNeill and Tewdwr-Jones, 2003). It suggests a tendency for cities to adopt singular and largely glossy visions that might lead to economic growth and cultural development in the short term, but which tends to eclipse other attributes of those cities that may be worth supporting, and to clarify this the reader is referred back to our definition of city vision in Chapter 7. In this sense, a city vision must be more than place branding, but we must also remember, of course, that the ways cities transform and redevelop over time are likely to be beyond the initial expectations of any visioning exercise that might have occurred in a different context. The mayor of Barcelona during the 1980s and 1990s, Pasqual Maragall, had a vision for the redevelopment of the city through his government's successful bid for the Olympic Games (McNeill, 1999) (see Figure 10.2). Despite this, even he would not have foreseen how the city has become so successful through tourism, that it has become a problem for the wider social, economic and environmental benefit of residents across the city.

In reality, as a city changes, so do the attributes, attractiveness and entrepreneurialism of the city, in ways that are unforeseen at the outset. Barcelona, driven by the city government initially, then became a victim of its own success in ways beyond the control of that government. The rise of budget airlines and cheap flights made Barcelona a 'must visit' location for a wider cohort of people from across the European continent. The demand for tourist accommodation was met not only by the official provision of double the amount of hotel accommodation over a 10-year period, but also through the development in the 2010s of urban sharing platforms such as Airbnb (Lagonigro et al, 2020).

Figure 10.2: Annella Olympica, Barcelona

Source: https://unsplash.com/photos/h3Y0giOyK1s

This allowed individual property owners to turn their properties into short-term lets that returned significant income to their owners. The rise of Airbnb properties created a domino effect in the city for the availability of affordable homes for urban dwellers, as homes were converted into holiday property lets. Similarly, the rise of other digital-sharing economy platforms such as Uber, the taxi-sharing app, has had a demonstrable effect on the economy of taxi companies in not only Barcelona but also other places globally. These disruptive economies have, in turn, morphed into other businesses, including parcel and food delivery platforms, but have also been accompanied by accusations of exploitative labour practices and the rise of venture capitalism (Gurran and Phibbs, 2017; Cant, 2020). The regulation of the sharing economy is challenging, and tends to sit beyond politicians' and planners' notions of how a city progresses. Existing taxi companies have complained about Uber's practices and demonstrations have occurred in some cities. In 2019, Uber announced that it would no longer operate within Barcelona (Edelstein, 2019). These examples all illustrate the inherent complexity of cities and how unplanned actions can often create unforeseen and unintended consequences.

Therefore, in promoting the idea of an urban vision for a place, it has to be acknowledged that 'city states', unlike their historic forebears, for example during the renaissance, do not necessarily have the means by which a vision can be turned into a programmable phased form of implementation unfettered by ad hoc changes, both within and outside its control. Historically, as we saw in both Chapters 2 and 3, it may have been possible in past eras to have some degree of certainty that a vision, usually initiated by the state, with authority and legitimacy for its preparation and roll out, would be implemented providing the political support and financial resourcing were guaranteed in the following years. This was the case, for example, with Abercrombie and Forshaw's London Plan of 1943. Today, in a world of complexity and increased uncertainty, city leaders face the challenge that while they may develop a vision, there is less certainty that that vision will find acceptance among a wider group of city interests, especially where the market is charged in totality (or in part) with its translation to action, and where those opposed to its contents may resort to oppositional tactics to stop it from being implemented at all. The consequence of this changed attitude today towards urban visioning and planning is for a city vision, at least in places where it does exist, to perform the role as an initiator of debate through incremental change. As we argue in this book, city visions provide a valuable tool to develop long-term strategic thinking in cities, even if there are some who question their inherent value (Goodspeed, 2020). Despite this, in some instances, they may not have the same level of controlling force over consequential decisions that the earliest visions once had when political action was shaped and determined largely by government (or the state) alone.

Summary

In summary, the question is, what are the desirable ways that cities can enact vision and planning in the 21st century for their long-term benefit? The answers should surely be by:

- Utilising the idea of a vision as a way to bring disparate groups into a conversation about sustainable and inclusive urban change.
- Harnessing smart data and intelligence on different issues from different sources and finding ways for them to sit together.
- Taking a synoptic and strategic view of the city as a whole, made up of a multitude of inter-related systemic parts.
- Adopting long-term perspectives and reminding all agencies within the city to think of the long game, to overcome vested short-term interests.
- Accepting the need to be sensitive to place and to people.
- Identifying urban assets and urban distinctiveness as the foundation of change.
- Adopting a vision and planning approach that has a strong political force and intent.
- Appropriating an array of tools to enact change that may involve initiating engagement opportunities, social media platforms, circular economy opportunities, non-governmental initiated ideas, an emphasis on proof-of-concept projects and pilots.
- Accepting that no single agency or rigid single plan will be able to bring about action for change.
- Legitimising an agile, non-linear approach to urban intervention that is responsive, proactive and less institutionalised.

Neither a city vision nor an urban planning approach for any city should claim to be able to instantly solve complex problems. If politicians argue that their approach is instant and can guarantee immediate results, it is unlikely to truly address the fundamental challenges that cities are facing. Moreover, a city vision is not a masterplan, and strictly speaking it is not what we might call urban planning, although it can certainly link and support that activity. Rather, the approach in city visioning should be to help decision-makers and communities think clearly and logically about resolving their problems, and the primary structural matters that include issues to do with equity or growth. It should try to examine alternative courses of action and trace, through scenarios and modelling, as far as possible, the consequences of each of these for different groups of people, in different places. That, invariably, will take time and effort. It cannot avoid looking at the most difficult questions of power, exclusion, wellbeing and the legitimacy to act.

We should claim, modestly, that planners are more capable than the average person to conduct this kind of analysis, but we admit that they are not uniquely expert nor should their judgements drown out other voices from being heard. That is why a participatory approach, bringing together the four elements of the quadruple helix that we discussed earlier in this book, is much more likely to gain traction and support in a city than one led by a single stakeholder group. In effect, a desire for a city vision (as part of what we term 'urban futures' thinking), and a commitment to plan for that future, are fundamentally a resource for democratic and informed decision-making about the sustainability of our lives now and in the future. That, we argue, is in everyone's interest. As Herb Caen (1967) (the San Francisco journalist wrote): 'A city is not gauged by its length and width, but by the broadness of its vision and the height of its dreams.'

11

Conclusions: facing the urban future to 2050 and beyond

> Never let the future disturb you. You will meet it, if you have to, with the same weapons of reason which today arm you against the present.
> Marcus Aurelius, 2nd century AD, *Meditations*

Introduction

Throughout this book, our argument has been that we need to bring four main stakeholder groups together in cities – that is, the public (or civil society), academia, local government and business – to develop participatory-based, long-term city visions. Although not predictive, these city visions can help us to plan, prepare and manage a transition to a sustainable future for our cities. Developed using a range of city foresight methods, and recognising the value of a parallel 'science of cities' approach and the inherent complexity of cities, these visions can help to create support and mobilise action to tackle the pressing issues of climate change, resource depletion, health and wellbeing concerns, socioeconomic disparities and other major urban challenges at a crucially important time in humanity's history. They present us with a way of looking long term, beyond short-term crises and politics, to 2050 as part of an overall framework we have called urban futures (see Chapter 1).

As we were writing this book, the COVID-19 crisis was having a huge impact on cities across the world. Directly through the substantial number of deaths, and indirectly through social distancing and restrictions on work, industry, services, education and travel, COVID-19 has had far-reaching repercussions not only on people's lives, but also on the economic activities of countries and cities globally. Because we live in an interconnected and globalised world, it is not surprising that the crisis is having substantial impacts on Gross Domestic Product (GDP) and health and welfare systems, with people in poverty living in the world's urban areas suffering disproportionately (UN-Habitat, 2020).

But crises provide opportunities as well as risks, and there is an argument for suggesting that the COVID-19 crisis, and the continuing impact of climate change, provide us with a chance to think longer term beyond the present, and reimagine the way in which cities should be like further into the future to 2030, 2050 and beyond. In the rest of this chapter, therefore, we look at three main themes that have emerged from the book: (a) city foresight, transitions theory and city visions; (b) urban planning and governance; and (c) the future for cities. In doing this, we offer our view on the practical and pragmatic steps city leaders and other groups need to take to develop city visions and new forms of flexible governance as part of urban futures thinking.

City foresight, transitions theory and city visions: making the connections in practice

In earlier chapters of this book, we saw how transitions theory, encompassing both the multi-level perspective (MLP) and transition management (TM), could help us understand how to plan and manage an urban transition to a more sustainable future. Part of this process involves city visioning, which we outlined in Chapter 7. So how can this interconnectivity be encouraged and what steps are required to develop this at the city level?

In the context of the UK, the Future of Cities programme (GOfS, 2016a) called for cities to take action and establish platforms for city foresight or networks that connect cities locally and regionally with their universities, to establish best practice and transferable lessons. Cities need to exchange insights, experiment and be creative to develop city visions. National government was also exhorted in the programme report to encourage evidence-based explorations of cities' long-term futures by incorporating futures-based thinking into grants and funding such as city deals.

Ultimately, however, much will depend on city governments and their willingness to be involved and help co-produce city visions. In the UK, getting local government onside in an era of reduced spending and austerity-driven cutbacks in expenditure may be challenging; and in the global south, public participation and engagement may be an additional challenge. There is no doubt that fostering a culture in cities that recognises the importance of this urban futures thinking requires leadership, resourcefulness and determination. Table 11.1 shows the sequential stages that are most important in developing a city vision using city foresight techniques and the key questions that will need to be addressed. We have drawn directly on our own experience in developing this table and, where relevant, indirectly from other relevant literature.

Essentially, we see the city visioning process as being at the heart of urban futures, and involving five main stages (Table 11.1):

- Stage 1: Setting the baseline – where are we now?
- Stage 2: Developing the vision – where are we going?
- Stage 3: Identifying the roadmap and pathways to the future – how will we get there?
- Stage 4: Implementing the vision – how will we do it?
- Stage 5: Assessment and monitoring – how are we progressing?

In Stage 1, much of the process will involve setting up the city visioning process and deciding on the best leadership model. This requires an understanding of how ultimately power relations can influence and shape city visions, and how to best adopt an inclusive and co-produced approach to vision development. In Stage 2, as we saw in Chapters 7 and 8, how we frame the challenge is very important in determining the shape and form of the visioning process. This helps answer the question, 'where are we going?' and the key stakeholders involved in leading the process need to agree the details of how the process will work, how engagement and participation are embraced and how new digital platforms could help underpin this work. In Stage 3, detailed thought must be given to how the future vision can be achieved through detailed roadmapping and pathway analysis; in this respect, ownership of the plans and projects is crucial and understandings of how these will link with the wider vision will be important to think about. In Stage 4, the implementation of the vision is the primary focus and will be dependent on agreeing a detailed plan of action and promoting the vision and engagement for the vision. In Stage 5, assessment and monitoring will be important to determine, provide feedback on and influence any required changes to the vision. This may mean a revised organisational structure that brings on board other partners and new collaborations to tap into new funding streams.

City foresight and city visioning are therefore fundamental parts of urban futures thinking. This requires new ways of doing things and moving beyond simply the short term; it will mean the city vision partnership also fully engaging with teams in local government and beyond, in planning, economic development, sustainability, climate change and transport, and across a variety of service delivery providers in organisations. However, the watchwords must always be

Table 11.1: City visions: stages of development, key steps and key questions

Stage	Key steps	Key questions
Stage 1: Setting the baseline – where are we now?	• Set up the leadership team and determine who the champion(s) will be • Plan the process • Establish funding/in-kind contributions • Stakeholder analysis – determine the important stakeholders • Situation analysis – strategic context • Identify key urban challenges • Build the evidence base – understand the past, present and future of the city	• Who will lead the vision development process? • How is the programme funded/resourced? • How will the programme engage with the public? • How does the vision sit with other existing visions and strategies? • How can complexity and cross-cutting challenges be embraced?
Stage 2: Developing the vision – where are we going?	• Develop engagement and participation with key stakeholders • Develop and plan the details of the visioning process • Run workshops and other relevant urban foresight processes (including Delphi groups and scenario analysis)	• How will the urban challenge(s) in the city be framed? • How is the balance of stakeholder groups determined? • What are the trade-offs between diversity, breadth and scale in public engagement? • How can new technology/new digital platforms help? • How can dynamic co-production be ensured? • How can genuine engagement be best developed? • How can expectations be managed? • How much public participation is appropriate or possible? • Which city foresight methods best fit the individual city and its current circumstances?
Stage 3: Identifying the roadmap and pathways to the future – how will we get there?	• Develop projects, plans and roadmaps to the future • Identify the preferred pathway and vision • Use scenarios if needed as part of the visioning process	• How will the roadmaps identify key issues and challenges and milestones? • Who will 'own' the agreed actions and plans? • Which tangible physical spaces (innovation districts, living labs etc) and on-the-ground projects will work best in underpinning the vision and making it a reality?

Table 11.1: City visions: stages of development, key steps and key questions (continued)

Stage	Key steps	Key questions
Stage 4: Implementing the vision: how will we do it?	• Establish a process for continuous strategy/vision development • Use buy-in and engagement to launch the vision • Promote the vision • Engage and use participatory approaches for continuous feedback	• How will the vision be implemented and by whom? • How will the shared purpose(s) be communicated? • How will the process of feedback/consultation be developed? • Will new urban governance models be needed? • How will new funding streams be secured to underpin R&D in the 'experimental city'?
Stage 5: Assessment and monitoring – how are we progressing?	• Develop and put in place an appropriate body (e.g. a Futures Commission or Group) to monitor progress • Assess progress against predefined qualitative or quantitative indicators	• How can continuous and reflexive feedback loops be put in place? • How will assessment and monitoring work and who is responsible for this? • Can a long-term group be developed for this and what should its remit be? • How will appropriate changes be made to the vision if required?

'a participatory-based approach', irrespective of who leads the co-produced programme of visioning activities.

Urban planning and governance: democratising the future

Urban planning, and the governmental context within which it sits, has been one of the principal mechanisms used by city governments over the past 120 years to manage change and shape the future. As we saw earlier in this book, the concept of 'urban planning' has been bound up with utopic traditions, a wider concern with citizens and places, and strong political commitments to deliver action. During the 20th century, it led to the redesign of cities, either wholesale or incrementally, often achieving more immediate benefits for the delivery of homes, transport, commercial districts and jobs, while securing the provision of green spaces and the protection of historic buildings and landscapes.

By its nature, urban planning is meant to be multi-scalar, addressing wider and longer-term changes over larger territories that are often difficult to see, while managing short-term site-specific changes that are identifiable and visible. Its essence is to attempt to combine a range of often-competing sectoral demands, synoptically, in the same geographical location, with a multitude of different voices and interested constituencies who seek very specific outcomes and benefits. This incredible juggling act for professional planners and urbanists to manage makes it a unique function of government, on the one hand, and one that is overwhelmingly contentious, on the other. The same process of urban planning for a single city is meant, simultaneously, to deliver housing, jobs, transport and commercial development for the market, protect the environment, secure health and wellbeing for citizens and communities, stop flooding, deliver energy, secure historic buildings, enable the city to flow without impediment and reduce overt regulation and bureaucracy that might otherwise add costs and cause delay to the city's functioning trade and mobility. Urban planning is no easy feat, nor has it ever been, for any city that is undergoing any form of change because the expectations of city growth and city management are so vast for all concerned.

Of course, it is frustrating for city residents or city business people when things do not happen as quickly as one would expect, and it is annoying when personal interests and property freedoms are held back in the interests of the city as a whole. Urban planning, however, is still the most convenient political and organisational device we have available to manage a city's complex set of inter-relationships and inter-dependencies over time, and despite occasional and what seems never-ending noises from newly elected politicians across nations to 'do something' about urban planning, by reducing its statist control in favour of ad hoc and pragmatic intervention and introducing market freedoms, history has shown that urban planning usually survives the turmoil to live another day. Urban planning can also, therefore, absorb changing political expectations and priorities, as well as changing urban challenges and circumstances.

That is not to say that the components of urban planning have remained the same over decades. The tools at the disposal of politicians and planners, and the methods utilised to understand and consider different urban trajectories, have varied almost as much as the different urban trends that they have sought to manage. As a consequence, when we refer to urban planning, what we are actually referring to is a toolkit of political, systems-thinking, temporal and organisational devices that are available to any given city at a particular moment in time. Those devices change, and have to change, to remain relevant, usable and applicable. However, when set within governmental institutional contexts, they can be slow to adapt speedily enough to demand and circumstances. It is not urban planning that is necessarily too slow to deal with instantaneous problems in cities, but rather the legitimate legal, political, democratic, financial and institutional frameworks within which it sits, a fact compounded further by decisions about change being determined by changing behavioural and subjective preferences on the part of people. Competing issues, competing interests, contentious plans, politicised decision-making and scarce investment and resources, are all the factors in cities that urban planning has to navigate around.

Short-term needs have to be addressed. Equally, however, the long-term game is one feature of planning that has been neglected across nations as the decades have passed. If we are to make cities resilient against the threat of climate change, pandemic threats, economic uncertainty and poverty and deprivation, we need urban planning devices and toolkits that can think proactively about our urban futures, and not be caged in outdated urban planning concepts and methods that were designed in a different age, for different circumstances and for short-term concerns. This change requirement is as much about the democratic future of cities as it is about urban planning itself. We have to acknowledge that those older notions of urban planning have rarely addressed more fundamental structural urban needs, or been of benefit to the interests and welfare of all in society, especially those from disadvantaged minority ethnic groups in most acute need.

We need to start rethinking urban planning as a deliberative, democratic, inclusive and sustainable political programme that shapes urban futures. That may not involve a reliance on plans and strategies, or on zoning ordinances, or on land-focused development opportunities, and it may not be led by governmental bodies and property sector interests or, for that matter, by professional planners alone. These are the traits of an increasingly outmoded system. In its place, urban planning may involve a focus on urban programme and project management, with multi-sector actors working collaboratively, to secure multiple benefits for multiple audiences, and where the price of land and development is determined by societal benefits. There may be more of a focus on digital and data tools, to generate instantaneous information, accessible to all, with urban communities supported by professional advocates, and an optimisation of imagery and visuals as the language of inclusion and of debate across a range of public forums. Digital places might be shaped as much by consideration of their wider societal impact as their technological ability, to the point that we do not have to define the smartness (or sustainability) of our cities: rather, smart and sustainable cities are those that face the future with confidence as vibrant, creative, welcoming and inclusive places that offer good standards of living. There might be greater sensitivity given over to places as unique and different geographies, shaped by different histories and multi-ethnic communities, proud of their past but also open to the idea of change and rebirth. Indeed, at the time of writing, the planning system in England is under review (see MHCLG, 2020), but whatever the result of the consultation, thinking about the long-term future and developing a coherent city vision will remain vital ingredients to urban futures thinking.

All these traits may seem a world away to what urban planning, and even urban government, has become in many places; they may even seem fanciful, or even utopian. However, they are exactly what urban planning was always meant to address – harnessing open dialogue about possible long-term futures in ways that, presently, may seem startling. The switch in thinking towards a proactive and progressive form of urban planning, compared with what we presently have, is to dream the art of the possible, unfettered by institutional and professional sclerosis, overcoming narrow sectional interests, and relying on urban planning devices and methods – shaped for the 21st century – that embrace pluralism and urban liveability goals. Dig deeper into cities across the globe, and this art of the possible is already happening – it is just not happening yet *within* urban planning.

In short, our viewpoint differs from that of both Batty (2018) and Goodspeed (2020) for different reasons. We see city visioning for specific cities and the practice of urban futures as critical to the current and future development of urban planning. For us, and in contrast to Batty (2018), our perspective of city visioning (based on participatory approaches) can help city stakeholders reimagine the future of specific cities. Unlike Goodspeed (2020), we do not recognise city visioning (within the terms of our definition) as an incomplete technique, or a 'Pollyannish exercise'. Used in a formal way, which recognises the quadruple helix conceptualisation, city visioning can recognise the importance of external forces and, moreover, is not automatically confined to a single vision or indeed a predictive outcome. For us, city visioning is not about glossing over the harsh truths of urban living now and in the future. Far from it: city visioning can and should be about building participation and consensus within communities (while recognising different perspectives), as well as democratising urban futures in the context of a new and reimagined urban planning.

The future for cities: what lies ahead?

Throughout history, cities have frequently been at the centre of the spread of infectious diseases but have bounced back, often responding to such crises with increased economic growth, new infrastructure and new urban design. After the cholera outbreak of 1854 (see Figure 11.1), for example, London's sewerage system was transformed, and we can see the legacy of that today with the Victoria Embankment, which was completed in 1870; and, after the Spanish flu outbreak of 1918, which killed many millions of people, major cities such as London, New York and Paris all grew rapidly. The recent global COVID-19 crisis has placed our urban areas centre stage once again, as the major cities of the world have become the capitals of infection (see Figure 11.2): about 95 per cent of people with COVID-19 live in cities, including the one billion people who live in informal settlements and slums (Florida et al, 2020).

Many commentators have argued that the 'new normal' of increased home working, reduced travel, commuting and air pollution, and reduced energy consumption, provides us with opportunities to

Figure 11.1: The London cholera outbreak of 1854

Source: 'A court for King Cholera' – Illustration by John Leech. Wellcome Collection. Attribution 4.0 International (CC BY 4.0)

Figure 11.2: Shoppers in face masks during the Spanish flu pandemic (1918, San Francisco) and during the COVID-19 pandemic (2020)

Source: Wikimedia Commons and https://flickr.com/photos/111977604@N05/ 49726977771: Nickolay Romensky

reconfigure and reimagine what our cities should be like when the crisis is over. In the UK, for example, daily emissions fell initially by 36 per cent during the national lockdown in early 2020 (Parsley, 2020) before they started to rise again as people returned to work. It is certainly true that in the short to medium term, until a vaccine for COVID-19 is found, the world will be a very different place[1].

Yet it would be complacent to think that the new normal will automatically be a world of home working, cycling and sustainable living. Governments around the world will surely soon respond with 'boosterism' policies designed to refire and refuel economic growth, and the low price of oil (as at mid-2020) might actually increase environmental damage still further. Somewhat worryingly for air quality in the UK, at the time of writing, the extension of the Ultra Low Emission Zone in London will not take place until later in 2021, and Clean Air Zones (CAZs) in Birmingham, Leeds, and Manchester and the Zero-Emission Zone in Oxford will also not be rolled out before 2021 or later (Quinio, 2020), although there is also some optimism that other UK cities are rolling out new schemes (for example, Bath) over the next few years (Energy Saving Trust, 2020). There will, be, almost inevitably, a substantial rebound effect in terms of increased emissions and poorer air quality when economic recovery begins, which would be bad for the environment and people's lives in cities, especially people in poverty living in informal settlements in urban areas who may face rising food prices and perhaps increased disruption and social unrest. It would be very wrong, therefore, to waste the opportunity to do things differently now when we face not only the challenges of a global pandemic but also the continuing impact of climate change.

The COVID-19 crisis has also highlighted the importance of thinking about resilience, sustainability and complexity in our cities and ultimately how cities are governed (Batty, 2020a; Dixon, 2020; Hambleton, 2020; Parker, 2020). Resilience, or the ability of cities to respond to environmental and socioeconomic shocks, essentially operationalises sustainable development, which is the path to the ultimate goal of sustainability (Dixon et al, 2018b). Globally, larger cities have been hit the most by COVID-19 (Stier et al, 2020) and, in the UK, places with stronger highly skilled information-based economies (mainly in the greater South East) have been able to more easily adapt to working from home, ensuring that some parts of the economy continue to function. However, the north of England and the Midlands, with weaker low-skill service-based economies, have been less able to manage this (Centre for Cities, 2020). Recent work by Nathan and Overman (2020) in the UK suggests that in big cities, patterns of urban work, shopping and social interaction have all been impacted by COVID-19, but the longer-term impacts remain unclear, depending as they do on a complex web of factors, not least the time taken to find a vaccine. Similarly, Batty (2020b: 743) suggests that the pandemic is a reflection of the complexity and uncertainty inherent in our relationship with cities:

> The recent pandemic is likely to force us into new ways of dealing with the physical space of cities in terms of the way we connect with one another – social distancing and self-isolation may well turn into principles of spatial distancing that change the way we think of moving and locating in cities, to cities with lower densities where the local and the global mesh in ways that we have yet to invent.

Any future vision for a city must therefore consider how to develop and enhance its economy and infrastructure to make it resilient to pandemics as well as flood risk and extreme climate events. Urban preparedness (and being agile and adaptable for the 'next' crisis) must be an inherent part of our thinking for urban futures. This is as true of the global north as it is of the global south. Cities will not die, but we will need to be vigorously engaged in reinventing and reimagining how we want to live, work and play in our cities in the future. As Sadik Khan (Florida et al, 2020) suggested: 'the challenge we face isn't whether cities will survive. The question is whether we have the imagination and vision to transform streets to bring about the safer, more accessible, and more resilient cities we've needed all along'.

In a real sense, therefore, there is a very strong argument for governments now more than perhaps even before to encourage cities to seize the opportunity to develop long-term visions for their future. Moreover, this could be backed by a green stimulus for economic growth, or a green new deal at national level, which would make perfect sense in the current climate. This argument is strengthened by the fact that there is strong evidence suggesting that air pollution is linked to COVID-19 cases, death rates and the spread of the disease (Carrington, 2020). Clean energy systems, clean and green public transport, a retrofitted built environment and smart infrastructure will be vital elements of the way we reconfigure our cities in the medium to long term and will be required to cut emissions even more deeply to meet the required zero-carbon targets to 2030. Recent research has shown, for example, that green projects create more jobs, better returns and higher cost savings than a traditional fiscal stimulus (Hepburn et al, 2020). Indeed, the Committee on Climate Change (2020) wrote to the UK government stressing that any economic recovery package must focus explicitly on climate change and resilience. Not only are there positive benefits from cities committing to becoming more resilient and healthy, but there are also likely to be significant cost savings in terms of long-term health and social care costs. Nationally, there are some encouraging signs that the UK Government is starting to focus on a green economy recovery with the publication of its *Ten Point Plan for a Green Economy Revolution* (HM Government, 2020), although critics point out that stronger action and more funding is required.

At city scale, we are already seeing the growth of 'green shoots' of this sort of thinking, with cities such as Mexico City and Milan introducing hundreds of miles of new bike lanes and New York and Seattle widening pavements and pedestrianising neighbourhoods. In Milan, for example, there are 22 miles of transformed cycling streets; the Mayor of Paris has allocated 300 million euros for a cycle lane network as an alternative to public transport; and in Bogota, 75 miles of streets will be traffic free all week. In the UK, the Scottish government has allocated £10 million to create pop-up walking and cycling routes, and some London boroughs, such as Hackney and Lambeth, have announced measures to widen pavements (Taylor and Laville, 2020). It seems likely that city networks such as C40 could play a role in promoting global changes in thinking, and in the UK the devolved metropolitan areas could help drive similar changes.

Beyond the short term, however, and as the calls for economic recovery grow stronger, we will face the challenges of winning the arguments over green stimulus recovery and tackling the inherent carbon lock-in and path dependency that cities inherently have. Yet, as we saw earlier in this book, cities are complex and multifaceted. We have seen in the past, for example, how some suggested that new technologies would strengthen the 'death of distance' and lead to an overwhelming centrifugal effect, or decentralisation from cities, at the expense of the forces of continued agglomeration, or the pull of the city. In fact, technology ultimately not only re-enforced the 'sticky' centripetal pull that cities already had, but also contributed to decentralisation as well (Dixon et al, 2005). Part of the reason for this is that the built environment of cities is resistant to rapid change: patterns of land use and density are baked in or locked in, and wholesale change is difficult without a managed and planned transition for the long term. Similarly, we face the paradox of the COVID-19 crisis today: cities have been eerily quiet in lockdown as social distancing has been rolled out in urban centres, but it is the physical proximity in cities and their density that contributes to their economic strength and continuing pull. It is very unlikely that cities will magically de-densify as a result of COVID-19 because of the continuing benefits of agglomeration, although anecdotal evidence suggests that the powerful mix of COVID-19, agile home working and the aspirations of workers and some companies to move out of city centres could create churn and movement in office space and other types of land and property use over the short to medium term. On the other hand, carbon lock-in and infrastructure and institutional lock-in will continue to act as inhibitors to change unless national and city governments do things differently and develop new policy and practice guidance for cities and city-regions in a post-lockdown world. However, we will also need to be watchful for the increasing surveillance technology and its impact on privacy and data security in a world in which new apps to monitor health and track infections have far-reaching consequences for people living in cities.

Finally, there are several important reasons why we believe that cities should develop a more strategic view or vision for their long-term futures right now.

First, city visions are place-based and engender a spirit of co-production and cooperation, which is based on the observation that community spirit (or the concept of 'communitarianism') is alive and well in many cities around the world, as the COVID-19 crisis has shown. Plans based simply on numbers will not suffice; we need to understand the 'eigenart' of a place to develop a proper comprehension of a place's unique characteristics, and what it should be like in 2050.

Second, we have also seen the emergence of a new municipalism in many parts of the world, including the UK. Essentially, this provides local responses to austerity and the centralising tendencies of national government, and in England this has also been partly triggered by a 'devolution revolution', statutorily underpinned by the Cities and Local Government Devolution Act 2016 (Thompson, 2020). Combined with climate activism, this offers a potentially powerful mix, which will continue to provide the impetus for calls for a move away from business-as-usual models of economic growth.

Third, when we do return to a normality, we will need to be prepared to continue to tackle the growing threats of climate change and so, having a clear city vision in place, linked to climate strategy and ongoing ambitions for net-zero carbon emissions by 2030 and beyond, is crucial.

What is certain, in our view, is that city stakeholders and leaders need to seize the opportunity now and develop and implement clear city visions for the future. City vision development goes hand in hand with the need for translating a vision into on-the-ground implementation and new, fit-for-purpose urban governance and planning structures. In the words of Thomas Edison (1847–1931), the US inventor and businessman : 'Vision without execution is hallucination.'

Appendix: selected examples of city visions

In this appendix we provide a list of selected city visions – the list is not exhaustive. The list includes existing cities but not new cities. We have excluded more specialist visions focusing on a single element, such as those relating to smart cities, and we have also excluded what may be broadly defined as traditional 'masterplans'. We have included several examples of strategic city-wide or city regional plans where the view taken is long term, large-scale and visionary and/or may involve some degree of consultation with or participation by key stakeholders. The majority of the visions are local government-led, although in some instances, academia, citizens and business have played an important role in helping to shape or lead the vision.

Type of vision	World region	Vision	Period of development	Comments	Website (accessed February 2020)	Academic review/discussion papers
Planning-led and/or community-based	US and Canada	Atlanta 2020	1991–97	One of the earliest examples of planning-led visioning in the US. Led by local government.	Not available	Helling, 1998
		Portland 2030	2007–13	The Vision PDX project was a major community visioning exercise that underpinned the development of the city plan in its various forms from 2002 to 2013. Led by local government.	https://beta.portland.gov/sites/default/files/2020-01/portland2030-avisionforthefuture_visionpdx.pdf	Pettibone, 2016
		Phoenix 2050	2009–11	Work by Arizona State University helped develop a sustainability-based vision, which underpinned the city plan. Led by local government with input from the university.	https://www.phoenix.gov/pdd/reinvent-phx	Iwaniek and Wiek, 2014
		Metro Vancouver 2040	2011	Metro 2050 is currently updating Metro 2040. Both are examples of regional growth strategies with a high degree of visionary content. Led by local government.	http://www.metrovancouver.org/services/regional-planning/metro-vancouver-2040/Pages/default.aspx	John et al, 2015; Abbott and DeMarco, 2016
		York Region 2051	2010–12	Vision 2051 is York Region's (Toronto to Lake Simcoe) latest long-term strategy. It describes the region's ideal vision of the next 40 years and the necessary steps to see it through. Led by local government.	https://www.york.ca/wps/wcm/connect/yorkpublic/a6d9d1ce-0813-4376-a593-daccf2b7fd6e/vision+2051.pdf?MOD=AJPERES&CVID=muliVE5	John et al, 2015

Appendix

Type of vision	World region	Vision	Period of development	Comments	Website (accessed February 2020)	Academic review/ discussion papers
	Europe	Helsinki 2050	2013	The Helsinki City Vision Plan 2050 was launched in 2013. A Greater Helsinki 2050 design competition was also held in 2007. Led by local government.	https://www.hel.fi/hel2/ksv/julkaisut/yos_2013-23_en.pdf https://www.hel.fi/hel2/helsinginseutu/FINAL_GreaterHelsinki_200x200mm_english_03-09-2010_LOW.pdf	Ache, 2011
		Co-Create Copenhagen 2025	2015	'Co-Create Copenhagen' is a vision covering technical and environmental issues towards 2025. The vision is to create 'A Liveable City', 'A Bold City' and 'A Responsible City'. Led by local government.	https://urbandevelopmentcph.kk.dk/artikel/co-create-copenhagen	Huxley et al, 2019
	UK	Bristol One City 2050	2018–19	The One City Plan describes the 2050 vision, and how city partners will work together to create a fair, healthy and sustainable city. Led by local government.	https://www.bristolonecity.com/about-the-one-city-plan/	Hambleton, 2018
		Oxford 2050	2018–19	A city council-led vision with consultation on the vision.	https://oxford2050.com/	Not applicable
		Edinburgh 2050	2016–19	A major consultation exercise was undertaken and the vision was launched in 2019. Led by the council.	https://edinburgh.org/2050-edinburgh-city-vision/	Not applicable

(continued)

Type of vision	World region	Vision	Period of development	Comments	Website (accessed February 2020)	Academic review/ discussion papers
	Rest of world	Sustainable Sydney 2030	2006–08	The vision aims to make the city as green, global and connected as possible by 2030. Led by local government.	https://www.cityofsydney.nsw.gov.au/vision/sustainable-sydney-2030	Kornberger and Clegg, 2011; UN, 2012; Hu, 2015
		Sydney 2050	2019–ongoing	A new visionary plan for the city looking to 2050 is currently under development. Led by local government.	https://www.cityofsydney.nsw.gov.au/vision/planning-for-2050	Not applicable
		Johannesburg 2030	2002	Aimed to develop Johannesburg as a 'world-class African city'. Led by local government.	Not available	Robinson, 2008; Rogerson and Rogerson, 2015
		Johannesburg 2040	2011	A revised growth and development strategy that replaces the 2030 vision. Led by local government.	https://www.joburg.org.za/about_/Documents/joburg2040.pdf	Rampini and Vilela, 2014
		Johannesburg Spatial Development Framework	2016	The Spatial Development Framework 2040 (SDF) for Johannesburg is a metro-wide spatial policy document that identifies the main challenges and opportunities in the city, sets a spatial vision and outlines strategies to achieve that vision.	https://unhabitat.org/spatial-development-framework-2040-city-of-johannesburg-metropolitan-municipality	Abrahams and Everatt, 2019

Appendix

Type of vision	World region	Vision	Period of development	Comments	Website (accessed February 2020)	Academic review/ discussion papers
		Nairobi Metro 2030	2011	The vision of Nairobi is to be 'a world-class African metropolis by 2030'. Led by local government.	https://www.namsip.go.ke/wp-content/uploads/2018/05/Metro2030_Strategy.pdf	UN, 2012; Myers, 2014; Watson, 2013; Smith, 2017
		Hong Kong 2030+	2016	A planning vision and strategy looking beyond 2030 and building on the former Hong Kong 2030 vision. Led by local government.	https://www.hk2030plus.hk/	Teriman et al, 2009
Participatory and foresight-based	UK	Newcastle 2065	2016–or going	Newcastle City Futures (NCF) was established in 2014 by Newcastle University as a collaborative platform to bring together R&D potential with long-term policy trends and business needs in the city. The vision for 2065 was part of this programme and the UK Future of Cities work. Led by the university with local government, business and the community.	http://www.newcastlecityfutures.org/	Vallance et al, 2019, 2020; Tewdwr-Jones et al, 2020

(continued)

Type of vision	World region	Vision	Period of development	Comments	Website (accessed February 2020)	Academic review/ discussion papers
		Reading 2050	2013–ongoing	A vision to develop a smart and sustainable Reading by 2050. The vision was part of the UK Future of Cities work. Led by the university with business.	www.reading2050.co.uk	Dixon and Cohen, 2015; Dixon and Montgomery, 2015; Dixon et al, 2018a
	Rest of world	Gothenburg 2050	2002–05	This work was led by Chalmers University and used backcasting techniques to develop a vision with city stakeholders.	http://goteborg2050.nu/	Ramnero, 2005
		Queensland City Futures	2013	This work focused on four urban areas in Queensland (Maroochy, Logan, Gold Coast and Brisbane). Led by local government with input from futures specialists.	https://workingplanet.com.au/ portfolio-item/maroochydore-2025-sunshine-coast-vision-documentary-video-print-project/ https://www.yumpu.com/en/ document/view/4622686/logan-2026-city-directions-framework-logan-city-council https://www.brisbane.qld.gov. au/planning-and-building/ planning-guidelines-and-tools/ neighbourhood-planning-and-urban-renewal/neighbourhood-planning-and-urban-renewal-process/ brisbane-cityshape-2026	Russo, 2015, 2016a, 2016b

Notes

Chapter 1
1. More recently, the European Commission has proposed what it claims is a more accurate and consistent definition of urban settlement, using a new tool – the population grid – to help define spatial boundaries and densities. Based on this definition, 75 per cent of the world's population already lived in cities in 2015 (Dijkstra et al, 2019).
2. China has plans to build 400 new cities by 2020 (Bullivant, 2012).
3. Peter Drucker is credited with this quote.

Chapter 3
1. In Saudi Arabia, there are plans to build a new $500 billion futuristic city in the desert, called Neom, which literally means 'new future' (the first three letters are from the Ancient Greek prefix *neo-*, meaning 'new', and the fourth letter is from the abbreviation of *mustaqbal*, the Arabic word for 'future').

Chapter 5
1. This use of the term is different from the term 'urban futures' that we defined in Chapter 1 of this book. For us, 'urban futures' means: a term used to imagine what cities and urban areas will be like in the long term, how they will operate, what infrastructure and governance systems will underpin and coordinate them and how they are best shaped and influenced by their primary stakeholders (civil society, governments, businesses, investors, academia and others). Urban futures thinking should be analytical, investigative, diagnostic and participatory in its ambition by exploring the future through city foresight techniques, including city visioning.

Chapter 6
1. See https://climateemergencydeclaration.org/ and https://www.climateemergency.uk/blog/list-of-councils/

Chapter 7
1. www.readingmuseum.org.uk/get-involved/projects-consultation/where-s-reading-heading/
2. www.newcastlecityfutures.org/

Chapter 8
1. Perhaps even William Morgan's first large-scale accurate map of London in 1682, after the Great Fire, also contained elements of a reimagined or 'sanitised' London.
2. We have excluded any references to smart city visions or other types of 'specialist vision' that do not rely on some degree of consultation and participation in their development. Our list is not exhaustive, but we have attempted to highlight a range of the more important and well-documented city visions from around the world.

[3] This is now 'net-zero carbon' in the light of Reading Borough Council's Climate Emergency Declaration and a target of net-zero carbon emissions by 2030.

Chapter 11

[1] At the time of writing there is a great deal of optimism that a number of effective vaccines will be able to be rolled out during 2021.

References

Abbott, J., and DeMarco, C. (2016) 'Regional strategic planning and managing uncertainty in Greater Vancouver', in Albrechts, L., Balducci, A., and Hillier, J. (eds) *Situated Practices of Strategic Planning: An international perspective*, 1st edition, New York, NY and Abingdon: Routledge.

Abercrombie, P. (1945) *Greater London Plan 1944*, London: HMSO.

Abercrombie, P. and Forshaw, J. (1943) *County of London Plan prepared for the LCC, 1943*, London: Macmillan.

Abrahams, C., and Everatt, D. (2019) 'City profile: Johannesburg, South Africa', *Environment and Urbanization ASIA*, https://doi.org/10.1177/0975425319859123.

Ache, P. (2011) 'Creating futures that would otherwise not be' – reflections on the Greater Helsinki Vision process and the making of metropolitan regions', *Progress in Planning*, 75(4): 155–92.

Acuto, M., Parnell, S., Seto, K., and Contestabile, M. (2018) *Science and the Future of Cities*, Report of the International Expert Panel on Science and the Future of Cities, London and Melbourne, https://www.researchgate.net/publication/329717388_Science_and_the_Future_of_Cities (accessed April 2020).

Adam, B., and Groves, C. (2007) *Future Matters: Action, knowledge, ethics*, Leiden: Brill.

Agnew, J. (1999) 'Mapping political power beyond state boundaries: territory, identity and movement in world politics,' *Millennium*, 28: 499–521.

Agyeman, J. (2020) 'Urban planning as a tool of white supremacy – the other lesson from Minneapolis', *The Conversation*, https://theconversation.com/urban-planning-as-a-tool-of-white-supremacy-the-other-lesson-from-minneapolis-142249 (accessed 27 July 2020).

Alaily-Mattar, N., Dreher, J., and Thierstein, A. (2018) 'Respositioning cities through stararchitecture: how does it work?', *Journal of Urban Design*, 23(2): 169–92.

Albino, V., Berardi, U., and Dangelico, D. (2015) 'Smart cities: definitions, dimensions, performance and initiative', *Journal of Urban Technology*, 22: 1–19.

Albrechts, L. (2010) 'More of the same is not enough! How could strategic spatial planning be instrumental in dealing with the challenges ahead?', *Environment and Planning B*, 37: 1115–27.

Allmendinger, P., and Haughton, G. (2010) 'Spatial planning, devolution and new planning spaces', *Environment and Planning C*, 28(5): 803–18.

Allmendinger, P., and Haughton, G. (2012) 'Post-political spatial planning in England: a crisis of consensus', *Transactions of the Institute of British Geographers*, 37: 89–103.

Amin, A., and Thrift, N. (1995) 'Globalization, institutional "thickness" and the local economy', in Healey, P., Cameron, S., Davoudi, S., and Graham, S. (eds) *Managing Cities: The new urban context*, pp 91–108, Chichester: Wiley.

Amin, A., and Thrift, N. (2002) *Cities: Reimagining the urban*, Cambridge and Oxford: Polity Press.

Andersson, J. (2012) 'The great future debate and the struggle for the world', *American Historical Review*, 117 (5): 1411–30.

Angelidou, M. (2015) 'Smart cities: a conjuncture of four forces', *Cities*, 47: 95–106.

Arcadis (2018) *Citizen Centric Cities: The Sustainable Cities Index 2018*, Amsterdam: Arcadis.

Arnkil, R., Jarvesivu, A., Koski, P., and Piirainen, T. (2011) *Exploring Quadruple Helix: Outlining user-oriented innovation models*, Working Paper, Tampere: University of Tampere.

Arnstein, R.S. (1969) 'A ladder of citizen participation', *Journal of the American Planning Association*, 35(4): 216–24.

Athey, G., Glossop, C., Harrison, B., Nathan, M., and Webber, C. (2007) *Innovation and the City: How innovation has developed in five city regions*, London: NESTA.

Attenborough, D. (2020) *A Life on Our Planet: My witness statement and a vision for the future*, London: Penguin.

Bacon, F. (1627) *New Atlantis*, London: Watchmaker Publishing.

Bai, X. (2000) 'A comparative study of urban environment in East Asia: stage model of urban environment evolution', *International Review for Environment Strategies*, 1(1): 135–58.

Bai, X., McAllister, R., Beaty, R., and Taylor, B. (2010a) 'Urban policy and governance in a global environment: complex systems, scale mismatches and public participation', *Current Opinion in Environmental Sustainability*, 2: 1–7.

Bai, X., Roberts, B., and Chen, J. (2010b) 'Urban sustainability experiments in Asia: patterns and pathways', *Environmental Science and Policy*, 13: 312–25.

References

Baker, P.C. (2020) '"We can't go back to normal": how will coronavirus change the world?', *The Guardian*, 31 March, https://www.theguardian.com/world/2020/mar/31/how-will-the-world-emerge-from-the-coronavirus-crisis (accessed 27 July 2020).

Barbrook, R. (2007) *Imaginary Futures: From thinking machines to the global village*, London: Pluto Press.

Barnosky, A.D., Hadly, E.A., Bascompte, J., Berlow, E.L., Brown, J.H., Fortelius, M., Getz, W.M., Harte, J., Hastings, A., Marquet, P.A., Martinez, N.D., Mooers, A., Roopnarine, P., Vermeij, G., Williams, J.W., Gillespie, R., Kitzes, J., Marshall, C., Matzke, N., Mindell, D.P., Revilla, E., and Smith, A.B. (2012) 'Approaching a state shift in the Earth's biosphere', *Nature*, 486: 52–8.

Batty, M. (2013) *The New Science of Cities*, Cambridge, MA: MIT Press.

Batty, M. (2018) *Inventing Future Cities*, Cambridge, MA: MIT Press.

Batty, M. (2020a) 'The coronavirus crisis: what will the post-pandemic city look like?', *EPB: Urban Analytics and City Science*, 47(4): 547–52.

Batty, M. (2020b) 'Unpredictability', *EPB: Urban Analytics and City Science*, 47(5): 739–44.

Bazaz, A., Bertoldi, P., Cartwright, A., de Coninck, H., and Engelbrecht, F. (2018) *Summary for Urban Policymakers: What the IPCC special report on global warming of 1.5°C means for cities*, Geneva: Intergovernmental Panel on Climate Change.

Beauregard, R. (2015) *Planning Matters: Acting with things*, Chicago, IL: University of Chicago Press.

Beauregard, R. (2018) *Cities in the Urban Age: A dissent*, Chicago, IL: University of Chicago Press.

Beckert, J. (2013) 'Imagined futures: fictional expectations in the economy', *Theory and Society*, 42(3): 219–40.

Beckert, J. (2016) *Imagined Futures: Fictional expectations and capitalist dynamics*, Cambridge, MA: Harvard University Press.

Beer, A., and Clower, T. (2014) 'Mobilizing leadership in cities and regions', *Regional Studies, Regional Science*, 1(1): 5–20.

Beer, A., Ayres, S., Clower, T., Faller, F., Sancino, A., and Sotarauta, M. (2019) 'Place leadership and regional economic development: a framework for cross-regional analysis', *Regional Studies*, 53(2): 171–82.

Belfast City Council (2017) *Your Future City – The Belfast Agenda*, Belfast: Belfast City Council.

Belloso, J.C. (2011) 'The city branding of Barcelona: a success story', in Binnie, K. (ed) *City Branding: Theory and cases*, pp 118–23, New York, NY: Springer.

Bertolin, J. (2014) 'The essence of co-innovation generation: living labs in university environment', *Helice*, 3(4), https://www.triplehelixassociation.org/helice/volume-3-2014/helice-issue-4/essence-co-innovation-generation-living-labs-university-environment (accessed April 2020).

Bevilacqua, C., Ou, Y., Pizzimenti, P., and Minervino, G. (2020) 'New public institutional forms and social innovation in urban governance: insights from the "Mayor's Office of New Urban Mechanics" (MONUM) in Boston', *Sustainability*, 12(1): 23.

Bibri, S. (2018) 'Backcasting in futures studies: a synthesized scholarly and planning approach to strategic smart sustainable city development', *European Journal of Futures Research*, 6(13): 1–27.

Bibri, S. (2019) 'Generating a vision for smart sustainable cities of the future: a scholarly backcasting approach', *European Journal of Futures Research*, 7(5): 1–20.

Bibri, S., and Krogstie, J. (2017) 'Smart sustainable cities of the future: an extensive interdisciplinary literature review', *Sustainable Cities and Society*, 31: 183–212.

Bina, O., Inch, A., and Pereira, L. (2020) 'Beyond techno-utopia and its discontents: on the role of utopianism and speculative fiction in shaping alternatives to the smart city imaginary', *Futures*, 115: 1–14.

BIS (Department for Business Innovation and Skills) (2015) *Mapping Local Comparative Advantages in Innovation: Framework and indicators: Appendices*, London: BIS.

Booth, P. (2009) 'Planning and the culture of governance: local institutions and reform in France', *European Planning Studies*, 17(5): 677–95.

Bradbury, R. (1999) *Fahrenheit 451*, London: Harper Collins.

Bramah, M. (2019) 'Re-municipalisation of energy and how it can help to tackle climate change', *Town & Country Planning*, 88(9): 346–50.

Brandsen, T., and Honingh, M. (2018) 'Definitions of co-production and co-creation', in Brandsen, T., Steen, T., and Verschuere, B. (eds) *Co-Production and Co-Creation Engaging Citizens in Public Services*, New York, NY and Abingdon: Routledge.

Brenner, N. (2004) *New State Spaces: Urban governance and the rescaling of statehood*, Oxford: Oxford University Press.

Brenner, N., and Schmid, C. (2014) '"The urban age" in question', *International Journal of Urban and Regional Research*, 38(3): 731–55.

Brenner, N., and Schmid, C. (2015) 'Towards a new epistemology of the urban?', *City*, 19: 2–3.

Bristol One City/Bristol City Council (2020) *One City Plan 2020*, Bristol: Bristol City Council, https://www.bristolonecity.com/about-the-one-city-plan/ (accessed April 2020).

Brook, D. (2013) *A History of Future Cities*, London: W.W. Norton and Company.

Brown, R., Cox, G., and Owens, M. (2012) 'Bid, delivery, legacy – creating the governance architecture of the London 2012 Olympic and Paralympic Games legacy', *Australian Planner*, 49(3): 226–38.

Brundtland Commission (1987) *Our Common Future: Report of the 1987 World Commission on Environment and Development*, Oxford: Oxford University Press.

Buck, N., Gordon, I., Harding, A., and Turok, I. (eds) (2005) *Changing Cities: Rethinking urban competitiveness, cohesion and governance*, Basingstoke: Palgrave Macmillan.

Bulkeley, H., Castan Broto, V., Hodson, M., and Marvin, S. (eds) (2011) *Cities and Low Carbon Transitions*, Abingdon: Routledge.

Bullivant, L. (2012) *Masterplanning Futures*, Abingdon: Routledge.

Burgess, E.W. (1925) 'The growth of the city: an introduction to a research project', in Park, R., and Burgess, E.W. (eds) *The City: Suggestions for investigation of human behaviour in the urban environment*, pp 47–62, Chicago, IL: University of Chicago Press.

Butt, A. (2018) 'Endless forms, vistas and hues: why architects should read science fiction film', *Architectural Research Quarterly*, 22(2): 151–60.

C40 Cities (2019) *The Future of Urban Consumption in a 1.5^0 World*, London: C40 Cites and Arup, https://c40-production-images.s3.amazonaws.com/other_uploads/images/2236_WITH_Forewords_-_Main_report__20190612.original.pdf?1560421525) (accessed April 2020).

Cabet, E. (1848) *Voyage en Icarie*, Paris: Au Bureau du Populaire.

Caen, H. and Kingman, D. (1967) *San Francisco, City on Golden Hills*, New York, NY: Doubleday.

Callahan, G., and Ikeda, S. (2014) 'Jane Jacobs' critique of rationalism in urban planning', *Cosmos + Taxis*, 1(3): 10–19.

Candy, S., Larsen, K., Tworney, P., McGrail, S., and Ryan, C. (2017) *Pathways 2040: Results from Visions and Pathways 2040: Scenarios and pathways to low carbon living*, Melbourne: University of Melbourne.

Cant, C. (2020) *Riding for Deliveroo: Resistance in the new economy*, Cambridge: Polity Press.

Caprotti, F. (2018) 'Future cities: moving from technical to human needs', *Palgrave Communications*, 4(5), https://www.nature.com/articles/s41599-018-0089-5) (accessed April 2020).

Caprotti, F. (2019) 'From Shannon to Shenzen and back: sustainable urbanism and inter-city partnerships in China and Europe', in Zhang, Z. (ed) *Remaking Sustainable Urbanism: Space, scale and governance in the new urban era*, Singapore: Palgrave Macmillan.

Caprotti, F., and Cowley, R. (2017) 'Interrogating urban experiments', *Urban Geography*, 38(9): 1441–50.

Caprotti, F., and Cowley, R. (2019) 'Varieties of smart urbanism in the UK: discursive logics, the state and local urban context', *Transactions of the Institute of British Geographers*, 44: 587–601.

Carayannis, E., and Campbell, D. (2010) 'Triple helix, quadruple helix and quintuple helix and how do knowledge, innovation and the environment relate to each other?', *International Journal of Social Ecology and Sustainable Development*, 1(1): 41–69.

Carmichael, J. (2016) 'We're building urban dystopias on purpose', *Inverse*, 20 July, https://www.inverse.com/article/18488-science-fiction-future-city-planning-dubai-skyscrapers-dystopia (accessed April 2020).

Carmon, N., and Fainstein, S. (eds) (2013) *Policy, Planning, and People: Promoting Justice in Urban Development*, Philadelphia, PA: University of Pennsylvania Press.

Carrington, D. (2020) 'Take your breath away: early evidence links air pollution to Covid-19 risk', *The Guardian*, 4 May, pp 14–15.

Carson, R. (1962) *Silent Spring*, Boston, MA: Houghton Miffin.

Castan Broto, V., Trencher, G., and Iwaszuk, E. (2019) 'Transformative capacity and local action for sustainability', *Ambio*, 48: 449–62.

Centre for Cities (2015) *The Changing Geography of the UK Economy: A review of the primary urban area definition*, London: Centre for Cities, https://www.centreforcities.org/wp-content/uploads/2015/12/15-12-17-The-changing-geography-of-the-uk-economy.pdf (accessed April 2020).

Centre for Cities (2019) 'City definition', website article, https://www.centreforcities.org/city-by-city/puas/ (accessed April 2020).

Centre for Cities (2020) 'Coronavirus', webpage, https://www.centreforcities.org/coronavirus/ (accessed May 2020).

Champion, T. (2014) *People in Cities: The numbers*, Future of Cities Working Paper, London: Government Office for Science, https://www.gov.uk/government/publications/future-cities-people-in-cities-the-numbers (accessed April 2020).

Christaller, W. (1933) *Die zentralen Orte in Süddeutschland*, Jena: Gustav Fischer.

Cities Alliance (2016) *Future Cities Africa: Feasibility study*, Brussels: Cities Alliance, https://www.citiesalliance.org/future-cities-africa-outputs (accessed April 2020).

Cities Alliance (2017) *Cities Development Strategies 2.0: Cities growing with vision*, Brussels: Cities Alliance, https://www.citiesalliance.org/sites/default/files/CDS_Toolkit_Web.pdf (accessed April 2020).

City of Johannesburg (2011) *A Promising Future: Joburg 2040*, Johannesburg: City of Johannesburg, https://www.joburg.org.za/about_/Documents/joburg2040.pdf (accessed April 2020).

City of Johannesburg (2016) *Spatial Development Framework 2040*, Johannesburg: City of Johannesburg, https://unhabitat.org/spatial-development-framework-2040-city-of-johannesburg-metropolitan-municipality (accessed July 2020).

City of Sydney (2019) *Sustainable Sydney 2030 Snapshot*, Sydney: Sydney City Council, https://www.cityofsydney.nsw.gov.au/__data/assets/pdf_file/0010/199495/2030-snapshot-booklet_FA1.1.pdf (accessed April 2020).

Claeys, G. (ed) (2010) *The Cambridge Companion to Utopian Literature*, Cambridge: Cambridge University Press.

Claeys, G. (2011) *Searching for Utopia: The history of an idea*, London: Thames and Hudson.

Claeys, G. (2017) *Dystopia: A natural history*, Oxford: Oxford University Press.

Clark, G. (2016) *Global Cities*, Washington, DC: Brookings Institution Press.

Clark, G., Moonen, T., and Peek, G. (2016) *Building the Innovation Economy: City-level strategies for planning, placemaking and promotion*, London: Urban Land Institute.

Clarke, I.F. (1992) 'The city: heaven-on-earth or the hell-to-come?', *Futures*, 24(7): 701–10.

Coenen, L., Benneworth, P., and Truffer, B. (2011) 'Towards a spatial perspective on sustainability transitions', paper presented at the Dynamics of Institutions & Markets in Europe (DIME) Final Conference, Maastricht, the Netherlands, 6–8 April.

Colding, J., Colding, M., and Barthel, S. (2018) 'The smart city model: a new panacea for urban sustainability or unmanageable complexity?', *Environment and Planning B: Urban Analytics and City Science*, 47(1): 179–87.

Collie, N. (2011) 'Cities of the imagination: science fiction, urban space, and community engagement in urban planning', *Futures*, 43: 424–31.

Colomb, C. (2013) *Staging the New Berlin: Place marketing and the politics of urban reinventon post-1989*, London: Routledge.

Committee on Climate Change (2019) *Net Zero: The UK's contribution to stopping global warming*, London: Committee on Climate Change, https://www.theccc.org.uk/publication/net-zero-the-uks-contribution-to-stopping-global-warming/ (accessed April 2020).

Committee on Climate Change (2020) 'Take urgent action on six key principles for a resilient recovery', 6 May, https://www.theccc.org.uk/2020/05/06/take-urgent-action-on-six-key-principles-for-a-resilient-recovery/ (accessed May 2020).

Concilio, G., Li, C., Rausell, P., and Tosoni, I. (2019) 'Cities as enablers of innovation', in Concilio, G., and Tosoni, I. (eds) *Innovation Capacity and the City: The enabling role of design*, pp 43–60, Cham, Switzerland: Springer Open.

Corporate Policy Unit (2009) *Imagine Durban: The power of imagination: 50 lessons (2007–2009)*, Durban: CPU.

Cote-Roy, L., and Moser, S. (2019) 'Does Africa not deserve shiny new cities? The power of seductive rhetoric around new cities in Africa', *Urban Studies*, 56(12): 2391–407.

Cottineau, C., Hatna, E., Arcaute, E., and Batty, M. (2017) 'Diverse cities or the systematic paradox of urban scaling laws', *Computers, Environment and Urban Systems*, 63: 80–94.

Cowie, P., Goddard, J., and Tewdwr-Jones, M. (2016) *The Role of Universities in City Foresight*, London: Government Office for Science.

Crawford, R. (2016) *What Can Complexity Theory Tell Us about Urban Planning? Research Note 2016/2*, Wellington, New Zealand: New Zealand Productivity Commission, https://www.productivity.govt.nz/working-paper/what-can-complexity-theory-tell-us-about-urban-planning (accessed April 2020).

Crowley, L. (2011) *Streets Ahead: What makes a city innovative?*, Lancaster: Lancaster University and The Work Foundation.

Crump, L. (2020) 'Meanwhile uses in the city – should this be the new normal?', LSE Blog, https://blogs.lse.ac.uk/progressingplanning/2020/07/06/meanwhile-uses-in-the-city-should-this-be-the-new-normal/ (accessed 27 July 2020).

Crutzen P. (2002) 'The "Anthropocene"', *Journal de Physique IV France*, 12(10): 11–15.

Cugurullo, F. (2018) 'Exposing smart cities and eco-cities: Frankenstein urbanism and the sustainability challenges of the experimental city', *Environment and Planning A: Economy and Space*, 50(1): 73–92.

CUT (Coalition for Urban Transitions) (2019) *Climate Emergency: Urban opportunity*, London: Coalition for Urban Transitions, https://www.globalcovenantofmayors.org/press/climate-emergency-urban-opportunity-report/ (accessed April 2020).

Daffara, P. (2004) 'Sustainable urban futures', in Inayatullah, S. (ed) *The Causal Layered Analysis (CLA) Reader: Theory and case studies of an integrative and transformative methodology*, pp 424–38, Taipei: Tamking University Press.

Daffara, P. (2006) 'Global and local (glo-cal) visions of human habitation for 2100 and their defining cultural paradigms', PhD thesis, University of the Sunshine Coast, Queensland, Australia.

Das, D. (2020) 'In pursuit of being smart? A critical analysis of India's smart cities endeavour', *Urban Geography*, 41(1): 55–78.

Davoudi, S. (2001) 'Planning and the twin discourses of sustainability', in Layard, A., Batty, S., and Davoudi, S. (eds) *Planning for a Sustainable Future*, pp 81–94, London: Spon.

Davoudi, S. (2018) 'Imagination and spatial imaginaries: a conceptual framework', *Town Planning Review*, 89(2): 97–107.

Dawson, R., Wyckmans, A., Heidrich, O., Kohler, J., Dobson, S., and Feliu, E. (2014) *Understanding Cities: Advances in Integrated Assessment of Urban Sustainability*, Final Report of COST Action TU0902, Newcastle: Centre for Earth Systems Engineering Research, Newcastle University, https://pure.qub.ac.uk/portal/files/15624481/Final_All_CoverLo.pdf (accessed April 2020).

de Jong, M., Joss, S., Daan, S., Changjie Z., and Weijnen M. (2015) 'Sustainable–smart–resilient–low carbon–eco–knowledge cities; making sense of a multitude of concepts promoting sustainable urbanization', *Journal of Cleaner Production*, 109: 25–38.

De Jouvenel, B. (1964) *The Art of Conjecture: Futurible*, Monaco: Editions du Rocher.

De Laurnetis, C., Eames, M., Hunt, M., and Lannon, S. (2018) 'City-regional futures in context: insights from the Retrofit 2050 Project', in Eames, M., Dixon, T., Hunt, M., and Lannon, S. (eds) *Retrofitting Cities for Tomorrow's World*, pp 207–26, Oxford: Wiley-Blackwell.

De Satgi, R., and Watson, V. (2018) *Urban Planning in the Global South: Conflicting rationalities in contested urban space*, Cham, Switzerland: Springer.

DeLanda, M. (2006) *A New Philosophy of Society: Assemblage theory and social complexity*, New York, NY: Continuum.

Deleuze, G., and Guattari, F. (1987) *A Thousand Plateaus: Capitalism & schizophrenia*, trans. Brian Massumi, Minneapolis, MN: University of Minnesota Press.

Dijkstra, L., Poelman, H., and Veneri, P. (2019) *The EU-OECD Definition of a Functional Urban Area*, Paris: OECD, https://www.oecd.org/cfe/regional-policy/THE%20EU-OECD%20DEFINITION%20OF%20A%20FUNCTIONAL%20URBAN%20AREA.pdf (accessed April 2020).

Directorate General for Internal Policies (2014) *Mapping Smart Cities in the EU*, Brussels: European Parliament.

Dixon, T. (2011) *Low Carbon Scenarios, Roadmaps, Transitions and Pathways: An overview and discussion*, project report, EPSRC Retrofit 2050, Cardiff: Cardiff University.

Dixon, T. (2018a) '"City-wide" or "city-blind?" An analysis of retrofit practices in the UK commercial property sector', in Eames, M., Dixon, T., Hunt, M., and Lannon, S. (eds) *Retrofitting Cities for Tomorrow's World*, pp 33–52, Oxford: Wiley-Blackwell.

Dixon, T. (2018b) 'Smart and sustainable? The future of "future cities"', in Dixon, T., Connaughton, J., and Green, S. (eds) *Sustainable Futures in the Built Environment to 2050: A foresight approach to construction and development*, pp 94–116, Oxford: Wiley-Blackwell.

Dixon, T. (2020) *What Impacts are Emerging from COVID-19 for Urban Futures?*, Oxford COVID-19 Evidence Service, Oxford: CEBM, University of Oxford, https://www.cebm.net/covid-19/what-impacts-are-emerging-from-covid-19-for-urban-futures/ (accessed July 2020).

Dixon, T., and Cohen, K. (2015) 'Towards a smart and sustainable Reading 2050 vision', *Town and Country Planning*, January: 20–7.

Dixon, T., and Montgomery, J. (2015) *Towards a Smart & Sustainable Reading UK 2050: Full report*, project report, Reading: Barton Willmore, www.reading.ac.uk (accessed April 2020).

Dixon, T., and Farrelly, L. (2019) 'Urban rooms: where people get to design their city's future', *The Conversation*, online version, 18 January, http://theconversation.com/urban-rooms-where-people-get-to-design-their-citys-future-109077 (accessed April 2020).

Dixon, T., Thompson, B., McAllister, P., Marston, A., and Snow, J. (2005) *Real Estate & the New Economy: The impact of information and communications technology*, Hoboken, NJ: John Wiley & Sons.

Dixon, T., Eames, M., Hunt, M., and Lannon, S. (eds) (2014a) *Urban Retrofitting for Sustainability: Mapping the transition to 2050*, London: Routledge.

Dixon, T., Eames, M., Britnell, J., Watson, G. B., and Hunt, M. (2014b) 'Urban retrofitting: identifying disruptive and sustaining technologies using performative and foresight techniques', *Technological Forecasting & Social Change*, 89: 131–44.

Dixon, T., Barlow, J., Grimmond, S., and Blower, J. (2015) *Smart and Sustainable: Using big data to improve people's lives in cities*, discussion paper, Reading: University of Reading, https://www.reading.ac.uk/web/files/cme/cme-Dixon_SCME_big_data_paper_AS_v_11_WEB_(1).pdf (accessed April 2020).

Dixon, T., Van de Wetering, J., Sexton, M., Lu, S.-L., Williams, D., Ulutas Duman, D., and Chen, X. (2017) *Smart Cities, Big Data and The Built Environment: What's required?*, research report series, project report, London: RICS.

Dixon, T., Montgomery, J., Horton-Baker, N., and Farrelly, L. (2018a) 'Using urban foresight techniques in city visioning: lessons from the Reading 2050 vision', *Local Economy*, 33(8): 777–99.

Dixon, T., Connaughton, J., and Green, S. (eds) (2018b) *Sustainable Futures in the Built Environment to 2050: A foresight approach to construction and development*, Oxford: Wiley Blackwell.

Dobraszczyk, P. (2019) *Future Cities: Architecture and the imagination*, London: Reaktion Books.

Dodds. M. (ed) (2014) *City of God: Vol 1 Aurelius Augustine*, Project Gutenburg, www.gutenberg.org

Doucet, B. (ed) (2017) *Why Detroit Matters*, Bristol: Policy Press.

Drucker, J., Kayanan, C., and Renski, H. (2019) *Innovation Districts as a Strategy for Urban Economic Development: A comparison of four cases*, Center for Economic Development Technical Report, Amherst, MA: University of Massachusetts Amherst.

Dunn, N., and Cureton, P. (2020) *Future Cities: A visual history and critical guide to how we will live next*, London: Bloomsbury.

Dunn, N., Cureton, P., and Pollastri, S. (2014) *A Visual History of the Future*, London: Government Office for Science (GOfS) Foresight for Cities.

Eames, M. (2011) *Developing Urban Retrofit Scenarios: An outline framework for scenario foresight and appraisal*, Retrofit 2050 Working Paper WP 2011/4, Cardiff: University of Cardiff, www.retrofit2050.co.uk (accessed April 2020).

Eames, M., and Dixon, T. (2012) *Visioning Retrofit Futures*, EPSRC Retrofit 2050 Working Paper 2012/1, Cardiff: University of Cardiff, www.retrofit2050.co.uk (accessed April 2020).

Eames, M., Dixon, T., May, T., and Hunt, M. (2013) 'City futures: exploring urban retrofit and sustainable transitions', *Building Research and Information*, 41(5): 504–16.

Eames, M., Dixon, T., and Lannon, S. (2014a) *Retrofit 2050: Critical challenges for urban transitions: Technical Report*, Cardiff: Cardiff University, www.retrofit2050.org.uk (accessed April 2020).

Eames, M.D., Laurentis, C., and Hunt, M. (2014b) *Cardiff 2050: City regional scenarios for urban sustainability*, project report, Cardiff: Cardiff University, www.retrofit2050.org.uk (accessed April 2020).

Eames, M., Dixon, T., Hunt, M., and Lannon, S. (eds) (2018) *Retrofitting Cities for Tomorrow's World*, Oxford: Wiley-Blackwell.

Eaton, R. (2001) *Ideal Cities: Utopianism and the (un) built environment*, London: Thames and Hudson.

Edelstein, S. (2019) 'Uber withdraws from Barcelona following violent pushbacks from taxi drivers', *The Drive*, 31 January, thedrive.com/news/26270/uber-withdraws-from-Barcelona-following-violent-pushback-from-taxi-drivers (accessed October 2020).

Edinburgh City Council (2017) *Edinburgh 2050 City Vision One Year On*, Edinburgh: Edinburgh City Council.

Ek, R., and Santamaria, F. (2009) 'Meanings for spatial/geographical visions', in Farinos J., Romero J., and Salom J. (eds) *Cohesión e Inteligencia Territorial: Dinámicas y procesos para una mejor planificación y toma de decisions*, pp 89–103, València: Instituto Interuniversitario de desarrollo local, Universitat de Vallòncia.

Elkington, J. (1997) *Cannibals with Forks: The triple bottom line of 21st century business*, London: Capstone.

Elmqvist, T., Bai, X., Frantzeskaki, N., Griffith, C., Maddox, D., McPhearson, T., Parnell, S., and Romero-Lankao, P. (eds) (2018) *Urban Planet: Knowledge towards sustainable cities*, 1st edition, Cambridge: Cambridge University Press.

Energy Saving Trust (2020) 'Low emission and clean air zones: all you need to know', blog, 27 October, https://energysavingtrust.org.uk/low-emission-and-clean-air-zones-all-you-need-to-know/ (accessed November 2020).

Engelbert, J., van Zoonen, L., and Hirzalla, F. (2019) 'Excluding citizens from the European smart city: the discourse practices of pursuing and granting smartness', *Technological Forecasting and Social Change*, 142: 347–53.

ENoLL (2016) 'Introducing ENoLL and its living lab community', web article, https://ec.europa.eu/digital-single-market/en/news/introducing-enoll-and-its-living-lab-community (accessed April 2020).

ESPON (2018) *Possible European Territorial Futures: Summary report*, Luxembourg: ESPON, https://www.espon.eu/territorial-futures (accessed April 2020).

Etherington, D., and Jones, M. (2018) 'Restating the post-political: depoliticization, social inequalities, and city growth', *Environment and Planning A*, 50(1): 51–72.

EU Parliament Directorate General for Internal Policies (2014) *Mapping Smart Cities in the EU*, Brussels: European Union.

European Commission (1990) *Green Paper on the Urban Environment*, Brussels: European Commission.

European Commission (2001) *Foresight for Regional Development Network: A practical guide to regional foresight*, Brussels: European Commission.

European Commission (2019) *The Future of Cities: Opportunities, challenges and the way forward*, Brussels: European Commission, https://ec.europa.eu/jrc/en/publication/eur-scientific-and-technical-research-reports/future-cities (accessed April 2020).

European Union (2011) *An Initial Assessment of Territorial Forward Planning/Foresight Projects in the European Union*, Brussels: European Union.

European Union (2016) *Urban Europe: Statistics on cities, towns and suburbs*, Brussels: European Union, https://ec.europa.eu/eurostat/statistics-explained/index.php/Urban_Europe_%E2%80%94_statistics_on_cities,_towns_and_suburbs (accessed April 2020).

Evans, J., Karvonen, A., and Raven, R. (eds) (2016) *The Experimental City*, Abingdon and New York, NY: Routledge.

Evans, J., Karvonen, A., Luque-Ayala, A., Martin, C., McCormick, K., Raven, R., and Palgan, Y. (2019) 'Smart and sustainable cities? Pipedreams, practicalities and possibilities', *Local Environment*, 24(7): 557–64.

Executive Office of the President (2016) *Report to the President: Technology and the future of cities*, Washington, DC: Executive Office of the President.

Eylers, E. (2015) 'Thomas More's utopia: amaurotum and the vision of a public life', paper presented at the RC21 International Conference on the Ideal City, Urbino, Italy, 27–29 August, https://www.rc21.org/en/wp-content/uploads/2014/12/B2_Eylers.pdf (accessed April 2020).

Farias, I. (2009) 'Introduction: decentring the object of urban studies', in Farías, I., and Bender, T. (eds) *Urban Assemblages: How actor-network theory changes urban studies*, pp 1–24, London and New York, NY: Routledge.

Farrell, T. (2014) *The Farrell Review of Architecture and the Built Environment*, London: Farrell Review, http://www.farrellreview.co.uk/ (accessed April 2020).

Firley, E., and Groen, K. (2013) *The Urban Masterplanning Handbook*, Hoboken, NJ: John Wiley and Sons.

Florida, R. (2002) *The Rise of the Creative Class: And how it's transforming work, leisure and everyday life*, New York, NY: Basic Books.

Florida, R., Adler, P., and Mellander, C. (2016) *The City as Innovation Machine*, Toronto: Martin Prosperity Institute, University of Toronto.

Florida, R., Glaeser, E., Sharif, M., Bedi, K., Campanella, T., Chee, C., Doctoroff, D., Katz, B., Katz, R., Kotkin, J., Muggah, R., and Sadik-Khan, J. (2020) 'How life in our cities will look after the coronavirus pandemic', *Foreign Policy*, 1 May, https://foreignpolicy.com/2020/05/01/future-of-cities-urban-life-after-coronavirus-pandemic/ (accessed May 2020).

Folke, C., Carpenter, S., Walker, B., Scheffer, M., Chapin, T., and Rockstrom, J. (2010) 'Resilience thinking: integrating resilience, adapatability and transformability', *Ecology and Society*, 15(4): 20, https://www.ecologyandsociety.org/vol15/iss4/art20/ (accessed April 2020).

Forster, E.M. (2011) *The Machine Stops*, London: Penguin.

Forum for the Future (2016) *Future Cities Dialogue*, London: Forum for the Future.

Frantzeskaki, N., and Tefrati, N. (2016) 'A transformative vision unlocks the innovative potential of Aberdeen city, UK', in Loorbach, D., Wittmayer, J., Shiroyma, H., Fujino, J., and Mizuguchi, S. (eds) *Governance of Urban Sustainability Transitions: European and Asian experiences*, pp 49–68, Cham, Switzerland: Springer.

Frantzeskaki, N., Holscher, K., Bach, M., and Avelino, F. (eds) (2018) *Co-creating Sustainable Urban Futures*, Cham, Switzerland: Springer.

Freestone, R. (2012) 'Futures thinking in planning education and research', *Journal for Education in the Built Environment*, 7(1): 8–38.

Friedmann, J. (1987) *Planning in the Public Domain*, Princeton, NJ: Princeton University Press.

Fu, Y., and Zhang, X. (2017a) 'Trajectory of urban sustainability concepts: a 35-year bibliometric analysis', *Cities*, 60: 113–23.

Fu, Y., and Zhang, X. (2017b) 'Planning for sustainable cities? A comparative content analysis of the master plans of eco, low-carbon and conventional new towns in China', *Habitat International*, 63: 55–66.

Future Cities Canada (2018) *Future Cities Canada Roadshow Report*, Toronto: Evergreen, https://futurecitiescanada.ca/resources/ (accessed April 2020).

Future Cities Catapult (2016) *Future of Planning – State of the Art Innovations in Digital Planning*, London: Future Cities Catapult.

GACGC (German Advisory Council on Global Change) (2016) *Humanity on the Move: Unlocking the transformative power of cities*, Berlin: Wissenschaftlicher Beirat der Bundesregierung Globale Umweltveränderungen (WBGU), https://www.wbgu.de/en/publications/publication/humanity-on-the-move-unlocking-the-transformative-power-of-cities (accessed April 2020).

Gaffikin, F., and Morrissey, M. (eds) (1999) *City Visions: Imagining place, enfranchising people*, London: Pluto Press.

Gaffikin, F., and Sterrett, K. (2006) 'New visions for old cities: the role of visioning in planning', *Planning Theory & Practice*, 7(2): 159–78.

Galvin, R. (2008) 'Science roadmaps', *Science*, 280(5365): 803.

Garcia, M. (2010) 'The breakdown of the Spanish urban growth model: social and territorial effects of the global crisis', *International Journal of Urban and Regional Research*, 34(4): 967–80.

Gebser, J. (1985) *The Ever-Present Origin*, authorised translation by Noel Barstad with Algis Mickunas, Athens, OH: Ohio University Press.

Geddes, P. (1915) *Cities in Evolution*, London: Williams and Norgate, https://archive.org/details/citiesinevolutio00geddu0ft/page/n9 (accessed April 2020).

Geels, F.W. (2002) *Understanding the Dynamics of Technological Transitions, A Co-evolutionary and Socio-technical Analysis*, PhD thesis, Enschede, NL: Twente University Press.

Geels, F. (2004) 'From sectoral systems of innovation to socio-technical systems: insights about dynamics and change from sociology and institutional theory', *Research Policy*, 33: 897–920.

Geels, F. (2010) 'Ontologies, socio-technical transitions (to sustainability), and the multi-level perspective', *Research Policy*, 39(4): 495–510.

Geels, F. (2011) 'The role of cities in technological transitions: analytical clarifications and historical examples', in Bulkeley, H., Castan Broto, V., and Hodson, M. (eds) *Cities and Low Carbon Transitions*, pp 13–28, Abingdon: Routledge.

Geels, F., Monaghan, A., Eames, M., and Steward, F. (2008) *The Feasibility of Systems Thinking in Sustainable Consumption and Production Policy: A report to the Department for Environment, Food and Rural Affairs*, London: Brunel University and DEFRA.

Geraghty, P. (2019) 'The NPPF 2019 – new urban agenda or a disappointing own goal?', *Town & Country Planning*, September: 354–66.

Gerlach, N., and Hamilton, S. (2003) 'Introduction: a history of social science fiction', *Science Fiction Studies*, 30(2): 161–73.

Gibney, J., Copeland, S., and Murie, A. (2009) 'Toward a "new" strategic leadership of place for the knowledge-based economy', *Leadership*, 5(1): 5–23.

Gidley, J. (2009) 'Another view of Integral Futures: de/reconstructing the IF brand', *Futures*, 42(2):125–33.

Gidley, J. (2017a) *The Future: A very short introduction*, Oxford: Oxford University Press.

Gidley, J. (2017b) 'Participatory futures methods: towards adaptability and resilience in climate-vulnerable communities', *Environmental Policy and Governance*, 19: 427–40.

Giradet, H. (2004) *Cities, People, Planet*, New York, NY: Academy Press.

Glaeser, E. (2011) *Triumph of the City*, London: Macmillan.

Gleeson, B. (2012) 'The urban age: paradox and prospect', *Urban Studies*, 49(5): 1–13.

Gleeson, B., and Low, N. (2007) '"Unfinished business": neoliberal planning reform in Australia', *Urban Policy and Research*, 18(1): 7–28.

Goddard, J., and Vallance, P. (2013) *The University and the City*, Abingdon: Routledge.

Goddard, J., and Kempton, L. (2016) *The Civic University: Universities in leadership and management of place*, Newcastle: Newcastle University/CURDS.

Goddard, J., and Tewdwr-Jones, M. (2016) *City Futures and the Civic University*, Newcastle: Newcastle University.

Goddard, J., Kempton, L., and Vallance, P. (2014) 'Universities as anchor institutions in cities in a turbulent environment: vulnerable institutions in vulnerable places', *Cambridge Journal of Regions, Economy and Society*, 7(2): 307–25.

Godin, B. (2008) *Innovation: The history of a category*, Montreal: INRS.

GOfS (Government Office for Science) (2016a) *Future of Cities: Foresight for cities*, London: GOfS, https://www.gov.uk/government/publications/future-of-cities-foresight-for-cities (accessed April 2020).

GOfS (2016b) *Future of Cities: an overview of the evidence*, London: GOfS, https://www.gov.uk/government/publications/future-of-cities-foresight-for-cities (accessed April 2020).

GOfS (2016c) *Future of Cities: Science of cities and future research priorities*, London: GOfS, https://www.gov.uk/government/publications/future-of-cities-foresight-for-cities (accessed April 2020).

GOfS (2017) *The Futures Toolkit: Tools for futures thinking and foresight across UK government*, London: GOfS, https://assets.publishing.service.gov.uk/government/uploads/system/uploads/attachment_data/file/674209/futures-toolkit-edition-1.pdf (accessed April 2020).

Gold, J.R. (2001) 'Under darkened skies: the city in science fiction film', *Geography*, 86(4): 337–45.

Gold, J.R., and Ward, S.V. (1997) 'Of plans and planners: documentary film and the challenge of the urban future, 1935–52', in Clarke, D.B. (ed) *The Cinematic City*, pp 59–82, London: Routledge.

Gonzalez, S. (2010) 'Bilbao and Barcelona "in motion": how urban regeneration "models" travel and mutate in the global flows of policy tourism', *Urban Studies*, 48(7): 1397–418.

Goodspeed, R. (2015) 'Smart cities: moving beyond urban cybernetics to tackle wicked problems', *Cambridge Journal of Regions, Economy and Society*, 8: 79–82.

Goodspeed, R. (2020) *Scenario Planning for Cities and Regions: Managing and envisioning uncertain futures*, New York, NY: Columbia University Press.

Graham, S. (2016a) *Vertical: The city from satellites to bunkers*, London: Verso.

Graham, S. (2016b) 'Vertical noir', *City*, 20(3): 389–406.

Graham, S., and Marvin, S. (2001) *Splintering Urbanism: Networked infrastructures, technological mobilities and the urban condition*, London: Routledge.

Granqvist, K., Sarjamo, S., and Mantysalo, R. (2019) 'Polycentricity as a spatial imaginary: the case of Helsinki City Plan', *European Planning Studies*, 27(4): 739–58.

Green, G., Haines, A., and Halebsky, S. (2000) *Building Our City Future: A guide to community visioning*, Madison, WI: University of Wisconsin.

Greenfield, A. (2013) *Against the Smart City (The City is Here for You to Use)*, New York, NY: Do Projects.

Gresle, A., Cigarini, A., de la Torre Villa, L., and Jimeno, I. (2019) 'An innovative online tool to self-evaluate and compare participatory research projects labelled as science shops or citizen science', in Yacoubi, E., Bagnoli, S., and Pacini, G. (eds) *Internet Science 6th International Conference, INSCI 2019, Perpignan, France, December 2–5, 2019, Proceedings*, Cham, Switzerland: Springer.

Griggs, S., Hall, S., Howarth, D., and Seigneuret, N. (2017) 'Characterizing and evaluating rival discourses of the "sustainable city": towards a politics of pragmatic adversarialism', *Political Geography*, 59(July): 36–46.

Grimm, N.B., Faeth, S., Golubiewski, N.E., Redman, C.L., Wu, J., Bai, X., and Briggs, J.M. (2008) 'Global change and the ecology of cities', *Science*, 317: 756–60.

Grin, J., Rotmans, J., and Schot, J. (2010) *Transitions to Sustainable Development: New directions in the study of long-term transformative change*, New York, NY: Routledge.

Guimarães, A. (2019) 'Community participation: how the population contributes to urban planning and cities' development in Brazil and Portugal', *Terra@Plural*, 13(3): 388–409.

Gunderson, L., and Holling, C. (2002) *Panarchy: Understanding transformations in human and natural systems*, Washington, DC: Island Press.

Gurran, N., and Phibbs, P. (2017) 'When tourists move in: how should urban planners respond to Airbnb?', *Journal of the American Planning Association*, 83(1): 80–92.

Gurran, N., Austin, P., and Whitehead, C. (2014) 'That sounds familiar! A decade of planning reform in Australia, England and New Zealand', *Australian Planner*, 51(2): 186–98.

Haarstad, H. (2017) 'Constructing the sustainable city: examining the role of sustainability in the "smart city" discourse', *Journal of Environmental Policy and Planning*, 19(4): 423–37.

Hall, P. (1998) *Cities in Civilisation*, London: Weidenfeld and Nicholson.

Hall, P. (2014) *Cities of Tomorrow*, London: Blackwell.

Hall, P., and Pain, K. (eds) (2006) *The Polycentric Metropolis: Learning from mega-city regions in Europe*, London: Earthscan.

Hall, P., and Tewdwr-Jones, M. (2020) *Urban and Regional Planning*, 6th edition, London: Routledge.

Hall, P., Thomas, R., Gracey, H., and Drewett, R. (1973) *The Containment of Urban England* (two volumes), London: Allen & Unwin.

Hambleton, R. (2014) *Leading the Inclusive City: Place-based innovation for a bounded planet*, Bristol: Policy Press.

Hambleton, R. (2018) 'Inclusive place-based leadership: lesson-drawing from urban governance innovations in Bristol, UK', *Metropolitics*, 9 October, https://uwe-repository.worktribe.com/output/859014 (accessed April 2020).

Hambleton, R. (2020) *Cities and Communities Beyond COVID-19: How local leadership can change our future for the better*, Bristol: Bristol University Press.

Hambleton, R., and Howard, J. (2013) 'Place-based leadership and public service innovation', *Local Government Studies*, 39(1): 47–70.

Harrison, J., Galland, D., and Tewdwr-Jones, M. (2020) 'Regional planning is dead: long live planning regional futures', *Regional Studies*, https://doi.org/10.1080/00343404.2020.1750580 (accessed April 2020).

Harvey, D. (1989) 'From managerialism to entrepreneurialism: the transformation in urban governance in late capitalism', *Geografiska Annaler. Series B, Human Geography*, 71(1): 3–17.

Hashim, A.R.B. (2019) *Planning Abu Dhabi: An urban history*, London: Routledge.

Hatch Regeneris (2019) *The Economic and Social Contribution of the University of Reading*, London: Hatch Regeneris.

Haughton, G., Allmendinger, P., Counsell, D., and Vigar, G. (2010) *The New Spatial Planning: Territorial management with soft spaces and fuzzy boundaries*, London: Routledge.

Haughton, G., Allmendinger, P., and Oosterlynck, S. (2013) 'Spaces of neoliberal experimentation: soft spaces, postpolitics, and neoliberal governmentality', *Environment and Planning A*, 45: 217–34.

Haughton, G., Gilchrist, A., and Swyngedouw, E. (2016) ' "Rise like lions after slumber": dissent, protest and (post) politics in Manchester', *Territory, Politics and Governance*, 4(4): 472–91.

Healey, P. (1997) *Collaborative Planning: Shaping places in fragmented societies*, Basingstoke: Palgrave Macmillan.

Healey, P. (2007) *Urban Complexity and Spatial Strategies*, London: Routledge.

Health Canada (2002) *Natural and Built Environments*, Ottawa: Division of Childhood and Adolescence Ottawa, Health Canada.

Helling, A. (1998) 'Collaborative visioning: proceed with caution! Results from evaluating Atlanta's Vision 2020 project', *Journal of the American Planning Association*, 64: 335–49.

Hepburn, C., O'Callaghan, B., Stern, N., Stiglitz, J., and Zenghalis, D. (2020) *Will COVID-19 Fiscal Recovery Packages Accelerate or Retard Progress on Climate Change?*, Oxford: Smith School, University of Oxford.

Herrschel, T., and Newman, P. (2002) *Governance of Europe's City Regions: Planning, policy and politics*, London: Routledge.

Hillier, B. (2009) 'The city as a socio-technical system: a spatial reformulation in the light of the levels problem and the parallel problem', keynote paper to the Conference on Spatial Information Theory, London, September.

Hillier, J. (2003) 'Agonizing over consensus: why Habermasian ideals cannot be "real"', *Planning Theory*, 2(1): 37–59.

HM Government (2020) *The Ten Point Plan for a Green Industrial Revolution Building - back better, supporting green jobs, and accelerating our path to net zero*, London: HM Government, https://www.gov.uk/government/publications/the-ten-point-plan-for-a-green-industrial-revolution (accessed November 2020).

Hockenos, P. (2017) *Berlin Calling: A story of anarchy, music, the wall, and the birth of the new Berlin*, New York, NY: The New Press.

Hodson, M., and Marvin, S. (2010) 'Can cities shape socio-technical transitions and how would we know if they were?', *Research Policy*, 39: 477–85.

Hodson, M., and Marvin, S. (eds) (2014) *After Sustainable Cities?*, London: Routledge.

Hodson, M., and Marvin, S. (2017) 'Intensifying or transforming sustainable cities? Fragmented logics of urban environmentalism', *Local Environment*, 22(suppl 1): 8–22.

Hogland, L., and Linton, G. (2017) 'Smart specialization in regional innovation systems: a quadruple helix perspective', *R & D Management*, 48(1): 60–72.

Hollis, L. (2013) *Cities are Good for You*, London: Bloomsbury.

Hoppe, T., and van Beuren, E. (2015) 'Guest editorial: governing the challenges of climate change and energy transition in cities', *Energy, Sustainability and Society*, 5(19): 1–9, https://link.springer.com/article/10.1186/s13705-015-0047-7 (accessed April 2020).

Hordijk, M., Sara, L., and Sutherland, C. (2014) 'Resilience, transition or transformation? A comparative analysis of changing water governance systems in four southern cities', *Environment & Urbanization*, 26(1): 130–46.

Horlings, L., Collinge, C., and Gibney, J. (2017) 'Relational knowledge leadership and local economic development', *Local Economy: Journal of the Local Economy Policy Unit*, 32(2): 95–109.

Howard, E. (1898) *To-morrow: A Peaceful Path to Real Reform*, London: Swan Sonnenschein & Co.

Howard, E. (1902) *Garden Cities of Tomorrow*, London: Swan Sonnenschein & Co.

Howie, F. (2020) 'What will urban planning look like after coronavirus?', *New Statesman*, 27 May, https:// newstatesman.com/spotlight/coronavirus/2020/05/what-will-urban-planning-look-after-coronavirus (accessed November 2020).

Hu, R. (2015) 'Sustainable development strategy for the global city: a case study of Sydney', *Sustainability*, 7: 4549–63.

Hunt, A., and Watkiss, P. (2011) 'Climate change impacts and adaptation in cities: a review of the literature', *Climatic Change*, 104: 13–49.

Huxley, A. (2007) *Brave New World*, London: Penguin.

Huxley, M. (2006) 'Spatial rationalities: order, environment, evolution and government', *Social and Cultural Geography*, 7(5): 771–87.

Huxley, R., Owen, A., and Chatterton, P. (2019) 'The role of regime-level processes in closing the gap between sustainable city visions and action', *Environmental Innovation and Societal Transitions*, 33: 115–26.

IEA (2008) *International Energy Agency World Energy Outlook*, Paris: IEA.

Inayatullah, S. (ed) (2014) *The Causal Layered Analysis (CLA) Reader: Theory and case studies of an integrative and transformative methodology*, Taipei, Taiwan: Tamkang University Press.

Ingeborgrud, L. (2018a) 'Learning urban sustainability: making visions and knowledge for cities of the future', PhD thesis, Norwegian University of Science and Technology, Trondheim, Norway.

Ingeborgrud, L. (2018b) 'Visions as trading zones: national and local approaches to improving urban sustainability', *Futures*, 96: 57–67.

Iossifova, D., Doll, C., and Gasparatos, A. (2018) 'Defining the urban - a quixotic pursuit?' in Iossifova, D., Doll, C., and Gasparatos, A. (eds) *Defining the Urban: Interdisciplinary and professional perspectives*, pp 283–95, London: Routledge.

ISO/IEC (International Organization for Standardization/International Electrotechnical Commission) (2014) *ISO/IEC JTC 1: Smart Cities – Preliminary Report*, Geneva: ISO/IEC.

ITU (International Telecommunication Union) (2014) *Smart Sustainable Cities—An Analysis of Definitions*, Geneva, Switzerland: ITU.

Iwaniec, D., and Wiek, A. (2014) 'Advancing sustainability visioning practice in planning: the General Plan Update in Phoenix, Arizona', *Planning Practice and Research*, 29(5): 543–68.

Jacobs, J. (1961) *The Death and Life of Great American Cities*, New York, NY: Random House.

Jennings, I. (ed) (2008) *Cities as Sustainable Ecosystems*, Washington, DC: Island Press.

Jessop, B. (2000) 'The crisis of the national spatio-temporal fix and the ecological dominance of globalizing', *International Journal of Urban and Regional Research*, 24(2): 323–60.

John, B., Keeler, W., Wiek, A., and Lang, D. (2015) 'How much sustainability substance is in urban visions? An analysis of visioning projects in urban planning', *Cities*, 48: 86–98.

Johnson, B. (2014) 'Cities, systems of innovation and economic development', *Innovation*, 10(2–3): 146–55.

Jones, C. (2019a) *Stillicide*, London: Granta.

Jones, M. (2019b) *Cities and Regions in Crisis: The political economy of sub-national economic development*, Cheltenham: Edward Elgar.

Jones, R. (2019c) 'Innovation, regional economic growth, and the UK's productivity problem', online blog, National Centre for Universities and Business, https://www.ncub.co.uk/blog/innovation-regional-economic-growth-and-the-uk-s-productivity-problem (accessed April 2020).

Jordan, E. (2019) 'Boston's Mayor's Office of New Urban Mechanics', Centre for Public Impact, web article, https://www.centreforpublicimpact.org/case-study/bostons-mayors-office-new-urban-mechanics/ (accessed April 2020).

Joss, S., Sengers, F., Schraven, D., Caprotti, F., and Dayot, Y. (2019) 'The smart city as global discourse: storylines and critical junctures across 27 cities', *Journal of Urban Technology*, 26(1): 3–34.

Justice, J.B., and Skelcher, C. (2009) 'Analysing democracy in third-party government: business improvement districts in US and UK', *International Journal of Urban and Regional Research*, 33(3): 738–53.

Kamai-Chaoui, L., and Robert, A. (2009) *Competitive Cities and Climate Change: OECD Regional Development Working Papers 2/2009*, Paris: Organisation for Economic Co-operation and Development.

Karuri-Sebina, G. (2019) 'Urban Africa's futures: perspectives and implications for agenda 2063', *Foresight*, December: 1–14.

Karvonen, A., and van Heur, B. (2014) 'Urban laboratories: experiments in reworking cities', *International Journal of Urban and Regional Research*, 38: 379–92.

Kattel, R., Randma-Liiv, T., and Kalvet T. (2011) 'Small states, innovation and administrative capacity', in Bekkers, V., Edelenbos, J., and Steijn, B. (eds) *Innovation in the Public Sector. IIAS Series: Governance and Public Management*, pp 66–81, London: Palgrave Macmillan.

Katz, B., and Wagner, J. (2014) *The Rise of Innovation Districts: A new geography of innovation in America*, Washington, DC: Brookings.

Keil, R., and Hertel, S. (2020) 'Climate emergency, COVID-19, Black Lives Matter: urban planning's insurgent moment', blog, University of Western Australia, https://www.news.uwa.edu.au/archive/2020070112198/uwa-public-policy-institute/covid-19-climate-emergency-covid-19-black-lives-matter-urb/ (accessed March 2021).

Keith, M., and Headlam, N. (2017) *Comparative International Urban and Living Labs: The urban living global challenge: A prospectus*, Oxford: University of Oxford.

Keith, M., O'Cleary, N., Parnell, S., and Revi, A. (2020) 'The future of the future city? The new urban sciences and a PEAK Urban interdisciplinary disposition', *Cities*, (105), https://www.sciencedirect.com/science/article/pii/S0264275119323716?via%3Dihub (accessed January 2021).

Kelly, R.A., Jakeman, A.J., Barreteau, O., Borsuk, M.E., El Sawah, S., Hamilton, S.H., Henriksen, H.J., Kuikka, S., Maier, H.R., Rizzoli, A.E., van Delden, H., and Voinov, A.A. (2013) 'Selecting among five common modelling approaches for integrated environmental assessment and management', *Environmental Modelling and Software*, 47: 159–81.

Kemp, R., and Loorbach, D. (2006) 'Transition management: a reflexive governance approach', in Voss, J.-P., Bauknecht, D., and Kemp, R. (eds) *Reflexive Governance for Sustainable Development*, pp 103–30, Cheltenham: Edward Elgar.

Khaldun, I. (1989) *The Muqaddimah: An Introduction to History* (new Edition), Princeton, NJ: Princeton University Press.

Kimatu, J.N. (2016) 'Evolution of strategic interactions from the triple to quad helix innovation models for sustainable development in the era of globalization', *Journal of Innovation and Entrepreneurship*, 5(16): 1–7.

Kinney, R.J. (2016) *Beautiful Wasteland: The rise of Detroit as America's postindustrial frontier*, Minneapolis, MN: University of Minnesota Press.

Kitchin, R. (2015) 'Making sense of smart cities: addressing present shortcomings', *Cambridge Journal of Regions, Economy and Society*, 8: 131–6.

Knox, P. (ed) (2014) *Atlas of Cities*, Princeton, NJ: Princeton University Press.

Kornberger, M. (2012) 'Governing the city: from planning to urban strategy', *Theory, Culture & Society*, 29(2): 84–106.

Kornberger, M., and Clegg, S. (2011) 'Strategy as performative practice: the case of Sydney 2030', *Strategic Organisation*, 9(2): 136–62.

Kostof, S. (1991) *The City Shaped: Urban patterns and meanings through history*, Boston, MA: Bullfinch.

Krawczyk, E., and Ratcliffe, J. (2006) 'Application of futures methods in urban planning processes in Dublin', *Fennia*, 184(1): 75–89.

Kuosa, T. (2011) *Practising Strategic Foresight in Government: The cases of Finland, Singapore and the European Union*, Nanyang, Singapore: S. Rajartnam School of International Studies, Nanyang Technological University, Singapore.

Lagonigro, R., Martori, J.C., and Apparicio, P. (2020) 'Understanding Airbnb spatial distribution in a southern European city: the case of Barcelona', *Applied Geography*, 115, https://doi.org/10.1016/j.apgeog.2019.102136 (accessed April 2020).

Lall, S., and Wahba, S. (2020) 'No urban myth: building inclusive and sustainable cities in the pandemic recovery', *World Bank*, https://www.worldbank.org/en/news/immersive-story/2020/06/18/no-urban-myth-building-inclusive-and-sustainable-cities-in-the-pandemic-recovery (accessed July 2020).

Landry, C. (2012) *The Creative City: A toolkit for urban innovators*, New York, NY and Abingdon: Routledge.

Latour, B., and Hermant, E. (1998) *Paris Ville Invisible: Les empêcheurs depenser en rond*, Paris: La Découverte.

Leach, J., Mulhall, R., Rogers, C., and Bryson, J. (2019) 'Reading cities: developing an urban diagnostics approach for identifying integrated urban problems with application to the city of Birmingham, UK', *Cities*, 86: 136–44.

Lee, J., Hancock, M., and Hi, M. (2014) 'Towards an effective framework for building smart cities: lessons from Seoul and San Francisco', *Technological Forecasting & Social Change*, 89: 80–99.

Lefebvre, H. (1991) *The Production of Space*, London: Basil Blackwell.

Leontidou, L., and Martinotti, G. (2014) 'The foundational city', in Knox, P. (ed) *Atlas of Cities*, pp 16–33, Princeton, NJ: Princeton University Press.

Levitas, R. (1990) *The Concept of Utopia*, Syracuse, NY: Syracuse University Press.

Loorbach, D. (2009) 'Urban Transition Management Presentation', https://www.slideshare.net/SustainabilityTransition/urban-transition-management.

Loorbach, D., and Rotmans, J. (2004) 'The practice of transition management: examples and lessons from four distinct cases', *Futures*, 42: 237–46.

Loorbach, D., Wittmayer, J., Shiroyma, H., Fujino, J., and Mizuguchi, S. (eds) (2016) *Governance of Urban Sustainability Transitions: European and Asian experiences*, Cham, Switzerland: Springer.

Lord, A., and Tewdwr-Jones, M. (2014) 'Is planning "under attack"? Chronicling the deregulation of urban and environmental planning in England', *European Planning Studies*, 22(2): 345–61.

Loveridge, D. (2009) *Foresight: The art and science of anticipating the future*, London: Routledge.

Lynch, K. (1981) *A Theory of Good City Form*, Cambridge, MA: MIT Press.

MacKinnon, D. (2011) 'Reconstructing scale: towards a new scalar politics', *Progress in Human Geography*, 35(1): 21–36.

MacLeod, G. (2013) 'New urbanism/smart growth in the Scottish Highlands: mobile policies and post-politics in local development planning', *Urban Studies*, 50(11): 2196–221.

Marom, N. (2019) 'Urban visions and divisions in the global south: comparing strategies for Mumbai and Cape Town', *Transactions of the Institute of British Geographers*, 44(4): 778–93.

Marshall, A. (2016) *Ecotopia 2121*, London: Arcade.

Martin, C., Evans, J., and Karvonen, A. (2018) 'Smart and sustainable? Five tensions in the visions and practices of the smart-sustainable city in Europe and North America', *Technological Forecasting & Social Change*, 133 (August): 269–78.

Marvin, S., Harding, A., and Robson, B. (2006) *A Framework for City Regions*, London: Office of the Deputy Prime Minister, https://webarchive.nationalarchives.gov.uk/20070507024923/http:/www.communities.gov.uk/pub/588/AFrameworkforCityRegionsResearchReportPDF814Kb_id1163588.pdf (accessed April 2020).

Marvin, S., Luque-Ayala, A., and McFarlane, C. (2016) *Smart Urbanism: Utopian vision or false dawn?*, Abingdon: Routledge.

Marvin, S., Bulkeley, H., Mai, L., McCormick, K., and Palgan, Y. (eds) (2018) *Urban Living Labs: Experimenting with city futures*, Abingdon: Routledge.

Massey, D. (2005) *For Space*, London: Sage.

Matsumoto, T., Allain-Dupre, D., Crook, J., and Robert, A. (2019) *An Integrated Approach to the Paris Climate Agreement: The role of regions and cities: OECD Regional Development Working Papers 2019/13*, Paris: OECD.

Matthews, K. (2020) '4 predictions for urban planning post-coronavirus', *Planetizen*, https://www.planetizen.com/blogs/109432-4-predictions-urban-planning-post-coronavirus (accessed July 2020).

McAdam, M., and Debackere, K. (2017) 'Beyond triple helix toward quadruple helix models in regional innovation systems: implications for theory and practice', *R & D Management*, 48(1): 3–6.

McCann, E.J. (2001) 'Collaborative visioning or urban planning as therapy? The politics of public-private policy making', *Professional Geographer*, 53(2): 207–18.

McFarlane, C. (2011) 'Assemblage and critical urbanism', *City*, 15(2): 204–24.

McNeill, D. (1999) *Urban Change and the New Barcelona: Tales from the European Left*, London: Routledge.

McNeill, D., and Tewdwr-Jones, M. (2003) 'Architecture, banal nationalism and re-territorialization', *International Journal of Urban and Regional Research*, 27(3): 738–43.

McPhearson, T., Iwaniec, D., and Bai, X. (2016) 'Positive visions for guiding urban transformations towards sustainable futures', *Current Opinion in Environmental Sustainability*, 22: 33–40.

Meadows, D., Randers, J., Meadows, D., and Behrens, W. (1972) *The Limits to Growth*, London: Macmillan.

Mendizabal, M., Heidrich, O., Feliu, E., Graci-Blanco, G., and Mendizabel, A. (2018) 'Stimulating urban transition and transformation to achieve sustainable and resilient cities', *Renewable and Sustainable Energy Reviews*, 94: 410–18.

Messina, J. (2008) *Álamos, Sonora: Architecture and urbanism in the dry tropics*, Tuscon, AZ: University of Arizona Press.

MHCLG (Ministry of Housing, Communities and Local Government) (2020) *Planning for the Future: White Paper*, London: MHCLG.

Miller, R. (2011) 'Futures literacy – embracing complexity and using the future', *Ethos*, 10: 23–8.

Millington, N. (2013) 'Post-industrial imaginaries: nature, representation and ruin in Detroit, Michigan', *International Journal of Urban and Regional Research*, 37: 279–96.

Milojevic, I. (2002) 'Futures of education: feminist and post-Western critiques and visions', PhD thesis, The University of Queensland, Queensland, Australia, https://www.meta-future.org/uploads/7/7/3/2/7732993/a_selective_history_of_futures_thinking.pdf (accessed April 2020).

Ministry of Local Government and Modernisation (2014) *The City as a Resource*, Oslo: Ministry of Local Government and Modernisation, https://www.regjeringen.no/contentassets/e1c2707b314141008f80673bba6b5639/h_2328_english_fb_2014.pdf (accessed April 2020).

Minkkinen, M. (2019) 'The anatomy of plausible futures in policy processes: comparing the cases of data protection and comprehensive security', *Technological Forecasting & Social Change*, 43(June): 172–80.

Mintzberg, H. (1994) 'The fall and rise of strategic planning', *Harvard Business Review*, Jan–Feb: 107–14.

MISTRA (2015) *Mid-term Evaluation 2015: Mistra Urban Futures*, Stockholm: MISTRA, https://www.mistra.org/wp-content/uploads/2018/01/Mistra-Urban-Futures.pdf (accessed April 2020).

MISTRA (2018) 'Co-creation: 'oining forces for change', https://www.mistraurbanfutures.org/en/about-us/about-mistra-urban-futures (accessed April 2020).

Moir, E., Moonen, T., and Clark, G. (2014a) *What are Future Cities? Origins, meanings and uses*, London: Future Cities Catapult/Government Office for Science, https://www.gov.uk/government/publications/future-cities-origins-meanings-and-uses (accessed April 2020).

Moir, E., Moonen, T., and Clark, G. (2014b) *The Future of Cities: What is the global agenda?*, London: Government Office for Science, https://assets.publishing.service.gov.uk/government/uploads/system/uploads/attachment_data/file/429125/future-cities-global-agenda.pdf (accessed April 2020).

Moonen, T., and Clark, G. (2013) *The Business of Cities 2013: What do 150 city indexes and benchmarking studies tell us about the urban world in 2013?*, London: Jones Lang LaSalle.

Moore, A., King, L., Dale, A., and Newell, R. (2018) 'Toward an integrative framework for local development path analysis', *Ecology and Society*, 23(2): 13.

Moore, C. (1921) *Daniel H. Burnham, Architect, Planner of Cities*, Boston, MA and New York, NY: Houghton Mifflin Company.

Mora, L., Deakin, M., and Reid, A. (2018) 'Strategic principles for smart city development: a multiple case study analysis of European best practices', *Technological Forecasting and Social Change*, DOI: 10.1016/j.techfore.2018.07.035.

More, T. (1516) *Utopia*, in Duncombe, S. (ed) (2012) *Open Utopia*, New York, NY: Autonemedia, http://theopenutopia.org/wp-content/uploads/2012/09/Open-Utopia-fifth-poofs-facing-amended.pdf (accessed April 2020).

Mumford, L. (1924) *The Story of Utopias*, New York, NY: Boni and Liveright.

Mumford, L. (1938) *The Culture of Cities*, New York, NY: Harcourt Brace and Co.

Myers, D., and Kitsuse, A. (2000) 'Constructing the future in planning: a survey of theories and tools', *Journal of Planning Education and Research*, 19: 221–31.

Myers, G. (2014) 'A world-class city-region? Envisioning the Nairobi of 2030', *American Behavioral Scientist*, 59(3): 328–46.

Naess, P., and Vogel, N. (2012) 'Sustainable urban development and the multi-level transition perspective', *Environmental Innovation and Societal Transitions*, 4: 36–45.

Nathan, M., and Overman, H. (2020) 'Will coronavirus cause a big city exodus?', *Economics Observatory*, 23 September, https://www.coronavirusandtheeconomy.com/question/will-coronavirus-cause-big-city-exodus (accessed September 2020).

National Civic League (2000) *The Community Visioning and Strategic Planning Handbook*, Denver, CO: National Civic League Press.

Natural Step Canada (nd) 'Backcasting', https://www.naturalstep.ca/backcasting (accessed December 2020).

Ndizera, V., and Muzee, H. (2018) 'A critical review of Agenda 2063: business as usual?', *African Journal of Political Science and International Relations*, 12(8): 142–54.

Neirotti, P., De Marco, A., Cagliano, A., Mangano, G., and Scorrano, F. (2014) 'Current trends in smart city initiatives: some stylised facts', *Cities*: 25–36.

NESTA (2019) *Our Future: By the people for the people*, London: NESTA, https://www.nesta.org.uk/report/our-futures-people-people/ (accessed April 2020).

Neuwirth, R. (2006) *Shadow Cities*, Abingdon: Routledge.

Nevens, F., Frantzeskaki, N., Loorbach, D., and Gorissen, L. (2013) 'Urban transition labs: co-creating transformative action for sustainable cities', *Journal of Clean Production*, 50: 111–22.

Newman, P., and Jennings, I. (2008) *Cities as Sustainable Ecosystems: Principles and practices*, Washington, DC: Island Press.

Newton, P. (ed) (2008) *Transitions: Pathways towards sustainable urban development in Australia*, Dordecht, NL: Springer.

Nguyen, N., and Moehrle, M. (2019) 'Technological drivers of urban innovation: a T-DNA analysis based on US patent data', *Sustainability*, 11(24): 6966.

NIC (National Infrastructure Commission) (2016) *The Impact of Population Change and Demography on Future Infrastructure Demand*, NIC Working Paper, London: NIC, https://www.gov.uk/government/publications/the-impact-of-population-change-and-demography-on-future-infrastructure-demand (accessed April 2020).

Nicholds, A., Gibney, J., Mabey, C., and Hart, D. (2017) 'Making sense of variety in place leadership: the case of England's smart cities', *Regional Studies*, 51(2): 249–59.

Nurse, A., and Dunning, R. (2020) 'Is COVID-19 a turning point for active travel in cities?', *Cities and Health*, DOI: 10.1080/23748834.2020.1788769 (accessed July 2020).

O'Callagham, C., Boyle, M., and Kitchin, R. (2014) 'Post-politics, crisis and Ireland's "ghost estates"', *Political Geography*, 42: 121–33.

O'Connor, J., and Gu, X. (2010) 'Developing a creative cluster in a postindustrial city: CIDS and Manchester', *The Information Society*, 26(2): 124–36.

Olazabal, M. (2019) 'Are our cities effectively planning for climate change?', World Economic Forum blog, March, https://www.weforum.org/agenda/2019/03/are-our-cities-effectively-planning-for-climate-change/ (accessed April 2020).

ONS (Office for National Statistics) (2013) *2011 Census: Characteristics of built-up areas*, London: ONS, https://www.ons.gov.uk/peoplepopulationandcommunity/housing/articles/characteristicsofbuiltupareas/2013-06-28 (accessed April 2020).

ONS (2017) *The 2011 Rural-Urban Classification for Output Areas in England*, London: ONS, https://assets.publishing.service.gov.uk/government/uploads/system/uploads/attachment_data/file/591462/RUCOA_leaflet_Jan2017.pdf (accessed April 2020).

ONS (2018) *Mid-year Population Estimates for Major Towns and Cities*, 2016, London: ONS, https://www.ons.gov.uk/peoplepopulationandcommunity/populationandmigration/populationestimates/adhocs/008264midyearpopulationestimatesformajortownsandcities2016 (accessed April 2020).

Orwell, G. (2004) *Nineteen Eighty Four*, London: Penguin.

Ostrom, E. (2009) 'A general framework for analysing sustainability of socio-ecological systems', *Science*, 325(5939): 419–22.

O'Toole, R. (2007) *The Best Laid Plans: How government planning harms your quality of life, pocketbook, and your future*, Washington, DC: Cato Institute.

Park, R.E. (1952) *Human Communities: The city and human ecology*, Glencoe, IL: Free Press.

Parker, M. (ed) (2020) *Life After COVID-19: The other side of the crisis*, Bristol: Bristol University Press.

Parrad, F., and Goux-Baudiment, F. (2001) 'Quand les villes pensent leurs futurs. Une enquête sur les démarches prospectives dans 18 villes européennes', *2001 plus*, 64(October): 1–96.

Parsley, D. (2020) 'Carbon emissions fall by a third but progress may be wiped out', *The i Newspaper*, 3 May, https://inews.co.uk/news/environment/coronavirus-lockdown-reduced-co2-emissions-third-2841152 (accessed May 2020).

Patterson, A., and Pinch, P.L. (1995) '"Hollowing out" the local state: compulsory competitive tendering and the restructuring of British public sector services', *Environment and Planning A*, 27(9): 1437–61.

Peach, K. (2019) 'New platforms for public imagination', NESTA blog, May, https://www.nesta.org.uk/blog/new-platforms-public-imagination/ (accessed April 2020).

Pearson, L., Newton, P., and Roberts, P. (eds) (2014) *Resilient Sustainable Cities: A future*, New York, NY: Routledge.

Peck, J. (2015) *Fast Policy: Experimental statecraft at the thresholds of neoliberalism*, Minneapolis, MN: University of Minnesota Press.

Peck, J., and Tickell, A. (2002) 'Neoliberalizing space', *Antipode*, 34: 380–404.

Pelling, M. (2010) *Adaptation to Climate Change: From resilience to transformation*, London: Routledge.

Pereira, L.M., Hichert, T., Hamann, M., Presier, R., and Biggs, R. (2018) 'Urban futures methods to create transformative spaces: visions of a good Anthropocene in southern Africa', *Ecology and Society*, 23(1): 1–13.

Perry, B., and Atherton, M. (2017) 'Beyond critique: the value of co-production in realising just cities?', *Local Environment*, 22(suppl 1): 1–16.

Pettibone, L. (2016) *Governing Urban Sustainability: Comparing cities in the USA and Germany*, New York, NY and Abingdon: Routledge.

Phaal, R., and Probert, D. (2009) *Technology Roadmapping: Facilitating collaborative research strategy*, Cambridge: Centre for Technology Management, Department of Engineering, University of Cambridge.

Phelps, N. (2012) *Anatomy of Sprawl: Planning and politics in Britain*, London: Routledge.

Pike, A., MacKinnon, D., Coombes, M., Champion, T., Bradley, D., Cumbers, A., Robson, L., and Wymer, C. (2016) *Uneven Growth: Tackling city decline*, York: Joseph Rowntree Foundation.

Pike, A., O'Brien, P., Strickland, T., Thrower, G., and Tomaney, J. (2019) *Financing City Statecraft and Infrastructure*, Cheltenham: Edward Elgar.

Pinderhughes, R. (2004) *Alternative Urban Futures: Planning for sustainable development in cities throughout the world*, Lanham, MD: Rowman & Littlefield.

Place Alliance (2020) Urban Rooms website, https://placealliance.org.uk/working-groups/urban-rooms/ (accessed April 2020).

Plaza, B., and Haarich, S.N. (2013) 'The Guggenheim Museum Bilbao: between regional embeddedness and global networking', *European Planning Studies*, 23(8): 1456–75.

Polak, F. (1955) *The Image of the Future: Vols 1 and 2*, New York, NY: Oceana.

Poli, R. (2017) *Introduction to Anticipation Studies*, Cham, Switzerland: Springer.

Policy Exchange (2016) *Smart Devolution: Why smarter use of technology and data are vital to the success of city devolution*, London: Policy Exchange.

Pollastri, S., Boyko, C., Cooper, R., Dunn, N., Clune, S., and Coulton, C. (2017) 'Envisioning urban futures: from narratives to composites', *The Design Journal*, 20(suppl 1): 4365–77.

Presidents' Research Committee (1933) *Recent Social Trends in the United States* (vol 2), London: Forgotten Books.

Proctor, K. (2020) 'Councils in England fear they will have to make cuts of 20%', *Guardian*, 14 May, https://www.theguardian.com/society/2020/may/14/councils-in-england-fear-they-will-have-to-make-cuts-of-20.

Popper, K. (1957) *The Poverty of Historicism*, Boston, MA: The Beacon Press.

Porter, M. (1998) 'Clusters and the new economics of competition', *Harvard Business Review*, 76: 77–90.

Quine, W. (1950) *Methods of Logic*, New York, NY: Holt, Rinehart and Winston.

Quinio, V. (2020) 'Air quality in cities: now is the time to take a step forward, not back', 30 April, London: Centre for Cities, https://www.centreforcities.org (accessed May 2020).

Ramnero, A. (2005) *Gothenburg 2050: Working with visions of sustainable society*, Gothenburg: Environment Administration, http://www.goteborg2050.se/pdf/InfosheetGbg2050engweb.pdf (accessed April 2020).

Rampini, J., and Vilela, C. (2014) *For Less Segregated BRICS-Cities: The experiences of Rio de Janeiro's favelas and Johannesburg's townships public policies*, Rio de Janeiro: BRICS Policy Center/BRICS-Urbe.

Raskin, P., Banuri, T., Gallopin, G., Gutman, P., Hammond, A., Kates, R., and Swart, R. (2002) *Great Transition: The promise and lure of the times ahead*, Boston, MA: Stockholm Environment Institute.

Ravetz, J. (2020) *Deeper City: Collective intelligence and the pathways from smart to wise*, London and New York, NY: Routledge.

Ravetz, J., and Miles, I. (2016) 'Foresight in cities: on the prospect of a "strategic urban intelligence"', *Foresight*, 18(5): 469–90.

Reading 2050 (2020) 'Reading 2050', website, https://livingreading.co.uk/reading-2050 (accessed April 2020).

Reading Borough Council (2019a) *Local Plan*, Reading: Reading Borough Council, https://www.reading.gov.uk/media/10410/Reading-Borough-Council-Local-Plan/pdf/Local_Plan_Adopted_November_2019.pdf (accessed April 2020).

Reading Borough Council (2019b) *Corporate Plan*, Reading: Reading Borough Council, http://www.reading.gov.uk/media/4621/Shaping-Readings-Future-Our-Corporate-Plan-2018-21/pdf/CouncilCorporate_Plan_refresh_130619website.pdf (accessed April 2020).

Reading, M. (ed) (2015) *Nostradamus: The Complete Prophecies for the Future*, London: Watkins Media.

Reckien, D. et al (2018) 'How are cities planning to respond to climate change? Assessment of local climate plans from 885 cities in the EU-28', *Journal of Clean Production*, 191: 207–19.

Register, R. (1987) *Ecocity Berkeley*, Berkeley, CA: North Atlantic Books.

Rescher, N. (1967) *The Future as an Object of Research*, Santa Monica, CA: RAND Corporation, https://apps.dtic.mil/dtic/tr/fulltext/u2/651425.pdf (accessed April 2020).

Rhodes, R.A.W. (1988) *Beyond Westminster and Whitehall: Sub-central governments of Britain*, London: Unwin Hyman.

RIBA (2013) *City Health Check: How design can save lives and money*, London: RIBA, https://www.architecture.com/-/media/gathercontent/city-health-check/additional-documents/ribacityhealthcheckpdf.pdf (accessed April 2020).

Rickards, L., Gleeson, B., Boyle, M., and O'Callaghan, C. (2016) 'Urban studies after the age of the city', *Urban Studies*, 53(8): 1523–41.

Rip, A., and Kemp, R. (1998) 'Technological change', in Rayner, S., and Malone, L. (eds) *Human Choice and Climate Change: Resources and technology*, pp 327–99, Washington, DC: Batelle.

Ritchie, H., and Roser, M. (2018) 'Urbanisation: our world in data', Oxford University website, https://ourworldindata.org/urbanization (accessed April 2020).

Rittel, H., and Weber, M. (1973) 'Dilemmas in a general theory of planning', *Policy Sciences*, 4(2): 155–69.

Robins, N., Brunsting, V., and Wood, D. (2018) *Investing In a Just Transition: Why investors need to integrate a social dimension into their climate strategies and how they could take action*, London: LSE, http://www.lse.ac.uk/GranthamInstitute/wp-content/uploads/2018/06/Robins-et-al_Investing-in-a-Just-Transition.pdf (accessed April 2020).

Robinson, J. (2008) 'Developing ordinary cities: city visioning processes in Durban and Johannesburg', *Environment & Planning A*, 40: 74–87.

Rockefeller Foundation (2020) '100 Resilient Cities', website, http://100resilientcities.org/resources/#section-1 (accessed April 2020).

Rode, P. (2019) *Climate Emergency and Cities: An urban-led mobilisation?*, LSE Cities Discussion Papers, Research Strand 02, Cities, Climate Change and the Environment, London: LSE, https://lsecities.net/archives/climate-emergency-and-cities-an-urban-led-mobilisation/ (accessed April 2020).

Rode, P., Heeckt, C., Ahrend, R., Melchor, O., Robert, A., Badstuber, R., Hoolachan, A., and Kwami, C. (2017) *Integrating National Policies to Deliver Compact, Connected Cities: An overview of transport and housing*, Cities Working Papers, Washington, DC: Coalition for Urban Transitions, https://lsecities.net/wp-content/uploads/2018/01/NCE2017_OECD_LSE_NationalPolicies.pdf (accessed April 2020).

Rogers, C. (2018) 'The value of foresight and scenarios in engineering liveable future cities', in Eames, M., Dixon, T., Hunt, M., and Lannon, S. (eds) *Retrofitting Cities for Tomorrow's World*, pp 139–50, Oxford: Wiley-Blackwell.

Rogers, R. (1998) *Cities for a Small Planet*, London: Faber and Faber.

Rogers, R., and Power, A. (2000) *Cities for a Small Country*, London: Faber and Faber.

Rogerson, C., and Rogerson, J. (2015) 'Johannesburg 2030: the economic contours of a "linking global city"', *American Behavioural Scientist*, 59(3): 347–68.

Roorda, C., and Wittmayer, J. (2014) *Transition Management in Five European Cities: An evaluation*, Rotterdam: DRIFT, Erasmus University Rotterdam, https://drift.eur.nl/ (accessed April 2020).

Roorda, C., Wittmayer, J., Henneman, P., Steenbergen, F., van Frantzeskaki, N., and Loorbach, D. (2014) *Transition Management in the Urban Context: Guidance manual*, Rotterdam: DRIFT, Erasmus University Rotterdam, https://drift.eur.nl/) (accessed April 2020).

Rosenau, H. (2010) *The Ideal City*, Abingdon: Routledge.

Rotmans, J. (2005) *Societal Innovation: Between dream and reality lies complexity*, Erasmus University of Rotterdam, inaugural address, Rotterdam: Erasmus University, https://econpapers.repec.org/paper/emseuriar/7293.htm (accessed April 2020).

Rotmans, J., Kemp, R., and Asselt, M.V. (2001) 'More evolution than revolution: transition management in public policy', *Foresight*, 3(1): 15–31.

Rowe, C., and Koetter, F. (1978) *Collage City*, Cambridge, MA: MIT Press.

Roy, A., and Ong, A. (eds) (2011) *Worlding Cities: Asian experiments and the art of being global*, New York, NY: Wiley.

RSA (Royal Society for the Arts) (2014) *UniverCities: The knowledge of the power metros*, London: RSA.

Rudlin, D. (2020) 'Learning from lockdown: what are city centres for now?', *Building Design*, https://www.bdonline.co.uk/opinion/learning-from-lockdown-what-are-city-centres-for-now/5107062.article (accessed July 2020).

Russo, C. (2015) 'A critical analysis of four south east Queensland city futures initiatives', *Journal of Futures Studies*, 19(3): 29–48.

Russo, C. (2016a) 'Mapping outcomes of four Queensland city futures initiatives', *Foresight*, 18(6): 561–85.

Russo, C. (2016b) 'Mapping planning and engagement systems applied by four Queensland city futures initiatives: how city futures tools and methods engage across multiple contexts', *Journal of Futures Studies*, 21(2): 1–20.

Ryan, C., Twomey, P., Gaziulusoy, A.I., and McGrail, S. (2015) *Visions 2040: Results from the first year of Visions and Pathways 2040: Glimpses of the future and critical uncertainties*, Melbourne, Australia, University of Melbourne.

Ryan, C., Twomey, P., Gaziulusoy, I., McGrail, S., Candy, S., Larsen, K., Tudgeon, M., and Chandler, P. (2019) 'Visions, scenarios and pathways for rapid decarbonisation of Australian Cities by 2040', in Newton, P., Prasad, D., Sproul, A. and White, S. (eds) *Decarbonising the Built Environment: Charting the transition*, pp 507–28, Singapore: Springer Singapore.

Said, E.W. (1994) *Culture and Imperialism*, New York, NY: Vintage Books.

Saijo, T. (2019) 'Future design', keynote speech, Future Earth Philippines Program Launch, Manila, 19 November, http://www.souken.kochi-tech.ac.jp/seido/wp/SDES-2019-5.pdf (accessed April 2020).

Sanders, D. (2012) *Arrival City*, New York, NY: Vintage Books.

Sargent, L.T. (2010) *Utopianism: A very short introduction*, Oxford: Oxford University Press.

Saritas, O., and Aylen, J. (2010) 'Using scenarios for roadmapping: the case of clean production', *Technological Forecasting & Social Change*, 77: 1061–75.

Satherthwaite, D. (1992) 'Sustainable cities; introduction', *Environment & Urbanisation*, 4(2): 3–8.

Schubert, D. (2019) 'Cities and plans - the past defines the future', *Planning Perspectives*, 34(1): 3–23.

Schultz, W. (2016) 'A brief history of futures', *World Future Review*, 7(4): 324–31.

Sengers, F., Berkhout, F., Wieczorek, A., and Raven, R. (2016) 'Experimenting the city: unpacking notions of experimentation for sustainability', in Evans, J., Karvonen, A., and Raven, R. (eds) *The Experimental City*, pp 15–31, Abingdon and New York, NY: Routledge.

Sesay, A., Oh, O., and Ramirez, R. (2016) 'Understanding socio-materiality through the lens of assemblage theory: examples from police body-worn cameras', *Conference on Information Systems*, Dublin, December, https://pdfs.semanticscholar.org/fb36/a4bee7da43a42a5f2f26b4dc99b19ee0d22d.pdf (accessed April 2020).

Shaw, K., and Tewdwr-Jones, M. (2017) 'Disorganised devolution: reshaping metropolitan governance in England in a period of austerity', *Raumforschung und Raumordnung: Spatial Research and Planning*, 75(3): 211–24.

Shearmur, R. (2012) 'Are cities the font of innovation? A critical review of the literature on cities and innovation', *Cities*, 29(2): s9–s18.

Shelley, M. (2008) *The Last Man*, Oxford: Oxford University Press.

Shipley, R. (2000) 'Origin and development of vision and visioning in planning', *International Planning Studies*, 5: 225–36.

Shipley, R. (2002) 'Visioning in planning: is the practice based on sound theory?', *Environment and Planning A*, 34: 7–22.

Shipley, R. (2004) 'Evaluating municipal visioning', *Planning, Practice and Research*, 19(4): 193–207.

Shipley, R., and Newkirk, R. (1999) 'Vision and visioning in planning: what do these terms really mean?', *Environment and Planning B: Planning and Design*, 26: 573–91.

Shipley, R., and Michela, J. (2006) 'Can vision motivate planning action?', *Planning, Practice and Research*, 21(2): 223–44.

Shove, E., and Walker, G. (2007) 'Caution! Transitions ahead: politics, practice and sustainable transition management', *Environment and Planning A*, 39(4): 763–70.

Silva, C. (2020) *Citizen-Responsive Urban E-Planning: Recent developments and critical perspectives*, Hershey, PA: IGI Global.

Simone, A., and Pieterse, E. (2017) *New Urban Worlds: Inhabiting dissonant times*, Cambridge: Polity Press.

Smith, C. (2017) 'Our changes? Visions of the future in Nairobi', *Urban Planning*, 2(1): 31–40.

Smith, M. (2019) *Cities: The First 6,000 Years*, New York, NY: Viking.

Smith, M.E., and Lobo, J. (2019) 'Cities through the ages: one thing or many?', *Frontiers in Digital Humanities*, June, https://www.frontiersin.org/articles/10.3389/fdigh.2019.00012/full (accessed April 2020).

Sobchak, V. (2004) 'Cities on the edge of time: the urban science fiction film', in Redmond, S. (ed) *Liquid Metal: The science fiction film reader*, London: Wallflower.

Soja, E. (1996) *Thirdspace: Journeys to Los Angeles and other real-and-imagined places*, Cambridge: Blackwell.

Son, H. (2015) 'The history of Western futures studies: an exploration of the intellectual traditions and three-phase periodization', *Futures*, 66: 120–37.

Sotarauta, M. (2016) *Leadership and the City: Power, strategy and networks in the making of knowledge cities*, Abingdon: Routledge.

Srinivasan, S., O'Fallon, L., and Deary, A. (2003) 'Creating healthy communities, healthy homes, healthy people: initiating a research agenda on the built environment and public health', *American Journal of Public Health*, 93(9): 1446–50.

Steffen, W., Broadgate, W., Deutsch, L., Gaffney, O., and Ludwig, C. (2015) 'The trajectory of the Anthropocene: the great acceleration', *Anthropocene Review*, 2(1): 81–98.

Stier, A., Berman, M., and Bettencourt, L. (2020) *COVID-19 Attack Rate Increases with City Size*, Chicago, IL: Mansueto Institute for Urban Innovation, https://papers.ssrn.com/sol3/papers.cfm?abstract_id=3564464 (accessed May 2020).

Storper, M. (1997) *The Regional World: Territorial development in a global economy*, New York, NY: Guilford Press.

Storper, M., and Venables, A. (2004) 'Buzz: face-to-face contact and the urban economy', *Journal of Economic Geography*, 4: 351–70.

Sturzaker, J., and Nurse, A. (2020) *Rescaling Urban Governance: Planning, localism and institutional change*, Bristol: Policy Press.

Swain, C. (2016) *Understanding Current City Foresight Practice*, London: Government Office for Science.

Swilling, M. (2020) *The Age of Sustainability: Just transitions in a complex world*, Abingdon: Routledge.

Swyngedouw, E. (2018) *Promises of the Political: Insurgent cities in a post-political environment*, Cambridge, MA: MIT Press.

Taylor, M., and Laville, S. (2020) 'City leaders aim to shape green recovery from coronavirus outbreak', *The Guardian*, 1 May, https://www.theguardian.com/environment/2020/may/01/city-leaders-aim-to-shape-green-recovery-from-coronavirus-crisis (accessed May 2020).

Teriman, S., Yigitcanlar, T., and Mayere, S. (2009) 'Urban sustainability and growth management in South-East Asian city-regions: the case of Kuala Lumpur and Hong Kong', *Planning Malaysia*, 7: 47–68.

Tewdwr-Jones, M. (2012) *Spatial Planning and Governance: Understanding UK planning*, Basingstoke: Palgrave Macmillan.

Tewdwr-Jones, M. (2017) 'Health, cities and planning: using universities to achieve place innovation', *Perspectives in Public Health*, 137(1): 31–4.

Tewdwr-Jones, M. (2019) 'Michael Batty: inventing Future Cities – book review', *Urban Analytics and City Science*, 46(3): 595–96.

Tewdwr-Jones, M. and Allmendinger, P. (1998) 'Deconstructing communicative rationality: A critique of Habermasian collaborative planning', *Environment and Planning A*, 30(11): 1975–89.

Tewdwr-Jones, M., and Allmendinger, P. (eds) (2006), *Territory, Identity and Spatial Planning: Spatial Governance in a Fragmented Nation*, London: Routledge.

Tewdwr-Jones, M., and Galland, D. (2020) 'Planning metropolitan futures, the future of metropolitan futures: In what sense planning agile?', in Zimmermann, K., Galland, D., and Harrison, J. (eds) *Metropolitan Regions, Planning and Governance*, pp 225–34, New York, NY: Springer.

Tewdwr-Jones, M., Goddard, J., and Cowie, P. (2015) *Newcastle City Futures 2065: Anchoring universities in cities through urban foresight*, Newcastle: Newcastle Institute for Social Renewal, Newcastle University.

Tewdwr-Jones, M., Sookhoo, D., and Freestone, R. (2020) 'From Geddes' city museum to Farrell's urban room: past, present, and future at the Newcastle City Futures exhibition', *Planning Perspectives*, 35(2): 277–97.

Thompson, M. (2020) 'What's so new about new municipalism?', *Progress in Human Geography*, 1–26.

Thunberg, G. (2019) *No One Is Too Small to Make a Difference*, London: Penguin.

Tomalty, R. (2017) *Future Cities Canada: A systems approach to urban innovation*, Toronto: Future Cities Canada.

Townsend, A. (2013) *Smart Cities: Big data, civic hackers, and the quest for a new utopia*, London: W.W. Norton and Company.

Trencher G., and Karvonen, A. (2017) 'Stretching "smart": advancing health and well-being through the smart city agenda', *Local Environment*, 24(7): 610–27.

Trencher, G., Bai, X., Evans, J., McCormick, K., and Yarime, M. (2014) 'University partnerships for co-designing and co-producing urban sustainability', *Global Environmental Change*, 28: 153–65.

Truffer, B., and Coenen, L. (2012) 'Environmental innovation and sustainability transitions in regional studies', *Regional Studies*, 46(1): 1–21.

Tuiskunen, S., Rytkonen, E., and Nenonen, S. (2015) 'Urban vision – a static destination or a dynamic process?', *Procedia Economics and Finance*, 21: 346–54.

Twomey, P., and Gaziulusoy, I. (2014) *Review of System Innovation and Transition Theories: Visions and Pathways 2040 Project working paper*, Melbourne: University of Melbourne.

UK Trade and Investment (2015) *India's Smart Cities Programme*, London: UK Trade and Investment, https://assets.publishing.service.gov.uk/government/uploads/system/uploads/attachment_data/file/460151/UKTI_-_The_UK_offer_to_build_together__1_.pdf (accessed September 2020).

UK2070 Commission (2018) *UK 2070 – An Inquiry into Regional Inequalities Towards a Framework for Action-Prospectus*, London: UK2070 Commission.

UKRI (UK Research and Innovation) (2018) *The Urban Living Partnership*, London: UKRI, http://urbanliving.epsrc.ac.uk/files/ulpbooklet/ (accessed April 2020).

UN (United Nations) (1976) *United Nations Conference on Human Settlements – Habitat I*, Vancouver, Canada, 31 May–11 June, https://www.un.org/en/conferences/habitat/vancouver1976#:~:text=It%20took%20place%20in%20Vancouver,especially%20in%20the%20developing%20world (accessed January 2021).

UN (2002) *Sustainable Cities Programme – 1990-2000*, Nairobi: UN.

UN (2012) *Shanghai Manual: A guide for sustainable urban development in the 21st century*, New York, NY: UN, https://sustainabledevelopment.un.org/index.php?page=view&type=400&nr=633&menu=35 (accessed April 2020).

UN (2013a) *World Economic and Social Survey*, New York, NY: UN.

UN (2013b) *Science, Technology and Innovation for Sustainable Cities and Peri-urban Communities*, Geneva: UN Economic and Social Council, Commission on Science and Technology for Development.

UN (2016) *Project Document: Supporting Saudi Future Cities Program*, New York, NY: UN, https://www.sa.undp.org/content/dam/saudi_arabia/docs/Projects/161011%20Signed%20PD%20-%20Future%20Cities.PDF (accessed April 2020).

UN (2018a) *The World's Cities in 2018*, New York, NY: UN, https://www.un-ilibrary.org/human-settlements-and-urban-issues/the-world-s-cities-in-2018_c93f4dc6-en (accessed April 2020).

UN (2018b) *World Urbanisation Prospects: The 2018 revision: Key facts*, New York, NY: UN, https://population.un.org/wup/Publications/Files/WUP2018-KeyFacts.pdf (accessed April 2020).

UN (2018c) *The World's Cities in 2018: Data booklet*, New York, NY: UN, https://www.un.org/en/events/citiesday/assets/pdf/the_worlds_cities_in_2018_data_booklet.pdf (accessed April 2020).

UN (2018d) *World Urbanization Prospects: The 2018 revision – methodology*, New York, NY: UN, https://population.un.org/wup/Publications/Files/WUP2018-Methodology.pdf (accessed April 2020).

UN (2018e) *World Urbanization Prospects: The 2018 revision - full report*, New York, NY: UN, https://population.un.org/wup/Publications/Files/WUP2018-Report.pdf (accessed April 2020).

UN (2019) 'Sustainable Development Goals', website, https://sustainabledevelopment.un.org/?menu=1300 (accessed April 2020).

UNDP (United Nations Development Programme) (2018) *Foresight Manual: Empowered futures for the 2030 agenda*, Singapore: UNDP.

UN-Habitat (2012) *Better Cities for Kosovo – Visioning as Participatory Planning Tool*, Nairobi: UN-Habitat.

UN-Habitat (2016) *World Cities Report*, Nairobi: UN-Habitat.

UN-Habitat (2020) *UN-Habitat COVID-19 Key Messages*, Nairobi: UN-Habitat, https://unhabitat.org/sites/default/files/2020/03/covid19_key_messages_eng_1.pdf (accessed April 2020).

University of Sheffield (2017) 'New land cover atlas reveals just six per cent of UK is built on', https://www.sheffield.ac.uk/news/nr/land-cover-atlas-uk-1.744440 (accessed 30 October 2020).

UPP Foundation (2019) *Truly Civic: Strengthening the connection between universities and their places*, London: UPP Foundation.

Urban Foresight (2018) *Newcastle's System of Systems: The journey towards smart and innovative urban living: Report for Newcastle City Futures and Newcastle University*, Newcastle: Newcastle University, www.newcastlecityfutures.org/wp-content/uploads/2018/07/Newcastle-City-Futures-Systems-Report.pdf (accessed April 2020).

Urry, J. (2016) *What is the Future?*, Cambridge: Polity Press.

Urry, J., Birtchnell, T., Caltrio, J., and Pollastri, S. (2014) *Living in the City Future of Cities Working Paper*, London: Government Office for Science, https://assets.publishing.service.gov.uk/government/uploads/system/uploads/attachment_data/file/336660/14-801-living-in-the-city.pdf (accessed April 2020).

Valencia, S., Simon, D., Croese, S., Nordqvist, J., Oloko, M., Sharma, T., Taylor Buck, N., and Versace, I. (2019) 'Adapting the sustainable development goals and the new urban agenda to the city level: initial reflections from a comparative research project', *International Journal of Sustainable Development*, 11(1): 4–23.

Vallance, P., Tewdwr-Jones, M., and Kempton, L. (2019) 'Facilitating spaces for place-based leadership in centralised governance systems: the case of Newcastle City Futures', *Regional Studies*, 53(12): 1723–33.

Vallance, P., Tewdwr-Jones, M., and Kempton, L. (2020) 'Building collaborative platforms for urban innovation: Newcastle City Futures as a quadruple helix intermediary', *European Urban and Regional Studies*, 1–17, (https://journals.sagepub.com/doi/abs/10.1177/0969776420905630 (accessed April 2020).

Van der Heijden, J., Patterson, J., Juhola, S., and Wolfram, M. (2019) 'Special section: advancing the role of cities in climate governance – promise, limits, politics', *Journal of Environmental Planning and Management*, 62: 365–73.

Van der Helm, R. (2009) 'The vision phenomenon: towards a theoretical underpinning of visions of the future and the process of envisioning', *Futures*, 41: 96–104.

Van Dijk, T., and Weitkamp, G. (2017) 'What defines success when visions compete: lessons from post-Katrina New Orleans', *International Planning Studies*, 22(4): 350–65.

Van Waart, P., Mulder, I., and de Bont, C. (2015) 'A participatory approach for envisioning a smart city', *Social Science Computer Review*, October, 1: 15.

Varzi, A.C. (2019) 'What is a city?', *Topoi*, https://link.springer.com/article/10.1007/s11245-019-09647-4 (accessed April 2020).

Verne, J. (2019) *20,000 Leagues under the Sea*, Ottawa: East India Publishing Company.

Vigar, G., Healey, P., Hull, A., and Davoudi, S. (2000) *Planning, Governance and Spatial Strategy in Britain*, Basingstoke: Palgrave Macmillan.

Voce, A., and Van Mead, N. (2019) 'Cities from scratch', *The Guardian*, 15 February, https://www.theguardian.com/cities/ng-interactive/2019/jul/09/cities-from-scratch-100-and-counting-new-cities-rise-from-the-desert-jungle-and-sea (accessed April 2020).

Volpicelli, G. (2020) 'How London's Silicon Roundabout dream turned into a nightmare', *Wired UK*, https://www.wired.co.uk/article/silicon-roundabout-tech-city-property (accessed July 2020).

Walt, N., Doody, L., Baker, K., and Cain, S. (2014) *Future Cities: UK capabilities for urban innovation*, London: GOfS Foresight Future of Cities.

Ward Richardson, B. (2015) *Hygeia: A city of health*, Buffalo, WY: Creative Media Partners.

Ward Thompson, C., Aspinall, P., Roe, J., Robertson, L., and Miller, D. (2016) 'Mitigating stress and supporting health in deprived urban communities: the importance of green space and the social environment', *International Journal of Environmental Research and Public Health*, 13(4): 440.

Watson, V. (2009) '"The planned city sweeps the poor away...": urban planning and 21st century urbanisation', *Progress in Planning*, 72(3): 151–93.

Watson, V. (2013) 'African urban fantasies: dreams or nightmares', *Environment & Urbanization*, 26(1): 215–31.

Watson, V. (2016) 'Planning: mono-culture or planning difference?', *Planning Theory & Practice*, 17(4): 663–7.

Weber, M. (1921) *The City*, New York, NY: Free Press.

WEF (World Economic Forum) (2016) *Inspiring Future Cities and Urban Services*, Geneva: WEF.

Wells, H.G. (1902) *Anticipations*, London: Chapman and Hall.

Wells, H.G. (2017) *The Time Machine and Other Works*, London: Wordsworth Classics.

Wells, H.G. (2017) *The War of the Worlds*, London: Collins Classics.

West, G. (2018) *Scale: The universal laws of life and death in organisms, cities and companies*, London: Weidenfeld and Nicolson.

Whitehead, M. (2003) '(Re)analysing the sustainable city: nature, urbanisation and the regulation of socio-environmental relations in the UK', *Urban Studies*, 40(7): 1183–206.

Whitehead, M. (2011) 'The sustainable city: an obituary? On the future form and prospects of sustainable urbanism', in Flint, J., and Raco, M. (eds) *The Future of Sustainable Cities*, pp 29–46, Bristol: Policy Press.

Wiek, A., and Iwaniec, D. (2014) 'Quality criteria for visions and visioning in sustainability science', *Sustainability Science*, 9: 497–512.

Wiener, N. (1948) *Cybernetics: Or control and communication in the animal and the machine*, Cambridge, MA: MIT Press.

Wilde, O. (1891) *The Soul of Man Under Socialism*, Whitefish, MT: Kessinger Publishing.

Williams, R. (2019) *Why Cities Look the Way They Do*, Cambridge: Polity Press.

Wilson, A., Tewdwr-Jones, M., and Comber, R. (2019) 'Urban planning, public participation and digital technology: app development as a method of generating citizen involvement in local planning processes', *Environment and Planning B: Urban Analytics and City Science*, 46(2), DOI: 101177/2399808317712515.

Wirth, L. (1938) 'Urbanism as a way of life', *American Journal of Sociology*, 44: 1–24.

Withycombe Keeler, L., Beaudoin, F., Wierk, A., John, B., Lerner, A., Beecroft, R., Tamm, K., Seebacher, A., Lang, D., Kay, B., and Forrest, N. (2019) 'Building actor-centric transformative capacity through city-university partnerships', *Ambio*, 48: 529–38.

Wittmayer, J., Roorda, C., and van Steenbergen, F. (2014) *Governing Urban Sustainability Transitions: Inspiring examples*, Rotterdam: Dutch Research Institute for Transitions (DRIFT).

Wolfram, M. (2016) 'Conceptualizing urban transformative capacity: a framework for research and policy', *Cities*, 51: 121–30.

Wolfram, M. (2018) 'Urban planning and transition management: rationalities, instruments and dialectics', in Frantzeskaki, N., Holscher, K., Bach, M., and Avelino, F. (eds) *Co-creating Sustainable Urban Futures*, pp 103–25, Cham, Switzerland: Springer.

Wolfram, M., and Frantzeskaki, N. (2016) 'Cities and systemic change for sustainability: prevailing epistemologies and an emerging research agenda', *Sustainability*, 8: 144–62.

Wolfram, M., Borgstrom, S., and Farrelly, M. (2019) 'Urban transformative capacity: from concept to practice', *Ambio*, 48: 437–48.

World Bank (2019) *Urban Development*, Washington, DC: World Bank, https://www.worldbank.org/en/topic/urbandevelopment/overview (accessed April 2020).

Wu, F. (2015) *Planning for Growth: Urban and regional planning in China*, London: Routledge.

Yigitcanlar, T., and Kamruzzamann, M.D. (2018) 'Does smart city policy lead to the sustainability of cities?', *Land Use Policy*, 73: 49–58.

Yigitcanlar, T., Kamruzzamann, M.D., Foth, M., Sbatini-Marques, J., da Costa, E., and Iopollo, G. (2019) 'Can cities become smart without being sustainable? A systematic review of the literature', *Sustainable Cities and Society*, 45: 348–65.

Young, R., and Lieberknecht, K. (2017) 'From smart cities to wise cities: ecological wisdom as a basis for sustainable urban development', *Journal of Environment & Planning*, 62(10): 1675–92.

Yu, W., and Xu, C. (2018) 'Developing smart cities in China: an empirical analysis', *International Journal of Public Administration in the Digital Age*, 5(3): 76–91.

Zegras, C., Eros, E., Butts, K., Resor, E., Kennedy, S., Ching, A., and Mamum, M. (2015) 'Tracing a path to knowledge? Indicative user impacts of introducing a public transport map in Dhaka, Bangladesh', *Cambridge Journal of Regions, Economy and Society*, 8: 113–29.

Zhou, N., and Williams, C. (2013) *An International Review of eco-City Theory, Indicators and Case Studies*, Berkeley, CA: Ernest Orlando Lawrence Berkeley National Laboratory.

Zimmernann, K., Galland, D., and Harrison, J. (eds) (2020) *Metropolitan Regions, Planning and Governance*, London: Springer.

Index

References to figures appear in *italic* type; those in **bold** type refer to tables. References to endnotes show both the page number and the note number (231n3).

20,000 Leagues Under the Sea (Verne) 49

A

Abercrombie, Patrick 63–4
Aberdeen 120, 121–2
actor network theory (ANT) 81
adaptation action cycle 108
adaptive change 106
adaptive governance 108
Africa 2, 23, 24, 70, 93, 128–9
African Agenda 2063 125
agonism 72
air pollution 228
air quality 227
Airbnb 212–3
airports 74
alignment 38
Allmendinger, P. 72–3
Amin, A. 81
Annella Olympica, Barcelona *212*
Anthropocene 8
anticipation 124–5
arcology 86
Arcosanti complex 86
Asia 23, 24, 70, 93
assemblage theory 81–2
Atlanta 129
Atlanta Vision 2020 158, 175
Augustine 49
Australia 119–20, 163
Australian Stocks and Flows Framework (ASFF) 120

B

backcasting 115, 134–6
  participatory 139
Bacon, Francis 49
Bai, X. 107
banal nationalism 211–2
Barcelona 93, 154, 211, 212–3
Barcelona Innovation District 188
Barcelona Plan *155*
Bassett, Edward M. 154
Batty, M. 4, 6, 19, 82, 227–8
Belfast 127, **187**

Berlin 211
big plans 154
Bilbao 211
Birmingham
  Bournville 60
  Clean Air Zones (CAZ) 227
  Future of Cities (FoC) Programme 127
  population growth **25**
  productivity 27
  urban diagnostics 29
  Urban Living Partnership programme 128, 191
Blade Runner (Ridley Scott) 55, 57
Bogota 229
Boston 189
Boyle, Robert 49
Brazil 130
Brenner, N. 5
Brexit 79
BRIC countries 93
Bristol
  city vision 160, *162*, **187**
  Future of Cities (FoC) Programme 127
  population growth **25**
  smart city 94
  Sustainable Development Goals (SDGs) 33
  Urban Living Partnership programme 128, 191
Buckingham, James Silk 61
built environment 103
built-up areas 20

C

C40 Cities Climate Leadership Group 33
Cambridge 127, 183
  see also University of Cambridge
capitalism 70–1, 80–1
carbon discourse 89
carbon emissions 122
  COVID-19 226, 227
  net-zero 89, 90, 101, 104–5, 143
  see also greenhouse gas emissions
Cardiff 119, 127, 128, 139

Cardiff University 117
causal layered analysis 51
Centre for Cities 20, 27
Chalmers University 163
Chicago 11, 154, 210
Chicago Plan *155*
Chicago School of Urban Sociology 80
China 19, 24, 57, 67, 93, 107, 239n2
cities
  challenges for 27–34
  as complex systems 2–3, 17, 21, 82, 102–3, 202–5
  definitions 18–22, 80
  functions 9
  innovation. *see* urban innovation and experimentation
  narratives of 4–8, 79–99
    evolution 80–5
    smart and sustainable cities 97–9
    smart cities 91–7
    sustainable cities 85–91
  science of 2, 6, 7
  transformational changes 205–7
  see also future cities; garden cities; smart cities; sustainable cities
Cities Alliance 128, 131, 163, 175
Cities of the Future programme, Norway 99, 128
citizen participation 157, *158*
city beautiful movement 35
city development strategies (CDSs) 131, 175
city foresight 12, 14, 52, 109, 124–30, 156
city foresight methods 133–8, 163, 218–21
  see also city visions / visioning
City Futures Development Group, Newcastle 172–3
City of God (Augustine) 49
City of London 76
city of visions 59
city plans 154
city proper 19, 20
city statecraft 71
city states 213
city visions / visioning ix–x, 10, 11, 14, 38, 130–3, 230
  city foresight methods 133–138, 218–21
  evolution 153–63
  examples *162*, 233–8
  future cities 224
  and future studies 52–3
  global south 149–50
  good practice 174–7, 179–80

Newcastle City Futures 2065 (NFCF2065) 143–9, 167–74
  opportunities and challenges 177–9
  Reading 2050 138–43, 163–7, **168**, 194–5
  Retrofit 2050 118–9
  stages 218–21
  sustainability 90, 99
  transition management (TM) 110
  typology 83–4
  UK 12
  in an uncertain age 210–15
city-regionalism 72
city-regions 19
civic universities 192
Clean Air Zones (CAZ) 227
clean-tech corporate living 120
climate activism 104–5
climate change x, 75, 101–2, 103, *104*, 105, 218, 229
  see also global warming
climate change research community 108
climate emergencies 105
co-creation 156–7
collaborative planning 71
Committee on Climate Change (CCC) 105, 228–9
community balanced living 120
commuting 74–5
compact city 119
complex systems 2, 82
  cities as 2–3, 17, 21, 82, 102–103, 202–5
computerised visualisation *171*
Comte, Auguste 49
concrescence 81
conflict 72
contemporary cities 4
contingency futures 125
co-production 156, 157, 177, 194
cosmic cities 82
COVID-19 x, 74–5, 76, 79, 217–8, 225–30
cycling 229

D

Daffara, P. 83–4
data 205–6
Davoudi, S. 52
demographic changes 73
Detroit 54, 210
Dhaka 93
digital transformation 205–7
digitalisation 223–4
  see also smart cities
discourses 84

disposable spatial rationalities 84
Dubai 57, *58*
Durban 149
dystopia 54
dystopic literature 54

E

East Asia 2, 107
eco-city 84, 86–7, 88–9
  see also sustainable cities
eco-communities 86
ecological cities 59
ecological crisis 86
ecological modernisation 89
ecological utopia 49
economic cycles 73
economic growth 89
economic recovery 229
economy 120
Edinburgh 160, **187**
energy supplies 75
energy use 98
England 1
environmental problems 107
Ethiopia 129
euchronia 41
Europe
  climate change 101
  smart cities 93
  urban challenges **29**
  urban governance 70
  urbanisation 2, 23, 24
European Commission 87
European Network of Living Labs (ENoLL) 189
European Sustainable Cities Campaign 87
European Sustainable Communities Programme 87
European Union 79, 129
experiential futures 137–8
experimental cities 185
experimentation *see* urban innovation and experimentation
exploratory futures 125

F

Farias, I. 80–1
Farrell Review 189–90
fate 42
film 49, 55–57
Findhorn project 86
flexible cities 59
forecasting 124
foresight 11, 124
  see also city foresight
foresight studies 11–12
foresight-based thinking 156, 176

functional urban areas 20
future 1, 42, *133*
  historic interpretations 42–3
  see also urban futures
future cities 59, 225–31
  see also urban futures
Future Cities Africa 128–9
Future of Cities (FoC) Programme 12, 29, 125–128, 161–2, 218
futures studies 48–54, 124–5
futures thinking x, 49, 50–1, 52, 64, 124, 128–9, 163
Futures Toolkit (GOfS) 134, **135**
fuzzy boundaries 72

G

Gaian city 84
garden cities 4, 35, 61–2
garden city movement 35, 59
Geddes, Patrick 2, 5, 63–4, 85, 202
genealogical classification 83–4
generative spatial rationalities 84
Gerlach, N. 55
German Advisory Council on Global Change (GACGC) 125
Germany 60, 67
Ghana 129
Ghent 120, 121
Gibney, J. 78
Gidley, J. 11, 42, 47–8, 50–1, 124
Glaeser, Edward 6, 18
Glasgow **25**
global cities 81
Global Goals *see* Sustainable Development Goals (SDCs)
global Gross Domestic Product (GDP) 1, 22
global north / global south 2, 149, 178, 179
global sustainability challenges 9
global warming 28
  see also climate change
governance 67–71
  adaptive 108
  place-based leadership 193, 194
  post-political era 71–4
  smart and sustainable cities 99
  smart cities 94–5, 96
  transformational changes 206
  transition management (TM) 114–5
  and urban planning 221–4
  and urban sustainability 107
governance systems 106
Government Office for Science (GOfS) 12, 125–6, 134, **135**, 138, 144, 161
Graham, S. 57

Greater London Plan 63–4
Greek tragedy 42
green economic recovery 229
Green New Deal 89
greenhouse gas emissions 101, 105, 119–20
    see also carbon emissions
Grin, J. 113–4

H

Habitat Conference 86
Habitat II 87
Hambleton, R. 78
Hamilton, S. 55
Harris, Britton vii
Harvey, D. 71
Haughton, G. 72–3
health 29–30, 74
Hermant, E. 81
Hong Kong 160
horizons *see* time horizons
housing 197
Howard, Ebenezer 60–2, 63, 64, 85
Howard, J. 78
human ecology 63
Huxley, M. 84
hybrid cities 59

I

Imagine Durban initiative 149
India 24, 93, 129
informal cities 59
information and communications technology (ICT) 92, 95, 96, 97, 139, 184
infrastructure 75
innovation 92
    see also urban innovation and experimentation
innovation districts (IDs) 187–8
insurance industry 75
integral futures 51
integration 30, 38
internet of things 37
Iossifova, D. 80
Iwaniec, D. 134

J

Jacobs, Jane 2, 5, 17, 184
Japan 23, 107, 138
Johannesburg 160–161, *162*
Jones, C. 54–5

K

Kemp, R. 12
knowledge 92
Korea 23, 94, 107, 138

L

land use 6, 28
Las Vegas 210
Latour, B. 81
layered cities 59
Le Corbusier 3, 4, 5, 57
leadership 77–8, 177, 193–5
Leeds **25**, 128, 191, 227
Les Prophéties (Nostradamus) 49
Letchworth Garden City 62
limitations 8
Limits to Growth report 86
literature 54
Liverpool **25**, 27, 127, 128
Local Agenda 21 87
localisation economies 184
London
    centralisation 27
    cholera outbreak 1854 *225*
    Greater London Plan 63–4
    green recovery 229
    innovation 183
    Newcastle City Futures 2065 (NFCF 2065) 170
    population growth **25**, *26*
    Silicon Roundabout 76
    smart city 93, 94
    sustainability 91
    Ultra Low Emission Zone 227
long-term visioning 132–3
Loorbach, D. 13
Ludwigsburg 120, 121
Lynch, K. 82

M

Manchester
    Clean Air Zones (CAZ) 227
    Cottonopolis 210
    Future of Cities (FoC) Programme 127
    northern powerhouse 170
    Northern Quarter 76
    population growth **25**
    productivity 27
    Reading 2050 119
    Retrofit 2050 **117**
Marquis de Condorcet 49
Marshall, Alfred 61
Masdar City 94
masterplans 154–6
Matrix (Wachowski) 55
McPhearson, T. 130
mechanistic cities 83
megacities 24
Metropolis (Lang) 55, *56*, 57
metropolitan areas 19, 20
Mexico City 229

Index

micropolitan areas 19
Middle East 70, 93
Milan 229
Milton Keynes 27, 94, 127, 161, 163
Mitchell, William J. 188
Moir, E. 33–4
Montreuil 120, 121
MONUM (Mayor's Office of New Urban Mechanics), Boston 189
More, Thomas 44–6, 47
Mozambique 129
multi-level perspective (MLP) 13, 109, 110–3, 118, 186
Mumford, Lewis 63
municipalism 230
MUSIC (Mitigation in Urban Areas: Solutions for Innovative Cities) project 120–2

N

Nairobi 160
narratives of the city 4–8, 79–99
  evolution 80–5
  smart and sustainable cities 97–9
  smart cities 91–7
  sustainable cities 85–91
needs 8
neoliberalism 70–1, 72
network entrepreneurial living 120
net-zero carbon emissions 89, 90, 101, 104–5, 143
New Atlantis (Bacon) 49
New Urban Agenda (NUA) 31
New York 55, 57, 105, 225, 229
Newcastle **25**, 127, 128, 161, 191
Newcastle 2020 172
Newcastle City Futures 2065 (NFCF2065) 143–9, 167–74, 177, 178
Newcastle City Futures Urban Living Partnership 195–9
Newcastle Policy Cabinet 172
Newcastle University 144, 146, 147, 149, 170–1, 178, 195–9
Nigeria 24
North America 2, 23, 24, 35, 93
  see also United States
Northern Quarter, Manchester 76
Northumbria University 144, 170
Norway 99, 128
Nostradamus 49
Nottingham *25*
novelty futures 125

O

Oceania 23
optimisation futures 125
oral tradition 48

organic cities 83
Our Futures (NESTA) 130
Oxford 27, 160, 183, 227
Oxford Brookes University 118

P

panarchy 108
paradox of the modern metropolis 6
Paris 5, 57, 81, 154, 225, 229
parks 74
participatory backcasting 139
participatory foresight-based thinking 156
participatory futures 129–30
persistent problems 103, *104*
Place Alliance 190
place branding 211
place-based leadership 78, 193–5
place-based university partnerships 192–3
planned regulated living 120
Plato 44, 47
pluralism 51
Poli, R. 124
political context 65–78
  future opportunities 74–6
  post-political era 71–4
  urban governance 67–71
  see also governance
population growth 24, **25**, *26*
Portland 129, 160
Portugal 130
positivism 51
possible futures 124
post-political era 69, 71–4
preferred futures 124
primary urban areas 20
prophets 42–3
prospective futures 124
public engagement 143

Q

quadruple helix 163–5, 168, 178
Quine, W. 21

R

radiant cities 4
RAND Corporation 50
Reading 27, 127, 184
Reading 2050 138–43, 163–7, 168, 177, 178, 179, **187**, 194–5
Register, Richard 86–7
regulated cities 59
Republic (Plato) 44, *45*, 46
research & development (R&D) 183–4
resilience 227, 229
resilient change 106

Retrofit 2050 117–9
roadmapping **135**, 137
Rochdale 127
Rockefeller Foundation 33
Rome 210
Rotterdam 121
rural areas 20
rural population *23*

S

Saudi Arabia 239n
Saudi Future Cities programme 128
Saudi Visions 2030 128
scenarios **135**, 136–7
Schmid, C. 6
Schulz, W. 48
science fiction film 55–7
science of cities 2, 6, 7
science shops 190
Scotland 229
security agencies 75
self-reliant city 119
Shanghai 57, *58*
sharing economy 212–3
Sheffield *25*, 27
Shipley, R. 129
shops 74
Silicon Roundabout, London 76
Singapore 93, 190
smart and sustainable cities 139–42, 223–4
smart cities 6–7, 37, 53, 79, 85, 91–9, 205–6
  India 129
  sustainability agenda 84
  UK 132
smart-networked city 118
social cities 4
social futures 47
socioecological system (SES) frameworks 108, 109–10
sociotechnical transition (STT) studies 108, 109–10
soft spaces 72
Son, H. 52
Songdo 94
South Africa 149
South America 93
South East Asia 2, 88–9, 93
Soviet Union 49
Spanish flue pandemic *226*
spatial imaginaries 53–4
spatial planning 71–2
spatial rationalities 84
spatial strategy 71
Stern, Nicolas 101
Stillicide (Jones) 54–5

Stockholm 91, 188
sustainability agenda 84
sustainable cities 32, 79, 85–91, 97–9, 131
  see also urban sustainability
sustainable development 8, 72
Sustainable Development Goals (SDCs) 30–2, 90
sustainable futures 130
Sustainable Sydney 2030 programme 160
Swinburne University of Technology 119
Sydney 105, 119, 129, 157, 160, *162*
systemic change 107–10

T

Taoyuan 93
taxes 67
technocity 84
technological advancements 205–7
technological change 75
technology *see* information and communications technology (ICT); smart cities
Thames Valley 184
Things to Come (film) 55
thought experiments 3, 4
three horizons model 136, *137*
Thrift, N. 81
Thunberg, Greta x
Tianjin project 89
time 47–8
time horizons 136, *137*, 147
Tobler, Waldo R. 6
Toronto 19–20, 188
tourism 75, 211–3
transformation 106
transformation theory vii
transition management (TM) 13, 109, 113–6, 118, 121–2, 177–8, 186
transitioning 106
transitions theory ix, 12–13, 109, 110–6, 218
  application 116–22
transportation 6, 197, 202, 229
travel 74–5

U

Uber 213
Uganda 129
UK
  carbon emissions 226, 227
  city visions 12, 160
  COVID-19 79, 226–7, 228–9
  garden city movement 35, 59

Index

governance 67, 69
Green New Deal 89
greenhouse gas emissions 105
place-based leadership 194
smart cities 94–5, 98, 132
Sustainable Development Goals (SDCs) 33
urban areas 20
urban challenges **29**
urban experimentation **187**
urban innovation 183–4, **187**
urbanisation 24–7
UK 2070 programme 128
UN Centre for Human Settlements Conference 86
UN Sustainable Cities Programme 87
UN Sustainable Development Goals (SDGs) 30–2, 90
UN-Habitat Urban Settlement Programme 28
United Arab Emirates 94
United States 49–51, 61, 67, 89, 129, 188
see also North America
universities 181, 189, 190, 191–5
University of Cambridge 118
University of Durham 117
University of Melbourne 119
University of New South Wales 119
University of Reading 117–8, 192, 194
University of Salford 117
urban agglomeration 19, 20, 24
urban areas 20
urban assemblages 81
urban challenges 27–34
urban consumption 28
urban crisis 86
urban cybernetics 92–3
urban diagnostics 29
urban entrepreneurialism 71
Urban Environment Green Paper (EC) 87
urban environmental evolution 107
urban experimentation *see* urban innovation and experimentation
urban futures ix, 7, 10, 14, 130–1, 239n1
and technology 92
and urban planning 207–10
see also political context: future opportunities
urban governance 67–71
adaptive 108
place-based leadership 193, 194
post-political era 71–4
smart and sustainable cities 99

smart cities 94–5, 96
sustainability 107
transformational changes 206
transition management (TM) 114–5
and urban planning 221–4
and urban sustainability 107
urban government 74
urban hubs 184
urban imaginaries 7, 41
urban innovation and experimentation 181–200
engagement spaces 187–91
Newcastle City Futures Urban Living Partnership 195–9
role of universities 191–5
urban innovation systems 184–5
urban living labs (ULLs) 98, 186, 188–9
Urban Living Partnership programme 128, 191
Newcastle City Futures Urban Living Partnership 195–9
urban paradox 27–8, 104
urban planning 3, 4–5, 10–11, 34–9, 205
masterplans 153–6
political context 65–78
future opportunities 74–6
post-political era 71–4
urban governance 67–71, 221–4
and transition management (TM) 114
and urban futures 207–10
utopic tradition 60–4
urban planning movements 65
see also garden city movement
urban population 9, *23*, **25**, *26*
see also urbanisation
urban regeneration 76
urban resilience 33
urban rooms 189–90
urban science *see* science of cities
urban sustainability 7, 9
pathways to 106–10
projects 117–22
zero carbon 104–5
see also sustainable cities
urban transformative capacity 9, 13
urban transition management 13
urban triumphalism 7
urban visions 47
urbanisation 1–2, 22–7
China 239n2
utopia 44, 46–7, 54, 55
ecological 49
Utopia (More) 44–6, 47, 54, 83
utopian thinking 41
utopic tradition 60–4

V

Van Dijk, T. 175
Vancouver Declaration 28
Verne, Jules 49
Vienna 154
vision planning 157
visionary thinkers 48–9
visioning 115, 127, 129, 130, 134, **135**
  see also city visions / visioning
visions 43–7, 153
  see also city visions / visioning
Visions and Pathways 2040 (VP2040) 119–120
vitalist spatial rationalities 84
Von Thunen, Johan Heinrich 6

W

Wakefield, Edward Gibbon 61
Wales 1
War of the Worlds (Wells) 49, 50
Weitkamp, G. 175
Wells, H.G. 6, 49, 124
  War of the Worlds 49, *50*
West, G. 2
wicked problems viii, 9, 12, 103, *104*
Wiek, A. 134
Wirth, Louis 18–9, 22, 81
Wolfram, M. 9, 10

Y

York 128, 191

Z

Zero-Emission Zone 227
  see also net-zero carbon emissions
Zipf's law of distribution 6, 26–7

www.ingramcontent.com/pod-product-compliance
Lightning Source LLC
Chambersburg PA
CBHW071150070526
44584CB00019B/2742